I0160498

The Snitch
Jeffrey L. Barnes
Published By Black Market Publications
Printed By CreateSpace, an Amazon.com Company

Manufactured in the United States of America

ISBN - 0692286748

Acknowledgements

In memory of my brother Larry Bruce Barnes, whose generous soul and benevolent spirit helped to shape not only my life, but my writing of *"The Snitch"* I love you big brother! I pray you find peace in your eternal sleep.

Debra McGee, my sister the guardian Angel in the flesh.

I am truly grateful to my friend Francis Jermaine Bell, who's advice and editing talents helped shape my writing.

The Snitch is the result of an effort that could not have been completed without prayer, support, time and encouragement provide by my God sent, my prayer warrior, Gwendolyn Wesley.

Peace, love and blessings to the all of you.

PROLOGUE

It's 1:30pm, March 4, 2013. I'm sitting with my attorney, Carl Grayford, in the courtroom of the Honorable James M. Goodfellow, U.S. District Court Judge for the District of Minnesota. Having cooperated and assisted the government in the prosecution of seven of my codefendants, who have all received the death penalty, I'm now awaiting sentencing. My name is Shanally Lamar Robinson III a.k.a. Sazzar--I'm *THE SNITCH!*

<u>**C H A P T E R   1**</u>

From the shadow of the warehouse Sazzar ran through the smoke, which obscured his getaway. His eyes caught movement to his right. He raised his weapon ready to fire only a second to late, as his body collided with a police cruiser, which sent him airborne over its hood and hard onto the street.

He stumbled to his feet prepared to run when several rounds fired from the police officers guns slammed into his chest and dropped him where he stood. Sazzar, who had been trained to ignore pain, jerked upright, aimed and fired four quick rounds from his Beretta at the two blurred blue figures.

When he rolled to his feet, there was no return fire. The two Policeman's bodies only trembled and convulsed, their eyes filled with the terror of death.

A Lincoln Navigator roared toward him on Milton Avenue and came to a screeching halt twenty-five feet from him in an attempt at his extraction, the smoke impeding its forward progress. Time crept slowly at first, and then rapidly, as a hailstorm of bullets pelted the front of the Navigator.

Sazzar did not see his team exit the vehicle with thirty-round magazines taped together, inverted, and attached to their AK-47's. Dazed and disoriented, he could hear them screaming for him to get down just as muzzle flashes lit up the night and tarred street flew up all around him.

Sazzar threw himself to the ground, rolling to his right to avoid the live rounds that hit inches from his head. He blinked his eyes repeatedly to clear his vision and watched through the smoke as his team engaged the police, a fierce battle underway. Pinned beneath the crossfire, he thought of his soon-to-be newlywed wife, and their daughter; to be captured would ruin it all-- death on Selby Avenue was not an option.

He heard a voice in his earpiece. "Sazzar, crawl toward us!"

He summoned his strength, crawling as fast as he could, his body as flat to the ground as he could manage. Several rounds hitting the ground before him forced him to crawl in the direction of the dying officers; he half-stood, pushing himself against the shelter of the police cruiser. Seeing an opening, he raised a hand to his face.

"Do your business, Six, and get out. I'll find you!" Sazzar said into his handmic as he took off running through the residential neighborhood on Hague and Milton.

"Escape and evade!" Six commanded into his handmic. His team began falling back in two-by-two cover fire, using cars and trees as shelter. Six jumped inside the Navigator as a tidal wave of hostile gunfire sprayed glass from the windshield throughout the interior of the truck, showering him with the shattered remains.

The police didn't see the second vehicle until it was too late. Its driver exited the vehicle and walked toward them. The PKS he held in his hand fired its 7.62 x 54 rounds from its two- hundred-and-fifty-round can. The rapid fire from the weapon paralyzed the police behind their temporary positions of shelter. Every fifth round fired from the PKS was an incendiary round that set fire to everything it hit.

Six clutched a smoke grenade, pulled the pin and tossed it into the rear of the Navigator. As he reached forward to open the driver's side door, he simultaneously kicked open the passenger's side door. Grabbing hold of the gear shift, he yanked it into the drive position and the Navigator lurched forward. From a knapsack he pulled another canister and pulled the pin.

"One-thousand-one," he said into his handmic. He heard the pop of the smoke grenade and watched as the smoke began bellowing out from the shattered windows and doors. Tina's voice sounded in his earpiece.

"One-thousand-two." He grabbed the knapsack full of smoke grenades and slammed them onto the accelerator. Releasing the trigger on the canister he held in his hand, he flipped it onto the roof of the Navigator and rolled to the ground from the smoke laden passenger door.

Smoke streamed from the tires and the interior as the Navigator lunged forward directly at the police gauntlet. Six scrambled to his feet running, his exit obscured by the plumes of belching smoke from the Navigator.

"One-thousand-three, one-thousand-four," he heard in his ear piece.

The police had caught a visual of him ducking below the dash board and continued to pump shot after shot into the body of the vehicle as it crashed through the barricades coming to an abrupt halt. Officers began to surround the smoking vehicle, guns at the ready. Six slammed the door of the second vehicle, a Cadillac Escalade, and it peeled off, leaving rubber on Hague Avenue.

"One-thousand-six, one-thousand-seven." The driver of the Escalade said, "Boom!"

The canister on the roof exploded into a cloud of streaming lines. Screams replaced the gunfire and commands, as uniformed officers ran about, their hair and clothing ablaze, like human roman candles. Six knew the canister on the roof was a white- phosphorous grenade and that when it landed on their flesh it would burn straight through.

"I hate phosphorous!" Six said.

"I hate the shit, too," barked Rasheed.

"I sure as hell love what the fuck it can do." K-Nine said.

It will burn itself out eventually, Six thought.

C H A P T E R 2

"Motherfuckers! They did it!" Sazzar mumbled as he moved quickly between the houses. He heard the countdown in his earpiece and the small-arms fire in the distance, His team was mobile with no pursuit. On Holly Avenue he doubled back after seeing several patrol cars. Crossing Milton and then Victoria, he ran flat out for four more blocks before finding temporary refuge in a garage off Summit Avenue.

After a moments rest, the area in which he had been hiding came alive with the sounds of police radios and dogs. Damn, I hate dogs! He thought. He checked his ammo belt; the damn thing was empty. He stepped from the cover of the garage and moved quickly, while between two houses removing his flack vest. Five rounds were lodged center mast, had the police been using armor-piercing rounds like those in his Beretta, he'd be dead too.

Sazzar tossed the vest, Motorola and Beretta on top of a two story house. Damn evidence: he knew it would be found sooner or later. He just hoped it would be later, much later.

The police were close, maybe a neighbor's yard away. From the sound of their radios, a massive manhunt was underway. No shit! he thought. He heard them before he saw them. They were blocking his only exit, a female and her male partner.

From his hiding place in the shadows, he could see her face. She was swallowing hard, her lips were trembling. He could almost visualize her discursive mind rewinding her inadequacies as a police officer. Bottom line, the night's events had the bitch scared shitless.

Her partner was black, tall and slender, a bit over two hundred pounds. He looked streetwise, tough; raised in the hood, Sazzar thought. He sized him up as the sharper of the two, and by far more lethal. He pushed the thought out of his mind and kept silent, watching their movements, estimating his chances. Their sudden change in direction had them coming directly to where he was hiding, the male leading the way, his female partner close behind him.

He had to make a move, just a few more steps. Sazzar wheeled to his right, the crescent kick swept from the ground in a vicious arc that caught the male officer on the jaw. He went down hard, his weapon bouncing harmlessly against a fence.

When the female officer swung her weapon chest high, his left hand closed around her gun as she pulled the trigger, the hammer snapping hard against the web of his hand.

He smiled at the surprised look in her eyes.

"Sorry baby," and with his right hand hit her with a hook to the jaw. She dropped like a ragdoll, lying unconscious and still.

Sazzar stuck her service weapon into the waist of his pants and took her radio from her hip. As quickly as he could, he undressed the male officer, replacing his own clothing with the officer's uniform. Nearly a perfect fit.

Leaving both officers handcuffed and gagged in a garage, Sazzar joined the other officers in search of the fugitive. He crossed Dale at Grand, weapon in one hand, flashlight in the other, as he carefully searched the shadows of an apartment complex and store fronts.

During his training he had learned that it was important to be unpredictable, to conceal his form in the face of danger or threat, making his movements seem natural. He was nearly blinded by all the flashing lights and nearly as shocked at the number of police vehicles from several of Minnesota's counties posted at all major intersections and the decline of civilian vehicles on the street.

Sazzar calmly walked up to the police checkpoint, his head held high. He holstered his weapon, nodded at a few of his fellow men in blue, and walked through the barrier, securing it behind him. He'd blended in, which was easy to do because his blue uniform carried with it the symbol of power. The image and presence of a policeman was the only matter of importance to any of the police around the checkpoint.

Having gone unnoticed, Sazzar walked to the end of the block while behind him a major commotion had erupted. His discipline helped him fight the inclination to turn around. He kept moving forward.

Just when he thought all was well his radio began to chirp, "Our suspect may be dressed as a St. Paul police officer. Suspect is armed and extremely dangerous. Identify all officers in your presence who are African American. Our suspect is six foot, 215 pounds, with close-cut hair. Should you come in contact with the suspect, deadly force has been authorized." Sazzar turned off the radio and once again fled to the alleyways for cover.

Searching a flatbed truck, he found a pair of overalls and changed out of the uniform leaving the weapon, radio, and uniform under a tarp on the truck. With his hands shoved deeply into the pockets of the overalls, Sazzar crossed Western Avenue at Summit Avenue, walking down Ramsey Hill just as he'd done many times as a kid.

At the bottom of the hill he crossed the bridge, smiling at the site of Children's Hospital, and the thought of his son. As he neared the end of the bridge, two police cruisers, four deep, pulled to the curb in front of him. All eight officers exited the vehicles cautiously, weapons pointed directly at him.

"It's been a real fucked up night, buddy. We're arresting anyone walking around until we can get to the bottom of this shit and get it sorted out. Unless you want to get shot, I suggest you kiss the concrete. On the ground ...Now!" One of the officers shouted, his tone deadly serious. All eight officers stood over Sazzar, weapons trained on the back of his head, as one of them knelt down and cuffed him,

C H A P T E R 3

Sitting in the bullpen of the St. Paul Police Department, Sazzar raised up from the seat on the cement slab to look at the clock on the wall. It had been nine hours since the police had taken his fingerprints. He'd called his attorney in New York, who assured him that by morning he would be released. An attorney from their Minneapolis based firm, a woman with a solid reputation as a defense attorney would be there should the need for a court appearance arise.

Sazzar was about to return to his seat when three men in suits appeared at the holding cell door. One of them called out his name.

"Mr. Shanally Robinson?"

"Yeah, that's me."

"Turn around, sir. I need to cuff you." The spokesman stated.

"For what? Who are you?" Sazzar responded.

"Please, Mr. Robinson, don't be alarmed, we know who you are. Right now your attorney is waiting for you in our conference room. Please, sir, all we need is a moment of your time."

"You still haven't answered my question. Who are you?"

"My name is Richard Donoghue, and I'm a homicide detective with the St. Paul Police."

"Homicide detective? Why do you want to talk to me?"

"If you come with us, Mr. Robinson, I'm sure we can get to the bottom of this matter and get you on your way."

Sazzar allowed himself to be cuffed and was led to an interrogation room, where he was uncuffed and seated next to an attractive brunette. She looked twenty years younger than her forty-plus years. Her long legs were lithe and very muscular. She stood, and he could see that she had an incredible body, her hips blending nicely with her firm backside; beautiful by all of his standards.

"Mr. Robinson, I'm Fanny Corning and I'm with Grayford-Dworkins. I was sent here directly by Mr. Grayford personally, to assist with your release. Please sir, allow me to speak on your behalf?"

Sazzar nodded his approval.

"First of all, let me say that I'm a huge fan of yours, Mr. Robinson," Donoghue began. "I watched the game Monday night against Chicago, where you rushed for one-hundred-seventy-five yards. You run just as hard in the league today as you did when you entered in 2000. It's a damn shame that you are going to have to retire."

"Detective Donoghue, we are all aware of Mr. Robinson's rushing records with the New York Giants. I'm sure he was not escorted here in cuffs for us to discuss his statistics."

"You are absolutely right, counselor. We are not here to discuss your famous client's stats. However, we are here to talk about why Mr. Robinson's bloody hand and fingerprints were all over the crime scene of a double homicide in 1994?"

"Excuse me, Detective, did I miss something? Are you charging my client with murder?"

"No, counselor. Because your client is a poster boy for the NFL and a local hero, I'm simply extending him the courtesy of answering a few questions in hopes of shedding some light on a twenty-year-old murder investigation." Speaking directly to Sazzar Detective Donoghue asked, "Did you come into Hellman's Market on the morning of August 1, 1994 and find the Hellmans murdered?"

"Don't answer that, Mr. Robinson," she said, placing her hand on his wrist. Turning towards Detective Donoghue and his men, her tone became very aggressive. "Unless you are charging my client with some type of crime, this interview is over. As of this moment Mr. Robinson has no official charges or warrants to justify him to continue to be held in custody. Other than being in the wrong place at the wrong time, which last I checked the statute is not a crime, I suggest that you charge my client with a crime or release him."

Detective Donoghue looked to his associates, then back to Sazzar. "You're free to go, Mr. Robinson, for now. Our investigators know where to find you."

C H A P T E R 4

Sazzar cupped Miss Corning's hand in his, and was about to thank her, when the interrogation room doors opened and several men entered.

"Mr. Shanally Robinson III?"

"Who's asking?" Miss Corning said.

"I'm Special Agent in Charge Russell McMurtry with the FBI, and I'm here to take Mr. Robinson into federal custody."

"On what charges?" She asserted.

"For starters, the murder of a federal undercover agent and several gangbangers from a local organization."

"Are you suggesting that my client was somehow a part of that fiasco on Selby Avenue that's all over CNN and every local news channel in the Twin Cities?"

"I'm not suggesting anything, counselor. I'm here as I've said to take Mr. Robinson into federal custody."

"What is your probable cause for detaining my client, Special Agent McMurtry?"

"We have a witness, counselor, who places your client at the scene," he said calmly.

"Witness to what? News reports say the police have no witnesses or suspects." She became angry, thrown off kilter with this news.

"Calm down, counselor. Last night while the locals were in pursuit of the persons responsible, two officers encountered a man they believed to be the fugitive of the manhunt.

Unfortunately, he managed to escape, only after he rendered both officers unconscious, and fled the scene with one of the officer's clothing and the others weapon and radio."

"That's all fine and dandy, but how does any of this information connect my client to this crime?"

"We retrieved the police uniform, the weapon, and the radio from the driver of a flatbed truck, named Harold Meyers. He says the only thing missing from his truck was a pair of overalls with the name 'Harold' on them."

Miss Corning looked at the nametag on the overalls her client was wearing and the name Harold flashed like a neon sign. For the first time in her professional career she was speechless.

"Is this all the evidence you have to connect my client to this matter?" She asked, somewhat cowed.

"No, like I said, counselor, I have a witness who can without doubt and complete certainty, identify your client as the fugitive of the manhunt this past evening."

"And when and where will this alleged witness make this identification, Special Agent McMurtry?"

"Right now, counselor. Officer Moran!" He called as he walked toward the entrance of the interrogation room. Officer Edith Moran stepped into the interrogation room and stood inches from Sazzar's face.

"I have been a huge fan of yours since you played football with my older brother at the U of M. Last night my partner and I approached the warehouse from the Hague side, and saw an armed suspect fleeing. We followed him for several blocks. At one point the suspect crossed the street and stood under a street light. He looked around to see if he was being followed, and that is when I saw your face. I almost went into shock when you grabbed my weapon before you struck me. It's going to break my brother's heart when I testify against you and you receive the death penalty for the murders of my fellow officers and friends."

She held her eye contact with him just as he'd done the previous evening with her, before he knocked her unconscious. Reaching inside her shirt pocket, she pulled out a photograph and laid it on the table.

"Sorry, baby!" She turned on her heels, leaving the interrogation room.

Miss Corning lifted the photo, and there, in between them, sitting on the shoulders of Sazzar and his teammate, her older brother, was a younger, smiling version of Officer Edith Moran.

"Cuff him!" said Special Agent in Charge McMurtry.

C H A P T E R   5

"I wouldn't do that if I were you!" shouted Detective Donoghue, stepping between Sazzar and the FBI agents. "Mr. Robinson is in the custody of the St. Paul police as a suspect in the murders of two of St. Paul's most respected citizens, Mr. and Mrs. Hellman, and the prime suspect in the murders of ten St. Paul police officers.

"Excuse me, Detective Donoghue is it?"

"Yes, and who are you?" Donoghue inquired.

"I'm the obnoxious sumbitch, known as the United States Attorney for the great State of Minnesota. I have very little, if any patience for nonsense. If you continue to interfere here, you and your men will be in cuffs, and I will personally seek charges of obstructions of justice against all of you. This is a federal matter and I suggest that you stand down." His southern drawl overwhelmed his speech.

"The fuck this is, you uppity motherfucking United States Asshole!" Donoghue was angry and holding his ground. "I don't give a shit who the hell you think you are, or what kind of titles you want to throw around. This man is under suspicion of murder, and now under arrest by the St. Paul Police Department for the brutal murders of ten," Detective Donoghue held up all ten fingers. "Count them Mr. U.S. Asshole, ten of St. Paul's finest, not to mention the injuries he caused to forty other officers."

"Let me tell you something, you pork belly piece-of-shit,

beat- walking flatfoot fuck!" The U.S. Attorney shouted, wagging his finger. "There were federal agents in that warehouse, not to mention a ton of cocaine, five hundred kilos of heroin, and enough Ecstasy to have your great-granddaughter doing the freaky-deaky with the neighbor's bulldog. With all the automatic gunfire, and the use of a phosphorous grenade, the St. Paul Police Department is out of their league. Now, I am going to give the order to cuff this man. Shall you and your men be joining him?" The U.S. Attorney's anger matched the detective's disposition.

Donoghue hated the idea of cowering before this son of a bitch, and Sazzar could sense it.

He turned and slammed his fist into the wall, punching a nice size hole in it.

"I take it from that body language that you don't wish to interfere?" The U.S. Attorney stated.

"Suck out the crack of my ass with a straw when I got diarrhea, you lousy cocksucker!" Donoghue punched another hole in the wall.

"Hot damn! Now that's a no for certain from this angry sumbitch. Special Agent McMurtry, cuff Mr. Robinson."

"Don't worry, Mr. Robinson. I'm going to call Mr. Grayford and inform him of this situation," said Miss Corning. "I'm sure he's going to want to deal with this matter personally." Directing her next statement to U.S. Attorney Hughes, she said, "Do not speak to my client outside of my presence. Do you understand that, Mr. United States Attorney?" She moved her fingers in the form of sign language.

"By golly, she's got a set of nuts on her the size of the IDS Building. Okay counselor, you want to play too? Alright; are you sleeping with your client?"

"What the fuck kind of question is that?" She stepped forward, her shoulders squared and head held high, looking the U.S. Attorney directly in his beady-ass little eyes.

"Besides the fact that when I came in you two were holding hands, it's been my experience that it is impossible for a criminal defense attorney to effectively represent defendants in a sophisticated organized crime or drug organization without getting into bed with them. Now!" He shouted. "Shall I launch an investigation against you as well, counselor?"

Ignoring him, she turned to Sazzar. "Whatever you do, Mr. Robinson, do not speak to this man under any circumstances without myself or Mr. Grayford present." She instructed before she opened her cell phone, then turned on her heels, like the shit was choreographed, and walked out the room.

C H A P T E R   6

Sazzar was seated in a large conference room in downtown St. Paul's Federal Building, which housed the offices of the FBI. He counted the marshals and the FBI agents present in the room. Ten in all, the United States Attorney making eleven.

"Listen, Sazzar. I can call you Sazzar, can't I?" United States Attorney Hughes said with a smile.

"Whatever floats your boat."

"Whatever floats my boat, I like that. A sense of humor. Let's see if you still feel that way after you hear what I have to say. When I get through with the grand jury, there will be fifty or more counts in the indictment related to the drug trafficking operation uncovered in the warehouse alone. With the murder of a federal agent, and the locals, I'm going to see to it that you get lethally injected. Do you understand what I'm saying, Sazzar?"

Sazzar said nothing. His silence prompted the U.S. Attorney to change direction.

"Sazzar, you are a professional athlete, adored by millions of fans. I can say that your career as an NFL running back has come to an end, as are your hopes of being inducted into the NFL Hall of Fame. However, I can save your life if you give me full and complete cooperation, and truthful testimony in helping to convict the others responsible. The government will agree to seek only ten years of prison time on your behalf. Furthermore, despite the drugs involved in this case, neither your homes, nor you fortune will be bothered."

Sazzar raised his head looking the U.S. Attorney in his eyes. "Isn't this something you should be discussing with my attorney?"

"Listen, Sazzar, ethics guidelines forbid contact between prosecutors and defendants unless the defendant's counsel is present. However, there is a loophole. It's called the Thornburg Rule. This rule allows you to talk to me without your attorney's knowledge."

"Let me get this straight. You're telling me that if I cooperate, all I will receive is a ten year prison sentence?"

"In the name of expedient justice, Sazzar. It's a one-time offer."

"Do I have time to think about it, talk it over with my attorney?"

"Sazzar, listen to me and listen good. Agent McMurtry can take your black ass back to the St. Paul police and turn you over to that nice detective. If you survive until tomorrow morning, and you're not swinging from the ceiling of your cell, you can take your chances with an all-white Minnesota jury of your peers. As I've said, this is the only offer you are going to receive from me."

Sazzar's eyes met the U.S. Attorney's. "I don't want any jail time, of any kind, and absolutely no prison sentence. Also, I want to be in protective custody starting right now with the ten men in this room, and lasting until the sentences are pronounced. Otherwise no deal!"

"Kiss my lily-white ass. You bargaining with me, Sazzar?"

"It's a one-time offer," said Sazzar.

"I can flush your superstar ass down the toilet and still be a hero in the headlines. The shit you'd have to tell me would have to be more precious than the Black Stone in the Kabba at Mecca for me to give you a deal like that," U.S. Attorney Hughes laughed.

Sazzar sat back and considered that the next sentence that flowed from his mouth would mean his life--or his death.

"What is your name, sir?"

"Evan Hughes, add the USA to it and that's who I am."

"Mr. Hughes, the statement I'm about to make, and the story I can tell, should you accept my proposal, will make your name a household word. The shit leading up to the warehouse is bigger, and far greater than anything you have encountered in your career. The trial would be epic. As a matter of fact, the O.J. Simpson case would pale in comparison."

"You have my attention, Sazzar." U.S. Attorney Hughes leaned across the table within inches of Sazzar's face.

"This case has several high-profile and very successful people involved. A leak from this room of their involvement, every man in this room would be dead within twenty-four hours. To get your juices flowing, I'll give you two titles only, no names. You give me my deal, I'll fill in the blanks."

U.S. Attorney Hughes laughed raucously, and when he finally calmed down he used a napkin to dab at the moisture in the corner of his eyes.

"I've got nothing to lose and everything to gain it appears, Mr. Shanally Robinson III."

Sazzar sat ramrod straight in his chair, taking his time to look each and every man in the room in the eyes. Saving Special Agent McMurtry for last, he held eye contact with him and said, "Tell your boss that one of the men involved in the warehouse was a United States Senator, and another an Assistant United States Attorney for the District of Minnesota.

"My bullshit alarm just went off big time. However, Sazzar, I'm inclined to give you the deal just to hear the names."

Sazzar remained quiet as the U.S. Attorney considered his offer. After a few minutes, Hughes sighed. "Two years of probation, no jail time whatsoever, and the immediate protective custody with the ten men in this room. You have my word."

Sazzar leaned forward on the table. "Your United States Senator is Kenneth Wendell, and the Assistant United States Attorney is Ronnie Green."

"Kiss my mother's beloved shriveled-up southern white ass, you better have one hell of a story to tell. Senator Wendell and his lovely wife Tanya have spent many a night at my dining room table, and so have the Greens. Goddammit Sazzar, Ronnie Green is one of my most aggressive prosecuting attorneys, and is the successor to my job. He's going to be the first black U.S. Attorney for the State of Minnesota."

"When I finish telling this story, the only concern you are going to have is the millions you are going to receive for the book rights." Sazzar sat back like the CEO that he was.

"McMurtry!" shouted the U.S. Attorney.

"Yes, sir."

"Let's get some cameras set up as soon as possible, and get my personal stenographer. I don't want this thing leaking before we can get this whole thing set up."

"Right away, sir," said Special Agent in Charge McMurtry.

* * *

Within the hour Sazzar was in a different conference room with the United States Attorney and a very angry defense counsel.

"Where do you want me to start?"

"The beginning has always been good for me, Sazzar. How about you, counselor Corning?"

"Go fuck yourself, Hughes!" She spat.

"Please counselor, you first. I'm sure it would be much more enjoyable to watch you perform an act of self-satisfaction than myself," U.S. Attorney Hughes said, as he poured himself a glass of water, then added. "Sazzar, while you're telling the story, don't skip around. Give every little detail, no matter how insignificant you may think they are. Let me and my staff sort out the details of the case."

"Is there any other way to tell a story?" Sazzar said.

C H A P T E R   7

My whole damn life changed on August 1, 1994, my sixteenth birthday, when I met J.L. I never knew his name until I heard it called in a courtroom months later. Most people around the hood just called him Three-Sixty or Three-Six.

Three-Six pulled up on the corner of Victoria and Selby Avenue in his 1991 Cadillac Sedan Deville, ice cream white with navy blue interior, sitting on gangster whitewalls.

I was on the corner with a few of the fellas who played with me on the St. Paul Central's high school football team. We were always awe-inspired to see this sixteen-year-old player. Now don't get me wrong, I had my own rep as a jock, but Three-Six had his own car, clothes, jewelry, furnished apartment, and the finest woman in the hood. I'd wanted desperately to see inside his world, so I damn near went into shock when the window of the Caddy rolled down slowly and Three-Six spoke.

"Shanally Robinson, can I have a word with you, brother?"

I was like a deer caught in the headlights of a speeding semi. There was a thunderous pounding in my heart. Maybe it was fear, maybe it was my heart warning me to just run away. But my dumb ass summoned up the courage and I recklessly stepped over to his car.

"Three-Six, what's up, my man?" I tried to sound cool.

"I need a favor from you, Shanally." He didn't even look in my direction.

Before I could think of what to say, my damn mouth betrayed me. "Sure Three-Six, I'll do you a favor."

"Get in." He pushed the power door-locks.

The damn pounding in my chest was warning me not to get into that Caddy, but all of my waking teenage life I had been fascinated by this rising ghetto star in front of me. My desire to be a part of his world ruled out my fears, and I opened the passenger door and slid in.

As soon as the door closed I knew I had to have one. Hell, I'd made up my mind right then that from that moment on I was going to be a player!

For five minutes we cruised the neighborhood, the Kenwood sound system pumping out the sounds of Public Enemy No. 1, until Three-Six pulled the Caddy over and killed the engine. There was an awkward silence that followed and then he spoke.

"You and I have something in common, Shanally. Do you know what that is?"

Perplexed at the question, I simply answered, "What's that?"

"Our girls, they're cousins."

"Lynn and Tina are cousins?" This was news that excited me.

"Calm down brother, it's not like I said that we're long-lost family reunited. Tina told me how Lynn has been playing you with regards to your newborn son. Shanally, her reasoning is lame for why she's refusing to allow you to see your son. I'm here to offer you my help. That is if you're game for it."

All the while Three-Six was talking about Lynn and our son, a wave of nausea churned in my stomach. I was glad I was sitting down, the sick feeling that had come over me had me light headed.

I regrouped and pulled myself together. "Yeah, I'm down for your help, Three-Six."

"Good!" He smiled flashing his pearly whites. "But do me a favor. From now on just call me Six."

"Sure, Six." I stared at him with adoration, experiencing a lot of emotions. I didn't know whether to laugh or cry; the feeling alone that someone was actually going to help me be a part of my son's life was overwhelming. Back then, you see, I sometimes felt like a whore being pimped for my athletic ability. The way I saw it this smooth-talking young black man sitting across from me had just released me from the nineties black trap. You know, born black, born male, and pimped by white America because of my athletic prowess.

Unfortunately, here it was, a third pitch to swing at, and it was being thrown by one of my own, and not by the white establishment.

"Can I ask you something, Six?"

"Sure, Shanally. What is it?"

"Do you know where my son is now?"

"Right now I do."

"Where?" Aware that I was shouting, I looked into my lap trying to find a place to calm myself.

After a few seconds of silence Six answered my question.

"Your son and Lynn are with Tina at Dunning Field watching this fool Marcus, who's pushed up on your girl, and the local B-Ballers run the court."

The disgust in his voice, and the way he said 'Marcus' ignited an immediate hatred for this nigga in my soul.

"Marcus? Who the fuck is Marcus?" I didn't know if I sounded hard or jealous.

Six faced me. "Marcus is about twenty-four, did some time in Stillwater Prison. Right now he works out at the auto plant in Highland Park. Lynn's gold-digging ass has latched onto Captain Save-A-Ho because the nigga wants to be you. He wants to be the one to buy your son clothes, diapers and shit. He's a no good mothafucka and I don't like him. Now, do you want to do me the favor I've asked of you?"

"Yeah Six, I'm ready. What's the favor?"

"You know old man Hellman's Market on Selby and Dale?"

"Sure Six, everybody knows Mr. Hellman. Good old man, he sponsors scholarships at the high school for us."

"Today is the day, my friend, that old man Hellman gets

the money from his bank to cash the weekly payroll checks for the people in the hood. I want to rob this bitch-ass old man, but he knows me because I work for him."

"So how can I help you, Six?" He might need a getaway driver, I thought.

"I want you to rob old man Hellman's Market for me."

"What's in it for me if it's a favor for you?" I witnessed a complete change in his facial expression.

"I'll kick shit down Marcus' leg when you give Lynn some of the money, help you get your family back together."

"I can rob the store and beat the hell out of this nigga Marcus who got my girl. I ain't no punk, Six," I was feeling a genuine need to pour out the vials of rage trapped inside of me.

"Calm down, big fella, nobody is testing your manhood. Plus I've seen the way you run on the football field. Takes heart to play the way you do, but this game is different." He handed me a .45 automatic.

C H A P T E R 8

I took the gun and held it in my hand. My dumb ass didn't even have the sense God gave me to feel the tiniest delicious tingle of fear. Instead, I devoured it with my eyes. In my hands was the first gun I'd ever held in my life, and I was about to point it at someone.

"Shanally! It ain't no woman, man. You ever shot a gun before?"

"Yeah, when my pops was alive I shot his gun lots of times. He had one just like this one," I lied.

"Good, there's a round chambered and the clip is full. Just release the safety if you need to fire the gun."

"Is this the safety?" I flipped the switch.

"Yeah Shanally. You sure you down for this lick, man?"

"Hell yeah, Six, this ain't the first time I've robbed a store. I've done this shit before," I lied again. The closest I'd ever come to robbing anything was my little cousin's piggy bank.

"Alright partner, here's my deal. You go into the market and just point the gun at old man Hellman. Shanally, he's a stone-cold coward, and will give up the money without any problems. The money is in a small box that he keeps under the counter in a safe. The door to the safe is always open, just pull the lever. Shanally, there is at least ten-thousand dollars in that box. When you come out with the box in hand, you will be four-thousand dollars richer."

"Four grand... For me?" I gripped the gun in my hand.

"Yeah, Shanally. Four grand, all yours." Six had this devilish grin on his face, which I learned later in our friendship meant fuck the whole wide world, and any living soul that got in his way.

Looking to my left for the first time, I could see that Six had parked the Caddy in the alleyway on Dale and Selby. Hellman's Market was less than thirty yards away. Reaching under the seat, he pulled out a mask. It looked like the kind we wore during the winters around Minnesota. When he passed the mask, he had a look on his face like a parent about to chastise a child.

"Make sure you put the mask on before you go into the market. Okay, Shanally?"

"Yeah Six, yeah!"

"Yeah what, Shanally?"

"Put the mask on before I go into the market. I got it, I got it!" I was irritated with his instructions, like I was stupid or something.

I exited the Caddy, mask in one hand, .45 in the other . I mumbled under my breath trying to find the most authoritative pitch. This is a mothafucking stick up, give me the fucking money, I growled as I neared the entrance of Hellman's Market.

"Shanally Robinson; how is my favorite high-school running back?" Mr. Hellman had a big smile on his face. "I was at the game against Highland Park. Two touchdowns, one from seventy-five yards out. Son, you run just like Walter Payton. One hell of a game, one hell of a game. What can I do for you son?"

I stood there frozen, just a foot inside the doorway. My dumb ass forgot to put on the mask.

"This is a stick up ... mo-money the gimme!" I stammered as I brandished the weapon that literally vibrated in my sweaty palms.

"Now son, just calm down. I won't give you any problems. Why don't you put the gun down and the two of us can talk about what it is that's troubling you," Mr. Hellman pleaded with me, just like Six said he would.

I've thought about it a million times since that day, but I guess it was the old man's cowering that renewed my self-confidence. I cocked the hammer back on the .45 and rushed the counter to try and put the fear of God in him. My thoughts were that if I roughed him up a bit, maybe threaten to kill him, he wouldn't call the police. I could then return my portion of the money ... give it back, you know, apologize and move on with my life, if that was possible.

I raised the .45 over my head, and with a sweep of my arm I slapped the gun against Mr. Hellman's head. When the .45 crashed into his head a deafening explosion filled the air. At first I thought he'd shot at me and I dropped to the floor trembling like a coward lying in the fetal position and stood, scanning the market's interior -- Mr. Hellman was nowhere in sight.

Fearing the worst, I leaned over the counter, and there on the floor was Mr. Hellman lying in a puddle of his own blood, the back of his head missing. The sight of his brains wasting away on the floor caused my stomach to do flips, and I ejected the White Castle hamburgers I'd eaten earlier all over the counter, and onto Mr. Hellman's lifeless body.

I heard a scream and went numb. I managed to turn around and was in the direct path of Mrs. Hellman, who had been in the butcher shop and was now shouting, "Shanally Robinson, you son-of-a-bitch, you killed my husband. I'm going to kill you!"

I just stood there as she charged me with the butcher knife in her raised hand. I was prepared to let her take my life for what I'd done, and let the .45 I was holding drop to the floor. Just when I'd closed my eyes and was asking God for forgiveness, I heard two quick shots. I opened my eyes to see Mrs. Hellman standing directly in front of me, her eyes wide open with surprise, and blood oozing from her forehead as she slumped to the floor in front of me.

Six stepped over her body and shouted for me to grab the box behind the counter. "I'm going for the videotape, grab the fucking money, Shanally. Now!" he moved to the back of the store.

I found my legs and crawled over the counter, slipping in Mr. Hellman's blood and falling on top of him. With blood-stained hands I frantically grabbed everything I could put my hands on to stand up. When Six returned with the surveillance tape, he picked up the .45 off the floor and speaking softly, coached me and the metal box from behind the counter and out of the market into our new lives.

CHAPTER 9

Six walked out of the market with the intention of killing any potential witness, but to his delight and surprise the parking lot was empty, not a single soul had been witness to our crime.

He led me back to the Caddy and opened the passenger door, pushing me inside. I immediately began to pray when Six closed the door.

"I didn't mean it, God, I didn't mean to kill Mr. Hellman. Please God, please forgive me," was all Six heard when he opened his door and sat behind the wheel, pulling off his mask and gloves and stuffing them under his seat.

Six started the Caddy and pulled into traffic. I sat there repeating my prayer over and over, as if the words themselves would bring the Hellmans back to life.

The shit must have really irritated Six. "Shanally, stop with all the melancholy shit, killer, we got out of there scot free, and we have to get rid of these guns and stash the money. You hear me, Shanally? Shanally!"

"Yeah, I hear you, Six. I'm just trying to understand what I've done to my life. It's over before it's even started. I'm going to prison." I dropped my head letting my face fall into my hands.

"What you've done!" He looked at me while laughing.

"Going to prison!" he shouted. "You don't feel this power? This guiltless freedom? You stupid mothafucka, we ain't going to prison, and yo' ass is four-thousand dollars richer. So snap out of it and open that damn box on your lap."

I dropped my hands, and shaking uncontrollably, I managed after several attempts to open the clasp on the box. I started to say something about how sorry I was for falling apart, but instead when I opened the metal box on my lap the sight of the money temporarily put a halt to my mourning, and I began pulling out neatly stacked twenties, fifties, and hundred-dollar bills. Together we counted the bundles individually wrapped, each with a sticker that read 'One thousand dollars'.

We spoke in unison, "Twenty thousand dollars!"

Six steered the Caddy into the nearest alley, next to a garage shielded by some overgrowth. "Look partner," he began, turning towards me as he draped the hand that held the .380 automatic over the seat. "It's you and me; we can split the money down the middle, or you can get out right here. It's your call, Shanally." He had a look in his eyes that even to this day I can't describe.

"That won't be happening, Six. I'm already too far in to turn back now." My voice seemed to betray my fear. Even Six did a double take as he let the hammer ease down on the .380 he held in his hand.

"Down the middle, partner. You've just made yourself ten thousand dollars. But you still have to do something to earn it."

"What's that, Six?" I became damn near jubilant.

"Damn man, what happened to I'm going to prison, boo-hoo-hoo?" Six teased.

"It was the moment. That moment is behind me now. What else do I have to do, Six?"

Six began shaking his head from side to side with a confused look on his face. "Inside of you is a heartless mothafucka, you know that, Shanally? Here, take these guns and pull some of those Kleenex out of the glove box and wipe the blood off of your face."

"What do you want me to do with the guns?"

"How is your arm?"

"Six, I'm a jock. I can throw a pigskin in the air sixty yards before it touches the ground."

"Damn homey, I just want you to throw them out the window when I tell you to."

"That's it?"

"Yep, that's it." He put the Caddy in gear and drove out of the alley.

We sat on Marshall Avenue at the entrance to the Lake Street Bridge which separates St. Paul from Minneapolis. "What are we waiting for, Six?"

"We need to be the last car on the bridge, don't want anyone in our business. You ready, Shanally?"

"For ten-thousand dollars, hell yeah!"

Six dropped the Caddy into gear and pulled onto the bridge. Nearing the center, he checked the traffic from behind and the oncoming traffic and shouted, "Now Shanally!"

I tossed the .45 first and then the .380. When I rolled up the window both of us breathed a sigh of relief. The murder weapons were resting indictment-free at the bottom of the Mississippi River. The videotaped evidence of our crime was lying atop a metal box with twenty-thousand dollars in it.

"Shanally."

"Yeah, Six?"

"We need to get you and this car cleaned up. We're about the same size ... I've got some clothes in the trunk for times like this."

"Is there anything you don't think of, Six?"

"Not really. I was taught by a very special man to always plan to the end."

Years later, during a conversation, 'from the heart' he called it, he confessed to me that on that day in the alley, he was going to shoot me in the head.

CHAPTER 10

"Yeaah Marcus!" Lynn bellowed as Marcus dunked the ball on an alley-oop pass from one of his teammates. "So Miss Tee, how do you like my new man?" Lynn nervously twirled her hair around her finger.

"What's not to like? Six-four, two-hundred pounds, solid, Fine as hell, has a job, hustles on the side, seems to like yo' stankin' ass, and doing all this while on parole from prison, I might add."

"Girl, that ain't nothing. Don't sweat the small stuff. He'll be off parole in eight months and we'll be moving to Indiana."

"Indiana!" Tina sat with a stunned look on her face, her eyes growing wide with surprise as she threw her hands in the air as a sign of exasperation, breathed a long sigh and rolled her eyes. "Besides being the home of the Ku-Klux-Klan with five-hundred-thousand card-carrying members, bitch, you'd have to be out of your white girl-hatin'-ass mind to move down there. Plus you don't know nothing about this man, besides the size of his dick. He's been to prison for God knows what: he could be a woman beater or a child molester for all you know. And on top of all that, yo' dumb ass is only sixteen and this man is twenty-four. If you ask me, the pretty nigga is trouble." Tina had gotten worked up and was aggressively sticking her finger in Lynn's face.

"Nobody's asking for your permission, bitch!" Lynn pushed Tina's finger from her face. "The brotha give up the money for me and my son, Tee. Just yesterday he took us shopping and spent nearly a thousand dollars on us."

"Oh yeah! I bet yo' ass fucked like a University Avenue hooker." Tina teased, thinking how a University Avenue hooker would suck a dog's dick for a hit of crack, or an Alexander Hamilton.

"Bitch please, all he wanted was for me to spend some time with him. Hell, he shows my fine high-yella ass off more than he wants sex."

"Damn Lynn, that's pathetic! You an arm candy ho', too? Your damn stitches ain't even healed yet, and you already doing the nasty with a man who might have just pulled his dick out of a man's ass. You know how these fools are coming out of prison. They like the dick more than we do."

"Stop that shit, Tina!" Lynn cautioned. "He's not like that girl, he's real cool. Truth is, because I just had the baby, he hasn't tried to get the kitty yet."

"See, that proves my point. Dude got to be on boys. Shanally had yo freaky-ass doing it doggy style within the first hour of knowing you."

"Fuck you, Cuz, Marcus ain't like that. He's just taking care of me and Corey, maybe make some babies of his own from these childbearing hips and ass." She gave herself a soft pat on her shapely derriere. "Besides," She grinned inscrutably, "Marcus ain't got nothing but some of my deep throat."

"You lying cow. Yo' monkey is glowing red hot in them Daisy Dukes old boy got you wearing."

"What, you jealous? Since yo' ass decided to stop grinding on Six and open your legs, yo' ass been walking around this bitch bowlegged. Six done gone and knocked the bottom out of that twat."

"Now I know yo' skank ass did not just go there." Tina was visibly irritated.

"What, bitch! You can dish it out but you can't take it?" Tina said nothing.

"Oh, now yo' ass is in yo' feelings. Stop being so damn sensitive, Tina. We talk this ghetto shit to each other all the time. Truth be told, Six probably dusted that twat off before he dropped yo' ass off. So who be calling who a ho, ho? Ohhhhh ... Ohhhhh! Did you see that? My man just went coast to coast and slammed that shit," Lynn bellowed.

Damn Lynn, dudes cum must be love potion number nine. You've swallowed it and yo' ass is madly in love. What about Shanally?"

"Shanally, ha! Cuz, that nigga ain't nothing but a sperm donor. Oooooh baby, go baby!" Lynn cheered as Marcus blocked a shot and was moving the ball down the court.

"Lynn, Shanally is your baby's daddy, and just before Corey was born he was the only man for you .Girl, remember when you said 'I could live happy homeless if I had to as long as I was living in that box with Shanally'?" Tina mocked Lynn.

"Little do you know Shanally, Cuz, he's only sixteen and is more of a kid than a man, he's not like Six or Marcus. He's not going to work a job, pay bills, hustle, nothing. Lynn leaned forward, arms resting on her knees, intent that every word she spoke pierced Tina's ears, as she rung home her truth. "That's why I left his ass at the hospital."

After giving Tina a minute to digest her version of the truth, she continued. "He ain't gonna be shit, Miss Tee, wishing and hoping for a scholarship to play football and go to college."

Duplicating Lynn's posture, mirroring her image, Tina responded, "Lynn, that shit you're talking is silly. Shanally loves you, and he has million dollar NFL contract and endorsements written all over him like tattoos. Not only is your ass dumb, you're impatient."

"Impatient my ass, Tina. Tell that shit to my son, your nephew, when he needs diapers, milk, baby food, clothing, and not to mention a little thing desperately needed during the forty-and fifty-below zero temperatures: shelter. Besides, I can't afford to wait eight years hoping and praying for an NFL contract."

"And why not, Lynn?"

"It's not a given, Tina. There's no guarantee that he'll even get a scholarship. What happens if he breaks something? Too many ifs, Miss Tee. So I'm going to latch on to me and Corey a future now before it's too late. Yeah, that's my baby!" Lynn shouted as everyone jumped to their feet screaming when Marcus slammed the ball over a seven footer. Lynn turned back to Tina. "Now that's a man!"

During a lull in the action and a short time out, Lynn broke the silence that had come between her and her only true friend.

"Listen Tina, you know I love you, don't you?"

"And I you." Tina watched the smile form on Lynn's face.

"When we were growing up in those foster homes everyone thought you and I were sisters. Two high-yella fine-ass bitches. Damn if we didn't drive the niggas crazy! Over the years you've become the only family I have. You'll always be a part of me, Tina, but right now I'm on my own with an infant son, and I need a man's help. I just pray the one I've found will love me as much as Six loves yo' stankin' ass. So please, Miss Tee, be happy for me and my son that we've found someone who wants to love and support us cause good for nothing Shanally Robinson can't make the rent, buy diapers, or give me anything except a little dick."

"And Marcus will give you what you think you need?"

"Yes Tina, he will."

The sound of loud voices caused Tina to look down in the baby- stroller to check on her nephew. She stifled a sigh. Young fools, she thought. So full of passion, so damn impulsive over a damn basketball game. She glanced at her watch, Six would be here any minute. He said he had a plan to get Shanally and Lynn back together for her nephew's sake.

CHAPTER 11

Six walked out of the Lyndale Motel and the air seemed to be electric with his plans. He had heard on the news of the Hellmans' deaths; no witnesses, no suspects. His focus was fixed and unshakeable. I closed the door standing next to Six, our shadows gradually blurring in the haze of the summer heat.

"Shanally, you drive, man?"

"What sixteen-year-old youngster in the State of Minnesota you know, don't drive?"

"You answered my question with a question, so I'm going to assume you do." He tossed me the keys and for the first time sat on the passenger side of his car.

"Thanks for the clothes and putting me onto this motel with the kitchenette, Six."

"What are friends for, my brother?"

"How'd you find this place anyway?"

"I get around, Shanally."

"I get around. That's all you got to say, I get around?" I teased him in a playful manner as I drove the Caddy onto Lyndale Avenue.

"It wouldn't matter if I told you how I found it anyway. Some things are better left unsaid."

"You think?"

"Cogito, ergo sum."

"What the fuck did you just say?"

"I said cogito, ergo sum. It's Latin. It means 'I think, therefore I am'. The phrase was coined by Rene Descartes."

"Rene De who?"

"Rene Descartes. He was a French philosopher."

"So how does a sixteen-year-old come to know the sayings of a French philosopher?"

"I spend a great deal of time with a man who shows me an existential way of thinking."

"A what?"

"Don't trip, Shanally, and watch the road, man. Potholes are vicious around here."

"I'm doing the driving, my man. Calm down, I'm not gonna fuck up your ride." I expertly maneuvered the Caddy around the hole in the street.

"You do and your ass is paying for the repairs."

"No problem Six, got plenty of cash. Now get back to this exist- whatever."

"Existential, means in layman's terms: one thinks for one's self, therefore one is responsible for one's own actions. Hence the phrase cogito, ergo sum. If you paid attention in class as hard as you do on the football field, you'd know this shit."

"Damn man, that was cold. Did you just call me stupid?"

"A mind is a terrible thing to waste, Mr. Shanally Robinson. And another thing, if we're going to hang out together you've to lose the slave name."

"Naw man, my grandfather and my father's name are Shanally Robinson. I'm third generation." I poked my chest out with pride.

"You still need a street name."

"So what do you suggest?"

"Well my brotha, first take the Snelling exit and drive straight down Concordia. We'll park on the dorm side of Concordia College and walk to the field. As for your name, deep inside you a warrior king has emerged, so I'm going to call you Sazzar. Phonetically pronouncing it Say-zar."

"Sazzar, I like it. What does it mean?"

"Magnate, Baron King, Merchant Prince, Mogul, Tycoon; take your pick."

"I like Sazzar. I think I'll keep it."

"Good, park here and we can walk to the park from here. Don't want people seeing what we're riding in if Marcus wants to be a problem."

CHAPTER 12

"Six, are you sure Lynn is here with my son?" I looked around as we walked onto Dunning Field.

"Absolutely, Lynn would never leave Tina alone or vice versa. They're so tight I sometimes have to pry them apart." Six's smile widened at the sight of his girl.

"Six!" Tina stood up doing a little shimmy before running from the bleachers and into her man's arms.

"Damn baby, I find you more beautiful every time I see you.

"Tell me, do you ever look at yourself to see how truly beautiful you really are?"

"You are such a romantic. Do you always say things to women with such complete endearment?"

"Only one." Six looked deeply into her eyes.

"Well, in that case, I see myself as being very beautiful every morning I wake up and see that smile on your face. Now kiss me!" she demanded.

"Hey Six," Lynn chimed.

"Hey Lynn, where's Corey?"

"In his stroller sleeping," Lynn responded, not having noticed Shanally.

"Hi Shannally, silk looks good on you, boy. You clean up well."

"Hey Miss Tee, and it's Sha-nally not Shannally, and thanks for the compliment."

"Boy, stop being so damn sensitive." Tina laughed at him.

"Not sensitive, Miss Tee, just growing up. Anyway as of today you can drop the Shannally and call me, Sazzar."

"Hello, Sazzar."

"Hey, Miss Tee." I walked over to the stroller while Six and Tina looked on and lifted the sleeping infant into my arms. "Hey, little man, my name is Shanally Lamar Robinson III, and I am your father." Corey's little eyes opened and a smile graced his precious face. The sight of my son smiling at me melted my heart. "I'm never gonna let you out of my sight, ever again. I promise."

Lynn took her eyes from the action on the basketball court and her casual gaze in my direction held that same unreadable expression I'd seen that night at the hospital when she walked out of my life with my newborn son. But that was about to change. I had my son in my arms and I had no intentions of giving him up.

"Shanally, give me my baby!" Lynn acted a bit more aggressively than she meant.

"Bitch!" I exploded. "My name is Sazzar, and I haven't seen your good dick-suckin', once a month bleeding, funky deserting- ass since our son was born, and all you got to say to me is give my baby?"

"Sazzar!" she hissed. "Who the fuck do you think you are calling your sorry-ass self Sazzar?"

"That's my name and this is my son, and I'm taking care of him now."

"With what, Shanally? Yo' broke ass ain't got nothing, nigga, and that precious bitch of a mother of yours don't give a fuck. Hell, she wouldn't even come to the hospital to meet her grandson. So fuck you and your family, Sazzar, and give me my mothafucking baby!"

"Listen Lynn," I began, my voice calm, my mind, body and soul under complete control. "I've got plenty of money for your materialistic ass. I've rented a kitchenette in South Minneapolis with a pool, so you, me, and our son can spend the summer together. By the time school starts in September we'll have our own place in St. Paul." Taking her hand in mine and looking into her eyes, I tried to locate the woman I'd made this beautiful baby boy with.

"Lynn, I just want the chance to take care of our son, to be the responsible father and man that I know I can be for you and our son."

"Nigga, please!" She spat the words at me snatching her hand from mine. "You show up here wearing Six's clothes, change your name, and feel this makes you a man ready to take care of your son? I saw yo' trifling ass walking down Selby the other day with the same old funky-ass clothes you had on the day I left yo' stankin' black ass at the hospital. Yo broke ass ain't got no mo-."

Before Lynn could get the word money out of her mouth, I slapped her with ten crisp one-hundred-dollar bills. "One-thousand dollars for your gold-digging ass. Don't worry about my son, I got him. This money is for you to do whatever you please." I stood proud as the money cascaded all around her.

The sting from the slap left Lynn momentarily stunned. She stared into my eyes with complete disbelief; a mixture of fear and respect. You see, I'd never struck Lynn before. I touched her hand gently and she began to kneel as if she were bowing before me. She began picking up the money, holding on to my hand, afraid to let go.

"You, me, and our son, Lynn. I can be his father and a man for you. But you have to trust me." I was enjoying the thrill of the moment.

From the basketball court all Marcus saw was a nigga slapping the dog shit out of his woman, and no man was gonna disrespect Marcus or his woman. I never saw Marcus coming. Lynn could see the look of murder in his eyes and jerked her hand from mine, frantically reaching for our son.

Marcus' forearm smashed into my head driving me face first into the ground. My son screamed in pain as his tiny body fell to the ground between his parents. Tina ran to Lynn's side to aid and assist Corey while Marcus commenced to kick my ass with his size 14 Air Jordan's.

In his rage Marcus could not hear Lynn screaming. "My baby, my baby!" All he could see was the nigga beneath him who had disrespected his woman. "Nigga, I'm gonna kill you!" Marcus gave me a vicious kick to my ribs, and then my jaw that splashed blood on Lynn, Tina, and my baby.

Frank Peterson, the custodian of the park, dialed 911 and reported the fight, and the possible injuries to an infant child. It seemed sirens sounded from all directions simultaneously, and with each second that passed they grew louder as police and ambulances emerged onto Dunning Field

C H A P T E R   1 3

Time stood still when the first shot rang out.

Everyone in the park turned to see the gunman walking towards Marcus firing his weapon. The first shot hit Marcus high in the right shoulder, the second in the hip, the third and fourth shots hit him, point blank range, at the base of his spine.

Officer Ronnie O'Neal had just pulled out of Hardy's restaurant on Hamline and St. Anthony when the call came across his radio.

No more than a minute away, O'Neal punched the accelerator and turned on his siren. His cruiser had just jumped the curb on Dunning Field when the first shot was fired.

O'Neal raced his cruiser across the field watching the gunman walking towards his victim. He broke hard and with dust flying O'Neal opened his door, weapon drawn, cocked and aimed at the back of Six's head just as he placed the .25 automatic to Marcus's temple.

"Drop the gun!" O'Neal commanded.

Tina saw O'Neal moving toward Six, and a swarm of police cars running the curb onto Dunning Field. With a look of pure pleading, she willed Officer O'Neal to temporarily stand down. As she moved toward Six, she heard Officer O'Neal, "Hold your fire!"

Everyone on the field that day will tell you that it was

Tina who saved Marcus' and her man's life that afternoon.
Whatever she whispered in Six's ear stopped him from pulling
the trigger.

    ***

Sitting in the waiting room of Children's Hospital, the
thought of our son being seriously injured tormented Lynn.

"Miss Lynn Carlson, would you please follow me." The
cute little white nurse led the way.

Every muscle in Lynn's body jumped at the sound of the
nurse's voice. She whirled around, her heart pumping at an
alarming rate.

Her breath caught midway in her throat at the sight of
being led to a wing marked Trauma Unit that had a doctor
waiting at the entrance.

"Miss Carlson, my name is Dr. Trotter and I am one of the
physicians assigned to your son's care. My main concern when
your son was admitted to the Trauma Unit was whether or not
during the fall he had sustained any head injuries.

Lynn began to cry before Dr. Trotter finished his
diagnosis. Tina embraced her and the two of them let the tears
flow. Being the professional, Dr. Trotter moved the two of
them to the reception area and patiently waited until. Lynn was
in control of her emotions before he continued.

"Miss Carlson, I've X-rayed your son from head to toe,
and did a full MRI scanning. Good news is he has no brain or
head injuries. Remarkable actually, the angels were protecting
him. However, he has sustained injuries to his left femur,
which is the long leg bone extending from his hip to his knee,
and the right tibia, which is the inner of the two bones
extending from the knee to the foot. The splintered fractures to
his arm and shoulder, thank God, were not compound
fractures, which means your baby will have a soft cast on his
body that will breath and expand during his growth.

"Now, I must caution you, when you see him it will look
worse than it is because the cast is a half-torso cast running
forty-five degrees from the shoulder to the waist, bracing the
injured arm to the chest area so there's no movement. Of
course, the same type of cast will be on his leg. Right now
your baby is resting comfortably, he has been medicated. If

you like I'll take you to see him."

Lynn stood and hugged Dr. Trotter and immediately the tears began to flow. Only this time Dr. Trotter allowed the tears to flow onto his white smock.

CHAPTER 14

"Ramsey County Hospital Emergency Room has by far the best gunshot trauma unit in the Midwest." The fat Nurse with the cigarette dangling from her lips told another nurse, as Lynn and Tina walked by her into the Emergency Room.

"Excuse me, Nurse, could you please tell me what room Shanally Robinson is in?" Tina asked the slightly plump Nurse behind the counter.

"Mr. Robinson ... ahh ... aaaaah, Mr. Robinson. Okay, he's no longer here."

"What the fuck do you mean he's not here?" Lynn asked, venting her frustrations.

"There's no need for you to take that tone with me, young lady. Mr. Robinson was treated and released to the St. Paul Police."

"Treated and released? What type of injuries did he have?" Tina wondered how bad Marcus had hurt him.

"I'm sorry, I can't give out patient information."

"Please, Nurse, he's my friend and I really need to find him.'

The Nurse looked at Tina and smiled. She looked around to see if any of her co-workers were in ear shot. "Well, Mr. Robinson had a fractured jaw and bruised ribs. As I said already he was treated and given medication for his pain."

"Why was he released to the police? Is he under arrest?" Lynn was hoping that he was.

"That's something you are going to have to ask Mr. Robinson. Sorry." She turned back to her work.

"Nurse, please excuse my rude behavior earlier, but could you please tell me what room Marcus Taylor is in?" Lynn whined like a child.

"Why sure. Are you a relative?"

"I guess you could say that. We are engaged to be married," Lynn lied through her teeth.

"So he's your fiancé?"

"Yes, he is."

"Well then, just follow this corridor to the bank of elevators Mr. Taylor's is on the fourth floor, room 4300."

"Thank you, Nurse. What is your name?"

"Ooooh my, I'm Nurse Hunt, honey. Margret Hunt."

"Thank you, Nurse Hunt, you're so nice," Lynn placed her hand on the nurse's hand.

"No problem, honey. Us girls have to stick together in this male dominated world."

"Tina, I'll only be a minute, wait for me please?" Lynn gave her best begging face to support her request.

"Lynn, walk your ass across the bridge, to the police department, it's only a few blocks away. I'll meet you there. I'm going to check on Shanally."

"Damn Tina, could you please just wait ten minutes? I promise I'll make it quick."

"Ten minutes, Lynn. After that I'm gone."

"Alright Cuz," she shouted back over her shoulder as she stepped lively toward the elevator, beaming at the thought of running her hand between Marcus's legs.

CHAPTER 15

The man at the Juvenile Detention Center just laughed when Tina asked if they were holding Jeffery Alexander Lane.

"Sorry, young lady, to be the bearer of bad news, but your friend has moved on up to the big leagues. He's being held by the St. Paul Police Department at the Ramsey County Jail. From what I'm hearing from my deputy friend, he is going to be charged, certified, and tried as an adult. Couldn't've happened to a nicer guy." He smiled sarcastically.

Before Tina could mount all the curse words in her vocabulary to serve this dumb ass man, Lynn asked, "Is Six's name Jeffery?"

"Yeah Lynn, you got a fucking problem with that?" Tina faced Lynn, her brown eyes burning with anger.

"Naw girl, just asking," Lynn cowed under her angry friend's stare.

When Tina just stood there saying nothing, Lynn asked in a soft girly voice, "So what do we do now, Tee?"

"We can't go back to the police department. They told us no to come back unless we were in the company of an adult."

Finding her confidence, Lynn pressed, "So I'll ask the damn question again. What do we do now?"

"We find a phone." Tina headed for the door.

C H A P T E R   1 6

The next morning, Six was escorted from the Ramsey County Jail to the courthouse by Sheriff's deputies. He had never seen anything like this. Inmates were being herded in an out of the holding cell speaking with public pretenders, probation officers, and of course, the snitch game: the secret selling of others' lives for freedom was being played at an all-time high, everybody was losing.

"Jeffery Lane!" bellowed a fat deputy.

"Yeah, that's me."

"Get yo' narrow ass out of that seat, boy. Judge wants to see ya."

Six figured he'd get with this trailer park trash later about his 'boy' comment, but he was confused. The old con on lock-down told him that he would speak to the public pretender first, then a probation officer, before going before the judge. Now here he was being seated in an empty courtroom with fat-ass Deputy Dawg standing guard over him.

A few minutes later a well-dressed white man with coal-black hair walked into the courtroom. He stopped at one of the tables, placed a briefcase atop it and looked directly at Six.

Six had always said that he'd seen this man's face somewhere before, but he couldn't remember where. The man motioned for him to come to his table. Reluctant, he looked to Deputy Dawg for approval. The old dude responded with a few shoulder shrugs and dismissing hand gestures, so Six moved from the jury box.

During his survival training, Six was taught that there is always a small window of opportunity, no matter the situation. On impulse he started to bolt, he knew old Deputy Dawg would never catch him, a few more feet and the hunt would be on.

Just when he was about to make his move, the courtroom doors opened, and standing directly in his path was Tina. Knowing him the way she did, she shook her head from side to side and placed four fingers to her breast. Six looked over her shoulder and saw four armed Sheriffs deputies in the hallway. He stopped dead in his tracks, where the well-dressed white man was seated.

Six said his attorney looked more like a rich playboy than a lawyer, not a trace of redneck anywhere; then he spoke.

"Mr. Lane, please have a seat."

"Who are you, and how do you know my name?"

"Well," He flashed his lustrous smile. "My name is Thomas Shaw and I've been retained by some good friends of yours, one being this lovely young woman sitting behind me. The other is Lafayette James, who happens to be a very good friend of mine. He asked me to represent you as counsel. Does that answer your question

"Yes sir." Hearing Lafayette's name allowed him to relax. He immediately abandoned his thought of running, taking a seat next to Thomas.

"Jeffery," he began, "The State of Minnesota will file a motion with the Juvenile Court for certification of your juvenile status to adult status, and it will be granted. Are you aware of this?"

"Yes sir. Jailhouse lawyers have advised me that the State will want to treat me as an adult and send me to St. Cloud Reformatory ."

"Did they also explain to you that you must make a choice as to who will have jurisdiction over your case?"

"Yes sir, I'm going to save the State a whole lot of trouble and waive my juvenile status and be tried as an adult."

"Absolutely! dog-gone-it! Lafayette said you were a quick study. Okay Jeff, let's get down to business. What I want to hear from you are answers only to the questions I ask of you, nothing more. Understood?"

"Yes sir."

"Is your name Jeffery Alexander Lane?"

"Yes sir." '

"Were you arrested August 1, 1994, for the alleged shooting of Marcus Taylor?"

"Yes sir."

"Did you make any statements to the police after your arrest?"

"No sir."

"Very good. How old are you Jeff?"

"Sixteen and a half."

"Have you ever been locked up in any of the State's juvenile facilities?"

"Yes sir. Totem Town when I was twelve."

"Okay Jeff, it's time for some reality. You were arrested by police with a gun in your hand, and a gunshot victim at your feet with multiple gunshot wounds to his body. I'm willing to bet my left testicle that a ballistic test will be a match. I'll also put the right one on the chopping block to say that the police have several witnesses who have given statements, and are willing to testify that you are the shooter. I want you to understand that whether you waive the certification hearing, or go through with it, you will be certified an adult and go to prison. As well you will go to prison if you accept what is called a 'plea bargain' from the State's prosecutor. Any questions at this point?"

"No questions, just a statement."

"What's your statement, Jeff?"

"You don't sound very promising, Mr. Shaw."

"I'm not a miracle worker, Jeff, but I am one of the best there is in the area of litigating and negotiating criminal matters in the Midwest. Any more questions or statements?"

"No sir."

"The statute you will charged under, Jeff, calls for a five-to-ten-year prison term. I believe I can persuade the prosecutor to drop the window dressing charge of 'attempted murder'. How are you following so far?"

"Well Mr. Shaw, you've said that I could spend the next ten years of my life in prison, five being the minimum, ten being the max. The attempted murder charges can be reduced to a lesser offense in the event that a plea be negotiated. Is that right?"

"It's fair to say, son, it's fair to say. Would you like for me to represent you as your counsel today and in any future proceedings?"

"Hell yeah! Now I remember where I saw your face!" Six became excited. "You're the attorney who defended that Oriental lady who murdered her lover. You were all over the news when the jury returned a not guilty verdict. People say you're the shit. I mean, you're the best attorney around."

"I take it that means yes?"

"Yes Mr. Shaw, it does."

"Very good. Deputy!" Thomas called out.

"Yes Mr. Shaw?" Deputy Dawg stood up.

"Please inform the clerk that Mr. Lane and his attorney are ready."

"Sure thing, Mr. Shaw." The old deputy waddled out of the courtroom.

"Thomas ... I mean Mr. Shaw, can I ask you a question?"

"Sure Jeff, and you can call me Thomas if you like."

"Okay Thomas. The Oriental lady that you defended, did you tell her the same thing you told me about going to prison?"

"As a matter of fact I did. However, she did not believe a word that I said."

"Should I?"

"Pretty much, Jeff. And by the way, do me a favor and sign this document."

"What is it, Thomas?"

"It's a waiver form, Jeff."

C H A P T E R   1 7

As Deputy Dawg stepped out of the courtroom, another deputy looking like he belonged in the World Wrestling Federation with a .357 revolver on his hip took his place.

A few minutes later, a man Thomas said was the prosecutor walked in followed by a court reporter. Thomas walked over and handed the prosecutor a copy of the signed waiver and returned to his seat.

Six swiveled in his seat to look at Tina, but she avoided his gaze. Slightly confused by her actions, he turned to face the bench when WWF stood up.

"All rise! This court is now in session, The Honorable Judge Clyde Davison presiding!"

Thomas and Six stood, when to Six's surprise a black man took the bench. Judge Davison nodded at Thomas and as cued he spoke.

"You Honor, if it please the court, my name is Thomas Shaw and I represent the defendant, Jeffery Alexander Lane, as counsel of record."

"Your Honor, if I may. I'm Eric Beise and I represent the great State of Minnesota."

"Let the record so reflect. Well, counsels, I understand this young man is a juvenile, and unless there is a signed waiver form as to his juvenile status, all of this is a waste of time."

"I have a waiver form signed by the defendant and his attorney, and a copy of the complaint, your Honor." Beise stepped forward and handed the documents across the bench to the judge.

"Okay Mr. Beise, looks like this young man is officially our business. I will now read the complaint. Mr. Lane, would you please stand? This is the State of Minnesota versus Jeffery Alexander Lane, SIP number 00033943, County Attorney File Number 94-3760. Mr. Lane, this morning the State has brought charges, a three-count complaint, against you. The first count is attempted first degree murder, stating that on August 1, 1994, in Ramsey County, Minnesota, Jeffery Alexander Lane, while using a firearm, attempted to cause the death of Marcus Taylor a human being, with the intent to effect the death of that person.

"Count two of the complaint is assault one, great bodily harm, stating that on or about August 1, 1994, in Ramsey County, Minnesota, Jeffery Alexander Lane, while using a firearm, caused great bodily harm to Marcus Taylor, a human being, when he intentionally shot the victim four times. Two of the wounds inflicted upon the victim were at the base of the spine causing paralysis of the lower extremities.

"Count three, Mr. Lane, is carrying a firearm without a permit, stating that on or about August 1, 1994, in Ramsey County, Minnesota, Jeffery Alexander Lane did in violation of Minnesota Statue 624.714, carry a pistol, namely a Beretta .25 automatic, model number 950, six-shot semi-automatic pistol.

Jeffery Alexander Lane, you've been read the charges against you. How do you plead?"

"Not guilty, your Honor."

C H A P T E R 1 8

"Thank you, Mr. Lane, have a seat. Alright counsels, I want motions filed before September 20th, trial starts November 1, 1994. In the meantime, Mr. Shaw, your motion for a reduction of bail is denied. I believe for Mr. Lane's alleged crime, fifty-thousand dollars is appropriate, you gentlemen know the drill, this court is adjourned."

Judge Davison slammed his gavel and walked out of the courtroom and into his chambers where his guest sat waiting. "Alright Captain James, what the hell is going on with you and this kid for Christ's sake?"

Colonel Davison Sir, if all goes well you've just helped an old friend save a young man's life."

"Bullshit Captain James! What I have just done is placed in your custody a young hoodlum who shot a man at point-blank range four times. Dammit man, are you crazy?" He slammed his fist on the desk.

"Colonel Davison, you've known me for years and I've always been a little off the beaten track. So when I asked you to trust my judgment of this kid, believe me sir, it's because I believe in this young man."

"I sure hope you're right, Lafayette," Judge Davison stated with a sigh.

"Okay, sir. That one-hundred-year-old bottle of Scotch you promised me a drink from? Well sir, I'm here to collect."

"Dammit James, that invitation was extended to you during my son's graduation two years ago. He's in town right now on summer vacation. He would love to see you, and so would Helen."

"All I need is an invite, sir."

"Tonight you fool, my house seven o'clock, and bring Helen some of those flowers she likes so much. What are they called?"

"Tiger Lilies, sir."

"Yes, that's it. And James?"

"Yes Colonel?"

"My son still loves to hear the story of how you saved his old man's life on the Ho Chi Minh Trail."

"Damn Colonel, that was in 1971, and we were in the web of the roads and jungle paths in the Laotian Panhandle. Why does your son love for me to tell that story, sir?"

"It's simple, Captain James. If you had not saved my life that day on the Ho Chi Minh Trail, there would be no story to tell."

"I guess you're right, sir. Plus I tell one hell of a war story."

"Captain James, you are a war story! Now go, get out of my chambers and collect your boy. And James?"

"Yes Colonel?"

"I didn't reduce his bail."

"Sir, I stood proudly with you during the war, and when you were sworn both as a prosecutor and a judge. I remember your slogan very well: 'If you commit a crime in Ramsey County, you will go to prison and I don't care who you know'. So I did not expect a reduction in the bail, sir, only a quick hearing. And that you provided. Thank you, sir." Captain James saluted his superior officer.

"You're welcome James. See you tonight, my house at seven."

"Wouldn't miss it for the world, sir."

"Captain."

"Yes Colonel?"

"Don't forget the flowers."

C H A P T E R 1 9

Back in the holding cell, Six was waiting to be released. Thomas had instructed him to be in his office at 1:00pm the following day, and strange as it seemed, Tina showed no emotion whatsoever.

After an hour of waiting a guard poked his head in the holding area. "Lane, let's go!" This skinny future prosecutor led him to a desk where he was given his property, signed release and bail bond papers, and buzzed out the door like he was being ejected.

Six was met at the exit of the holding area by Tina, Lynn and Lafayette James, who he affectionately called Fate. Fate spoke first.

"Dammit boy! I teach you how to survive in this fucked-up world and this is how you repay my efforts?"

"It's good to see you too, Fate."

"Boy, that's a damn lie and you know the truth ain't in you. What you are trying to do is give me a heart attack. Why didn't you call me? Yo' ass had my number, and unless the laws have changed you still get one phone call don't you?"

"Yeah Fate, you still get one call." Six knew he'd fucked up big time.

"Well who the fuck did you call? Ghostbusters Bail bondsman?"

Tina and Lynn were in tears with laughter because Fate

was doing his Redd Foxx impersonation. "I'm coming honey. This fool-ass boy is sending me to you."

"Thanks for bailing me out, Fate." Six hugged his mentor.

"Anything for you kid, but don't just thank me. It was Tina that put this whole thing in motion. Now enough of this shit. Let's get out of here and figure out what we need to do next."

* * *

When they left the county jail, Six insisted they take him straight to Children's Hospital to see Corey.

Six told me later that he had to hold back the tears when he saw father and son together, me with the horse-collar around my neck attached to my jaw, and my son wrapped in plaster.

Tina and Lynn joined me in tears as we looked at my son's fragile body. Six stood next to me and I could feel his body trembling when he saw the tubes running from Corey's ankles and wrist.

His expression told me that he wished he'd killed Marcus for the pain that he caused Corey. I was glad he didn't. If he had, he would have died August 1, 1994.

I still get goose bumps when I think of what Tina said to him when he had put the gun to Marcus's head. I'm sure she would have preferred to tell him under more romantic conditions, but she figured she would rather be a single-parent with the child's father in prison with an outdate than a single-parent with his father in the grave or prison for life. So she did the damndest thing.

In the midst of all the shit, with police screaming orders and death threats, she walked over, shielding Six's body from the police with her own, and whispered in his ear, "I'm carrying our first child. If you pull that trigger, our baby will be fatherless." All Six could do was lower his gun and stare into her eyes. He told me later, and I agree with him one thousand percent, Tina's vivid brown eyes would move any man walking on this earth to proudly give his life to save hers.

CHAPTER 20

Tina and Six needed some time alone, and against all of his principles he allowed Lynn to drive his Caddy, so that her and I could keep vigil over Corey during the night.

Tina kept up her silent treatment with Six, usually when neither of them was speaking to the other they would just lay holding each other until the negative energy would disappear, or as they would say 'pass through them'.

As soon as they walked into their apartment, Six pulled Tina to the sofa and wrapped his arms around her, then closed his eyes and took himself back to the first day he saw her face.

Tina was in the living room of the Columbus Group Home on the south side of Minneapolis. They were both thirteen and grown as hell. From the time Six spent in Totem Town lifting weights, he packed weight and muscle onto his nearly six-foot frame. Tina on the other hand, stood five-seven and weighed 110 pounds. All I can say is even today she's drop-dead gorgeous.

Every time I heard the story of how they met, Six would always say that there was never a time Tina was more beautiful than the first day he saw her face. She was young, and had this angelic glow that hung over her like a halo. Six believed that God Himself had put this masterpiece of His creation in his presence.

He swore that he didn't know if it was love at first sight, or if it was his mission in life to protect her from the boys in the neighborhood, or that old-ass nigga, Mr. Bowman, who along with his wife, ran the Group Home.

Six laid awake in his bed every night the first week wondering what kind of girl inhabited such a body: so young, so fresh, and so innocent. Maybe he was just a hopeless romantic, cause no matter how hard he tried he couldn't deny that he'd fallen madly in love with a girl he didn't know.

The Bowmans were a nightmare to the inner-city orphans in South Minneapolis. Mrs. Bowman was a mean-ass bitch of a woman who treated the children she took in like her personal slaves. While Mr. Bowman, a drunk and a border-line rapist and pedophile, had his way with all the young girls who stayed in the Group Home and the neighborhood using his famous wallet.

Six, who always had his finger on the pulse of the underground, heard that for a small fee young girls would sell themselves to Mr. Bowman sexually. One day while Six was doing one of the many odd jobs he did for Mrs. Bowman, scrubbing the upstairs bathroom, he heard what sounded like a moan from someone who was sick. Thinking one of the girls was ill, he walked to the door where he thought the sound had come from and checked the doorknob. The door opened slightly as he turned the knob, and Six could see Mr. Bowman sitting in a high-back-red-leather chair with his pants down around his ankles, and Linda a girl around fourteen, with her skirt pulled up over her hips, straddling his lap. Looking directly at Six, Linda began to gyrate her hips with the expertise of a seasoned hooker.

Six couldn't help himself and shouted, "You two nasty mother fuckers!"

"Gawdamn!" Mr. Bowman excitedly mumbled, feeling the weight of his sagging penis against his thigh as he pushed Linda off and grabbed his trousers off the floor and covered his member.

"Look ... look ... look here, son!" He began. "It's not what it looks like," he slurred.

"The hell it ain't!" Linda pulled her panties up. "You better pay me the money you promised!"

"You two nasty mothas, I'm gonna tell Mrs. Bowman." Six turned toward the door.

"Now wait a minute, son. Let's talk for a minute. You're growing up and it's about time for you to experience sex. You probably want some yourself. Here! he held out a twenty-dollar bill.

"Pay for some yourself ... or keep the money. It's tight and it's good, too." His eyes desperately pled with Six to take the money.

"Fuck you, you fat bastard. Give Linda the money and consider my silence paid in full." Six laughed at the top of his voice, as he walked out of the room.

Linda exited the room a few minutes later and entered the bathroom where Six was working. He looked up from the toilet he was cleaning when he heard the door close. Linda stood in front of the doorway undressing herself. Having never seen a real live naked woman before, he waited until she was completely undressed, allowing his eyes to casually appraise her attributes.

"I'll take care of you if you like, he gave me the twenty dollars."

"No thanks, Linda. Enjoy your money." He suddenly felt shy about her nakedness.

Linda smiled, cursing her desire to sex him down, and then closed the door behind him as he left. She thought about how nice it would have been to have had sex with someone her own age. Turning on the shower, she ran her finger across the two crisp twenty-dollar bills, "His loss."

Six walked down the stairs and into the kitchen to investigate the smell of something wonderful being baked. Lynn and Tina were baking cakes. Banana Nut cake is what they called it, and it was smelling awfully good.

"Mind if I taste a piece of your cake, Lynn?"

"Sure, why not?" Lynn had a devilish smirk on her face. "Tina, give this boy a piece of your Banana Nut cake."

Six didn't know Tina was in the kitchen and he was nervous as hell. This was as close as he'd ever been to her. She was more beautiful up close than he imagined, her face suggested character and grace far more than her thirteen years.

For a brief moment, when she raised her fork to his lips with a piece of the Banana Nut cake on its tip, his knees buckled slightly and his heart rate quickened, leaving him feeling emotionally butt-ass naked and exposed .

He knew at that moment that his secret was out. He began to visualize his lips on hers as the morsel of cake was evaporating on his tongue, when Lynn interrupted his fantasy.

"How was it?" Lynn put the next cake in the oven.

"The best." He stood there mesmerized by one of Tina's long bangs that dangled flirtatiously over one side of her face, creating a peek-a-boo effect.

She moved the fallen bang with the back of her hand and returned to the cake batter. Six took it for what it was worth and stepped out the back door to cut the lawn and earn his pay of ten dollars.

C H A P T E R   2 1

The following week around the Columbus Group Home was frantic, summer had ended, and school had begun. There were arguments and fights among the girls every morning over bathrooms and irons.

Mrs. Bowman had gone to the Welfare Office to discuss raising the monthly allotment of her food stamps with her case worker, and paid Six two dollars to make sure the younger girls in the Group Home caught the bus on time for school. He jumped at the chance to see Tina again and graciously accepted.

At 7:05AM on the nose, the school bus pulled up to the corner of Columbus and 31st Avenue, and the Columbus Group piled onto the bus. Relieved of his duties, Six headed back to the Group Home to retrieve the pastries that Mrs. Bowman had left out for him and bumped into Linda and Lynn leaving for school.

At first he thought, those two heifers liked to walk, but the truth was they were both hot between the legs and the high-school boys with cars would pick their hot asses up a few blocks away.

Six walked into the house and its emptiness was peaceful.

There was never any peace at the Group Home he stayed in down the street. He had twenty minutes before his bus came to enjoy the solitude, so he turned on the old school VCR, pushed play, grabbed the donuts off the dining room table, and sat down to watch Underdog.

Underdog was chanting his battle cry: "Have no fear, Underdog is here!" When the silence was broken by the sound of something breaking, he turned down the television to listen, but there was nothing.

He returned his attention to Underdog and heard Tina shout,

"Get your hands off of me!"

Six ran to the top of the stairs and pushed open the door.

There on top of Tina was Mr. Bowman, his hand under her skirt. He stood there stuck, not knowing if Tina had accepted Bowman's twenty- dollar bill. He was looking for some kind of sign when she screamed and began to struggle under the weight of Bowman's 275-pound frame.

Six remembered the Louisville Slugger behind Mrs. Bowman's bedroom door and quickly ran to her room, grabbed the bat and made his way back to Tina's room. The television downstairs was blaring and Underdog was at it again: "Have no fear, Underdog is here!"

On cue, Six swung the bat downward onto the lower-lumbar section of Bowman's back. Bowman howled like a wounded animal and rolled off Tina onto the floor. The sight of his hardened penis and Tina's torn panties on the floor fueled Six's anger. With all of his strength he swung the bat like a golfer and struck Mr. Bowman dead center in the groin.

The thud was sickening and Bowman expelled all the air from his lungs. Six could have sworn on a stack of Bibles that Bowman's skin color began changing before his very eyes. He screamed for Tina to grab her clothes and turned his attention back to Bowman.

The sight of his nakedness was repulsive, and made Six want to kick him in the crack of his ass. He looked at Tina, she was sitting on the edge of the bed trembling, her face stained with tears. He began kicking Bowman in the ass repeatedly, trying to get him to uncoil so he could hit him with the bat one more time.

Logic overruled his sense of anger and he reached for the famous wallet of Mr. Bowman. This wallet was said to hold at least a thousand dollars cash at all times, small bills. Six yanked the chain, and the wallet tore free from Bowman's pants. It could be said that it wasn't the physical pain Bowman was suffering from, but the pain of losing his wallet that caused the old nigga to catch his breath, because he began to scream in the range of a soprano.

Feeling the need to flee, Six ran back to Mrs. Bowman's bedroom and snatched a suitcase he'd seen lying against a dresser.

When he returned to the bedroom, Bowman had begun to scream in the range of an alto, and Tina was still sitting on the edge of the bed shaking. Six opened the suitcase on the floor and pulled the first dresser drawer open, praying it was the right one. He emptied its contents into the suitcase, then after doing the same with the clothes in the closet, he half-dragged half-carried Tina from the bedroom to the door. Bowman let out a blood-curdling scream that put Tina in stride with Six, and they ran from the Columbus Group Home, never to see it again--partners for life.

CHAPTER 22

Six and Tina ran for five blocks before they stopped to catch their breath on the stairs of an apartment building on Chicago Avenue. While Tina angrily smoothed out her skirt, and wiped the remnants of tears from her eyes, Six found Bowman's wallet.

Besides his identification and credit card, there was nine-hundred-and-forty-five dollars in cash and two-hundred dollars in food stamps. Tina looked to have gotten control of herself while Six counted the money in two separate piles, four-hundred seventy-five dollars in cash and one-hundred dollars in food stamps apiece.

Six told me that his instinct told him to share the booty. Bad move.

When he handed her the share he'd set aside for her, she looked at him and the money like she wanted them both dead. He wasn't in the mood to argue, nor did he know how to argue with a female, so he pocketed the money and held out his hand. She hesitated for a moment before placing her hand in his. They walked hand-in-hand to the 21 bus line and boarded the Lake Street bus headed for Calhoun Beach.

When they arrived at the beach, Tina held on to him as if her life depended on it. At one point she laid her head in his lap. She was so beautiful. He gently lowered his hand, allowing his finger to trace the lines of her face, the soft pout of her lower lip, the elegance of her neck. He felt as if his eyes had been cast upon the perfect face.

For hours they sat and watched the water, had lunch at a fast food Mexican restaurant, and later that evening had a pizza delivered to their bench on the beach for supper. By now they were talking about all kinds of things, but mostly how they would never go back into the system. Foster homes and group homes were a thing of the past. From this day forward they both vowed to remain together, on their own.

By ten that evening it had started to get chilly, and with no identification and too young-looking to get a motel room, they walked the streets of South Minneapolis looking for shelter. At nearly two in the morning having been on their feet for hours, both of them were exhausted. Six began looking between houses for a temporary place to rest. He spotted the top of a fifth-wheel.

Using a stick to unlatch the gated fence, he tried the handle on the door just as it started to rain. While the rain pounded the roof of their temporary home, they explored the interior. In the rear of the wheel was a bedroom with a queen-size bed, and between the bedroom and the kitchen was a bathroom with a shower. Up front was a small living-room area with a sofa. Six decided without argument that Tina would sleep in the bedroom while he took the sofa.

Tina closed the door saying goodnight when a deafening clap of thunder rattled the trailer. Minutes later, she came out with a blanket and pillow, lying down on the floor next to the small sofa. Their hands were automatic, finding each other's hand in the darkness and holding on.

C H A P T E R   2 3

Early the next morning a scratching noise at the door woke them. Six watched Tina as she walked to the window and peeked out from behind the curtain. Outside pawing frantically at the door was a miniature Collie, its owner frustrated that the little dog was scratching at his fifth-wheel.

"Dammit mutt, come here. I've got to get to work!" The little dog just ignored him and kept scratching. The owner said a few choice curse words and dragged the little dog clawing the ground all the way back to his house, before he pushed the mini Collie inside and closed the door.

By now Six had joined Tina at the window and they watched as the owner, a man sporting a starched military cover, walked to a halftrack Hemi Jeep and drove away. Once the Jeep was out of sight, they went back to sleep and slept until noon.

With daylight at hand, Six left the property to survey their surroundings finding that they had landed on 59th and Clinton Avenue in South Minneapolis. The owner of the wheel sure liked his privacy, because his backyard was fenced in by a 12-foot-high planked redwood fence with two-by-four supports.

The thirty foot wheel was also equipped with a generator for electricity. They found the operator's manual, and with a little effort connected the generator and the interior of the wheel came to life.

Six scanned the area around the wheel's exterior to see if any of the neighbors had a direct line of sight to the wheel's deepest recesses. Their new squatting place was free from visual intrusion. From what they could see, the only living creature that knew they were on the property was a Collie, who watched their movements intently from the windowsill as they moved about its owner's property.

Tina did an inventory of the wheel and found the cooking utensils in good shape. There were towels, bedding, and plenty of plates and silverware. In a storage area she found a space heater, microwave, and a ten-inch battery-powered television. They were in heaven.

Venturing out into the neighborhood, they found a local market and purchased some of the foods they liked to eat. On their way back to the wheel they used the alley for cover to avoid detection. Tina suggested that they set up an observation point to watch and learn the owner's daily and weekly routines.

This guy was like clockwork, a machine really. Every morning at 5:00AM, weekends included, he would start the day with some Yoga exercises on a mat in his yard. He would follow that up with five reps of push-ups, one hundred in a set.

If that wasn't enough, 5:30AM he would take off running, and at exactly 6:30AM he would return, go into his garage and beat the hell out of ten heavy bags he had suspended on chains from the rafters. By 7:00AM the beating would stop, and he would walk from the garage to the house, cursing his dog for scratching at his wheel.

Weekends were different. For fear of being detected they would leave the wheel during Sarge's run, a nickname they had given him, and return after 10:00PM when they knew he would be asleep.

One morning they were scared out of their minds when, right by the bedroom window of the wheel, Sarge was screaming at the Collie like the dog understood him.

"Okay Snuff, dammit you little shit! That's it, that's how you want it? Stay yo' little four-legged ass outside until I get home."

Tina felt sorry for the animal because Sarge would be gone twelve hours daily, giving the dog no attention at all. He would return home, shower, read until 9:50PM, and lights out.

As soon as Sarge drove away, Snuff the Collie, who was a boy and not a girl as they'd thought, continued to scratch on the door. Unable to take it any longer, Tina opened the door an Snuff ran inside the wheel jumping up and down, tail wagging. She caught him in midair and he began to lick her face. Tina had found her second best friend.

C H A P T E R   2 4

During the entire month of September Six and Tina maintained a clandestine schedule, not being seen by any of the neighbors or the owner. As an added measure of precaution, whenever they would leave the wheel, all appliances as well as their clothing would be stored away, and the electricity disconnected, just in case old Sarge got the urge to venture inside. Their life in the wheel had gotten so comfortable that at night they had begun to watch television. Of course, to keep their presence undetected, they would blacken the windows in the bedroom.

October came in with a bang, and at night temperatures dropped to the lower fifties. From their late night TV watching they developed the habit of cuddling with each other, and began sleeping in the protection of each other's arms.

When the temperature dropped on those cold nights it gave them all the more reason to cuddle, any concerns to keep the wheel heated were short lived because they found several propane tanks in the garage.

They decided to send October off with a party, and on Halloween they purchased two costumes, and crashed the local high school dance. Hell, they even trick-or-treated throughout the neighborhood. Six was the Count Blackula and Tina, well, she was more in the line of a diva witch than a good one. With their bags full of candy, they thought how funny it would be to ring Sarge's doorbell and yell "Trick or Treat!"

When he answered the door, they noticed he appeared to be younger than they thought. Sarge emptied his pockets of change in Tina's bag, and started to close the door when she asked real shitty like, "Is that all?"

He mumbled something about grown folks asses acting like kids and gave her a five dollar bill, then frowned and closed the door in their faces. They laughed all the way back to his wheel.

November first a snow storm began and lasted for three straight days and nights. Along with five feet of freshly fallen snow, the temperatures dropped to ten below zero. Only being able to run the heaters during the time that Sarge was either gone or asleep, they went through all but one of the propane tanks. Tina developed a cold on the second day of the storm. She claimed it was nothing, but it just got worse.

Minnesota winters can be cruel, and the morning of November fifth it was twenty below with a wind-chill factor of fifty below.

Six listened as the heater sputtered before dying. The wheel was freezing and the generator was not functioning properly; but he had a plan to heat it. He figured if he could run an extension cord from the garage to the wheel, he could run the space heaters. Besides being a squatter, he was about to attempt his first B&E.

His plan was to go through the basement window to search for more blankets and extension cords. He didn't know how long it was going to take him and the wheel was growing colder by the minute. Tina was sleeping under several blankets, and he needed to wake her so she could wait in the warmth of Sarge's house while he heated the wheel.

When he pulled the covers back from her head, she was shivering uncontrollably. He placed his hand on her forehead and she was burning hot to his touch. In a moment of complete panic, he ran to the door of the wheel to scream for help, but noticed Sarge's Jeep was still in the drive way. Without hesitation he opened the door of the wheel, and the force of the thirty-mile-an-hour wind blew him to the floor. He picked himself up off the floor and labored to Sarge's back door and rang the doorbell.

Sarge answered the door. "Boy, what the hell are you doing at my back door?"

Six tried to speak but his jaw was chattering so hard all he could do was point at the wheel. Sarge opened the storm door to see what he was pointing at and Snuff bolted from the door and into the wheel. Following Snuff's lead, Sarge ran to the trailer and stepped inside. A few minutes later he emerged, carrying Tina wrapped in a blanket.

C H A P T E R   2 5

Sarge carried Tina to an upstairs bedroom and laid her across the bed. When Six finally made it to the top of the stairs, Sarge was stripping Tina of her clothing. When he reached a pair of oversized long johns, he shouted, "Ha! I'll be damned. Not only are these long johns soaking wet, they're mine. What the hell!" He continued to pull the wet clothing from her body.

Leaving Tina in her bra and panties lying on the bed, Sarge walked by Six as if he were not in the room. Six followed him with his eyes, his body to numb from the cold to move. Sarge went into his bathroom and Six could hear several things hit the floor and some choice curse words fill the air. When he came out, he held a small box in his hand.

Sarge sat down on the bed next to Tina taking the thermometer from the box. He shook it several times and placed it under her tongue. He lifted her eyelids one by one, examining them as a doctor would. Turning a blanket over her he waited a minute and a half before removing the thermometer. He turned to Six.

"Listen up boy. This girl has a temperature of 103 degrees and we have to bring it down. Do you understand what I'm saying?"

"Yes sir, I do." Six's body was trembling, his hands and feet stinging from thawing in the warmth of the house.

"I need you to go to the refrigerator and bring me as much ice as you can find. Can you do that?"

"Will the ice help her, sir?"

"Boy, don't answer my question with a question. Just do it!" Sarge lifted Tina into his arms and carried her into the bathroom, shouting back over his shoulder for Six to move his ass and get the ice.

Six's hands and feet were stinging so badly he could barely walk as he made his way down the stairs. He reached the refrigerator, opened it and stood there with his mouth hanging open. Both ice trays were empty. His heart began racing for the second time that morning and he was again in a state of panic. Midway into his panic attack, he looked up and saw the most beautiful sight, then he rummaged through the drawers in the kitchen until he found what he was looking for.

Six grabbed the hammer, walked into the familiar backyard, and under the kitchen window there it was, the second most beautiful thing he'd ever seen -- an icicle! The damn thing had to be seven feet long. He pulled at the icicle and it tumbled to the ground. He gathered up the larger pieces, running with them back to the bathroom.

Sarge had placed Tina in the bathtub and was running water into the tub, which slowly submerged her body. He could hear Six stumble up the stairs and growled at the top of his lungs. "Where is that ice, boy?"

"Right here, sir." Six extended his arms with the icicles piled on them.

"I'll be a motha! Boy, you ain't so stupid after all, are you? May be some hope for you yet. Now break up that ice, boy, and let's get started bringing her fever down."

For the next forty-five minutes Six broke ice in the sink with the hammer while Sarge added ice to the water in the tub, checking Tina's temperature every five minutes. Finally after what seemed forever he held the thermometer up to Six. "Look at this boy. 98.5 ... ain't that a pretty sight?"

"98.5, what does it mean, sir?"

"It's a normal body temperature reading, but it don't mean much. For the time being she's out of the immediate danger that the fever presented." He tossed Six an oversized towel and instructed him to wrap the towel around her when he stood her up.

Six managed to get the towel around her without much effort, and Sarge carried her to the bedroom, again he laid-her across his bed. Without saying a word, he walked to the dresser and pulled out a pair of men's pajamas. From a hall closet he got three blankets and a large comforter. When he returned, he dropped a bomb.

"Hey boy, do you know how to pray?"

"Not really, sir. I just say a few words into the air to a God. I believe hears me."

"If that ain't praying, I don't know what is. Put a few words in the air that this girlfriend of yours doesn't have pneumonia."

"Pneumonia!" Six's fear clearly registered in his voice.

Sarge put the blankets down and stood inches from Six's face, looking him directly in the eyes. "Here's the deal, boy. After you've rid this girl of her wet bra and panties, you are going to dry her off real good. When you've completed that task you will rub this Vicks Vapor Rub on her chest. When this is done, you will dress her in these pajamas, and cover her with these blankets and comforter. Can you do that?"

"Yes, sir, I think I can."

"Don't think. Either you can or you can't. Which is it?"

"I can do it, sir."

"Good. While you're doing that, I'm going to call for an ambulance to take her to the hospital."

"No sir, I can't let you do that."

"Why not, boy?" Sarge was clearly irritated by Six's defiance.

"Because we're both orphans and I made a promise when we ran away that I mean to keep that we would never be separated ever, or go back into the foster care or group home system."

"Listen, boy. If she does not receive proper medical attention, returning to the 'system' as you call it won't be your only problem."

"Please sir, you've already helped her. I promise that when she's better we'll be out of your life."

Sarge scratched his head and walked silently out of the room.

Six went to Tina and began drying her off. During the past few months he'd held her in his arms many times, be he'd never seen her naked. He pulled the wet bra from her body, and his eyes followed the line of her collarbone to the curves of her shoulders, and finally rested on the tender valley between her breasts.

Pulling down her wet panties, he could see the soft push of her ribs under her skin, and curves of her hips below a nearly nonexistent waistline. She was a masterpiece, sculpted by God's own hand, and he wanted to hold her, to kiss her, to tell her how much he loved her. He let the thought stay with his heart while he dried her, rubbed the Vicks on her chest, then dressed her, and covered her with the blankets.

Six left the bedroom, closing the door behind him, and walked down the stairs into the kitchen where Sarge was waiting. When he spoke his voice was soothing, fatherly.

"She'll be fine until I get back. Inside the refrigerator there is some orange juice. I want you to do whatever you have to do to get her to drink some. We need to keep her from dehydrating."

"Are you still going to call for an ambulance, sir?"

"Naw son, I'm going to give her an old family remedy guaranteed to have her on her feet before you know it. When she's better we'll talk." Sarge grabbed his coat and walked out the door.

Six heard the familiar sound of the Jeep come to life, then Sarge scraping ice from the windshield. He poured two glassfuls of orange juice and hurriedly made his way back to Tina. He lifted her head and she managed a weak smile, then took a few sips of the juice, closed her eyes and drifted off to sleep. Six knelt down beside the bed on his knees and prayed into the air for Tina's life.

C H A P T E R   2 6

Six was still praying when he heard Sarge in the kitchen.
He looked at Tina and his heart told him that everything would
be okay. He walked down the stairs and into the kitchen where
Sarge had the kitchen table covered with various cough
medicines, aspirins, teas, honey, lemons and a fifth of brandy.

"Pay attention, boy!" Sarge was standing in front of the
stove. "This is a tea pot, tea kettle, whatever you want to call it.
Take it over to the sink, fill it with water and place it on the
burner. Do it!" He handed Six the tea pot. Then he pulled a
mug from a bag and placed it on the table. "Open that box of
tea." He ordered.

"Now take one of the bags and put it in the mug. On the
knife rack over there, grab one of those little ones and cut
those lemons into quarters. You do know how to use a knife
don't you?"

"Yes sir, I have one of my own." Six pulled the
switchblade from his pocket.

"Well, pop that damn thing and cut the lemon, boy.
Good." He added when Six flicked the blade and began cutting
the lemon.

"Okay, next." Sarge extracted a small glass from his
pocket. "This is a shot glass, boy. Break the seal on that brandy
there."

Six did what he was told. "What next?"

"Pour a shot of the brandy into the mug." Sarge placed the shot glass on the table in front of Six.

"What's a shot?" Six looked puzzled.

"The glass is a shot, boy. You can't go wrong, just fill it up. Now for the family secret. Pour the brandy into the mug." Six did as he was told.

"Okay, now dip the tea bag in an out of the brandy. Gives the tea more flavor."

Six began to laugh because Sarge was sounding just like Bill Cosby. Still in his Cos mode, Sarge continued. "I have to leave now and go earn a living. When the pot starts to boil it will whistle. When it does, fill the mug with hot water, add a quarter piece of lemon, squeeze and stir. If she won't drink it like it is, use a couple tablespoons of honey. No matter what she says, make sure she drinks the whole thing."

Although Sarge and Six were the same height and nearly the same weight, he was larger than life to Six, and he was going to follow his instructions to the letter. On his way out the door

Sarge looked back. "When the phone rings once, hangs up and rings back, answer it, it will be me. What's the signal?"

"Rings once, hangs up and rings back, sir."

"Alright soldier, I'll call every couple hours. I should be home around 8:00PM. The house is under your watch. Man your post well." He winked at Six.

"Yes sir!" Six saluted like a new recruit as Sarge walked out the backdoor. The tea pot screamed and Snuff wagged his tail then made two quick motions with his body as if he were saying 'Come on man, get the lead out yo' ass, let's move!' You would swear this damn dog understood the English language.

Six fixed the tea with two spoons of honey and Tina drank it without protest. A few hours later she asked for another. Sarge called to check on her, and Six informed him that she'd been to the bathroom a few times and went back to bed. All Sarge said was "Good."

By eight o'clock that evening Tina had put down four of the family remedies and was sound asleep. When Sarge walked in the door he noticed the brandy bottle was nearly half gone and asked Six if he had been tapping the booze. Six assured him that he did not drink liquor, and per his instructions had made Tina a total of four of the family remedies.

With Six in tow, Sarge walked into the bedroom and felt Tina's forehead. She was cool to his touch and sleeping so hard that a train wreck inside the room wouldn't've wakened her. Sarge laughed at the thought that Tina was now sleeping off a good drunk. All night long Sarge and Six kept vigil over Tina, at least Sarge did. By morning they were both exhausted.

Sarge awakened Six, looking him in the eyes. "Follow me, boy. I'm going to teach you how to prepare a first-class breakfast."

Tina awoke to find that she was wearing a man's pajamas, even more they were damp, and she'd be damned if she wasn't naked underneath them. The room she was in was ninety-plus degrees and she could smell food cooking. She stepped into the hallway feeling a little lightheaded, and then into the bathroom where she found shampoo, a new toothbrush, and something called Shower to Shower. She showered, allowing the water to massage her body. Retracing her steps back to the bedroom from where she'd come, she searched the room for her clothing.

Unable to find them, she opened the closet door and there on a hanger were several pairs of freshly pressed jungle fatigues.

She found a new pair of boxer shorts in a package and a safety pin, and she was in business. All she could locate was a wife-beater that she barely managed to cover herself with and dressed in the jungle fatigues, rolling the sleeves up unbuttoning the shirt to where the wife-beater was straining.

She walked the unfamiliar stairs and could hear Six and another man talking. Laughing, actually. Sarge saw her and smiled.

"See there, boy. I told you, family remedy works every time." He smiled proudly.

"Yes sir. I can see that. Hello Tee." Six pressed his hands together, silently thanking God for answering his prayer.

"Hey, Jay." Her voice sounded very weak.

"She speaks! Softly, but none-the-less she speaks. And

damn, damn, damn little girl, you done gone and ruined a perfectly good shirt. Now it's gonna have those sissy pinch marks you women are notorious for leaving behind. You might as well keep those, little girl. I'll never get those imprints out."

Tina began to laugh and cough, and Six though it was the sweetest sound he'd heard. Sarge joined her, and Six thought the both of them had lost their damn minds.

"What's for breakfast?" Tina took a seat at the table.

"Home fried potatoes with onions and bell peppers, fried chicken wings and waffles," Sarge bellowed out.

"Chicken and waffles?" There was a bit of confusion in her voice.

"Yes, little girl, chicken and waffles. I said the same damn thing and felt the same damn way you're feeling when it was suggested to me. But dog-gone-it, after I tasted it I've been in love ever since."

"Where in the world would any restaurant serve chicken and waffles for breakfast?"

"None other than Rosco's Chicken and Waffles in Los Angeles, California. Best damn breakfast spot on the face of God's green earth. Now sit down and have yourself a cup of tea."

"No thank you. I've had enough tea, thank you very much!" She punched Six in the arm.

When the breakfast was ready the three of them sat down at the table in silence, until Sarge broke the silence. "What are your names? All this boy, girl, Mr. crap is driving me crazy."

"Well, I'm Tina, and this handsome young man is Jeffery."

"Tina and Jeffery," he pronounced their names like they were foreign or something. "How old are the two of you?"

"Together we're twenty-six and grown. Apart we're only thirteen. "She had a chicken wing hanging from her mouth.

Sarge shook his head ten times, adding 'damn' each time he shook it. "How long have the two of you been living in my backyard?"

"Nearly two months now, Sarge." Tina shoved a piece of waffle into her mouth.

"What in the hell did you just call me, young lady?" Sarge slammed his silverware on the table.

"Oh, I called you Sarge. You know, short for Sergeant. It's a name we gave you when we were living in your wheel."

"Dammit!" He slammed his fist into the table, and stood up, bending forward over the table, teeth clenched "My name is Captain Lafayette James, attached to the 1-9 1st Battalion 9th Marine Regiment. I've fought battles, you two little shits, from the Halls of Montezuma to the shores of Tripoli. And I'll be damned," he once more slammed his fist on the table to drive his point home, "if two teenage squatters are going to call me a Sergeant!"

Six and Tina had tears streaming down their faces from laughter. Lafayette was still stone-faced with both fist resting on the table, his muscles bulging, and his nose flaring in a picturesque pose of a Silverback Gorilla. Tina, with the smile that would melt the heart of a savage beast, walked over and kissed him on the cheek, and hugged him until he softened. When he relaxed, he sat back down, her arms still wrapped around him. "Thanks for saving my life. Because fate brought us together, I won't call you Sarge anymore, nor will I call you Captain. But I will call you Fate, if you let me."

CHAPTER 27

They talked late into the night, he listened to their story and agreed that calling the authorities was no longer an option.

He said if they could live in his backyard for two months undetected, they deserved a shot. Fate was now their big brother, single foster: parent, unauthorized of course, and a friend.

Fate promised to make the record straight if the need for adoption arose in the future. Their cover story, should anyone ask, was that they were the son and daughter of his deceased cousin out of Kansas City. Since neither of them had ever been adopted by any of the many families that had taken them in over the years, they did not have last names. Fate gave them the name of a man he truly respected, a man who'd saved lives in Vietnam, a decorated war hero. Their last name was now officially Lane.

Fate accepted their nickname for him and he gave them nicknames as well. He called Tina 'Nakia', said her name was a code name and was to be spoken only in extreme circumstances. He named Six 'Three-Sixty' or 'Three-Six'; he said it was because he had come full circle from a boy to a man, kind of a rite of passage.

Fate picked up the telephone and dialed a number, and after a few rings he spoke into the phone.

"This is Lafayette. I need two birth certificates: one male, the other female, both kids are thirteen years of age. Girl's name Tina Marie Lane, and the boy Jeffery Alexander Lane. Yeah, I'm sure about the ages, Andre. What? You trying to hustle me? Since when does a thirteen year old need a social security card? I'll be damned! Might as well throw in a credit card as well. Hell no, fool, I don't want the credit cards. Listen Andre, do you still have the contacts in the Kansas City School District? Good, I need school records for both kids, and make them at least B-average students. Yes, the usual channels, no later than 1800 hours Sunday evening. School starts early Monday morning."

Six and Tina listened to the one-sided conversation, and when he hung up the phone they started to protest the names he'd given them. The look on his face said 'don't fuck with me.' Then he spoke.

"Nobody under the age of eighteen who does not work, pay bills, buy food, or put gas in my Jeep will live under my roof and not go to school. Is this understood?

"Yes, sir!" They shouted in unison.

"Now dammit, let's go shopping. From the looks of the rags your bags the both you could use some new clothing for school."

C H A P T E R 2 8

Fate pulled the Jeep to a halt on the corner of University and Western Avenue in front of Lady Vee's Beauty salon. "With new clothing one always needs a new hair style, or a new cut. Lady Vee is the best in the Twin Cities in makeovers." He shut the engine down.

Lady Vee was known for working magic on her clients. She once did a makeover for a young country girl whose mother insisted that she participate in the States beauty pageant. Vee did such a wonderful job, the girl went on to become Miss Minnesota.

"Lafayette James, long time no see." She tucked her shapely frame in his outstretched arms. "How are you, Mr. James?"

"I'm fine, Vee. The place looks good."

Six and Tina watched the exchange between them and noticed how Fate and Vee's eyes regarded each other with pride.

"Are these the two young people you told me about?"

"Yeah, Vee. Jeffery and Tina, I'd like for you to meet a good friend of mine, Lady Vee."

They shook her hand, and she gave Tina her bright smile, ran her fingers through her hair, shouted out a few commands and she was taken to the back of the salon. Lady Vee had ten styling stations, five shampoo chairs, a nail console and a room for facials and waxings. She took a look at the ten inches of wool on Six's head, and suggested that the look of the day was braids, and he'd look and feel much better with his hair washed, conditioned, oiled, and braided. She assured him when she started that his new look would drive the young girls crazy. When she finished she turned him around in her chair, and cupped her hand under his chin. "You know what baby? I think you're gonna drive some old girls crazy too."

An hour later Tina was nearly ready. Lady Vee took one look at her and grabbed her makeup case.

"Listen baby," she began. "Fate, as you call him, told me under no terms was I to give you any makeup, but what do men know? The eyes, honey, more than any other feature, are what makes a woman lovely. I'm going to show you a few tricks to bring out the beauty of your eyes. If he says anything, say to him, was it not Shakespeare who said, 'The eyes are doorway to the soul'?"

Tina walked out with Lady Vee, and there was no longer a young girl, but a woman standing beside her. It was if she had presented them with a portrait. When Tina smiled it was infectious, a vibrant smile that warmed their hearts.

"She's beautiful, Fate." Six eyes were locked on her perfect face.

"Yeah, I can see that. A touch of glamour with a hint of mystery. Lady Vee, you've outdone yourself."

"Thank you, Lafayette. I didn't do anything but put a perm in her head. This child was already rivetingly attractive. All I did was show her that her maturity is just as valuable as her innocence." Lady Vee sauntered up to Fate and kissed him boldly on the mouth. "I just couldn't stand it another minute, you fine-ass motherfucker." She pressed her body against his.

His eyes gleamed brightly. "What are you doing, Vee?" He was feeling so overwhelmingly taken aback by her actions.

Standing on her tiptoes she moved in closer, an inner warmth stealing her soul as she lifted her hand to his face, and stroked his clean shaven chin. "Now Lafayette," she purred. "Don't think, just go with it. It's about time that you and I spend some quality time together, don't you think?" She felt his response as their bodies continued to touch.

"If you're trying to get my attention, Vee, you're succeeding." He tightened his arms around her.

Vee's sister was unable to control herself any longer. "Get a fucking room, you too! This soft porn is making me and the customers horny as hell. Vee, let that man go, or you know what you got to do, dammit!" She fanned herself in an over-dramatic way.

The beauty shop erupted in laughter and Lady Vee whispered something in Fate's ear, then they separated. Six and Tina fell in stride behind Fate, and they walked across a wintery University Avenue to his Jeep. Lady Vee watched from her window as Fate drove away. Her sister moved to her side.

"That man is a handful, Sis, and you've already said he's bad for your heart. Don't set yourself up to get hurt."

"Girl, he's only different because of all the wars he's fought in. He wouldn't hurt anyone who wants to love him." A pang of sorrow pierced her heart at the thought of being hurt again. Naw! she thought, I sing and dance to a tune only I can hear every time he comes around. If all goes well she'd see him this weekend. Her desire for love and lust was overruled by her business sense and she shouted, "Who's next?"

CHAPTER 29

When they returned to Fate's home, he explained the house rules. "There are three bedrooms. Tina, yours is down the hall from mine on the second floor. Six, your bedroom is on the bottom floor, up front. No one goes into another person's bedroom, or violates that person's personal space without their permission." He pointed at Six. "Am I understood?"

"Yes Fate." They eyed each other.

"Now, I need to know something. All these nights you spent alone in my wheel, were you sleeping in the same bed?"

"Yes Fate." They replied barely above a whisper.

"Were you sexually active?"

They shook their heads so hard Fate probably thought they were gonna fall off. His second question jarred them even more.

"Are either of you virgins?"

They both nodded their heads yes. He clapped his hands together so loud both of them jumped up, ready to run for the front door.

"Good, both of you be in the living room at 1900 hours." He walked out the door singing a song.

Tina and Six looked at one another wondering what had just taken place. Although they cared deeply for one another, and had laid in each other's arms, they had never had sex with one another, nor anyone else for that matter. Until yesterday neither of them had seen the other naked. Their intimacy was precious to them, even more so today than it was back then.

Fate returned with an old school VCR and a videotape in his hand. After he connected it to the television he faced them. "I know the two of you are wondering what this is all about, but before you ask I'll tell. This is sex education, uncut and in the raw."

Tina protested, stating unequivocally that she was a virgin.

"Point taken and duly noted." He put the tape in the VCR, closed it, and pressed play. "But this is not about whether you are or not. It's strictly educational."

They sat through boring sex videos in school during sex education class, but those videos could never have prepared them for what they were about to see.

"I'll be back when the video is over." He turned out the light and walked out of the room.

They started out sitting in each other's arms just as they had during their late night movie watching in the wheel. The video they watched that night was 'Deep Throat' with Linda Lovelace in the starring role. When it was finished they were no longer entangled in each other's arms, and Fate stood before them. "There will be zero tolerance of that kind of foolishness in my house. Any questions?" He spoke to them in a fatherly tone.

"Yes!" Tina shouted, obviously upset.

"What is your question?"

"Why did you show us that disgusting video?" She was pissed that she was made to watch it.

Fate knelt down beside the couch to her eye level, and looked directly in her eyes. "Miss Tee, sex can be both beautiful and disgusting. Procreation, the creation of a child between two people who love each other is what our Creator had in mind. Not the act of lust and fornication the two of you witnessed firsthand in that video. To answer your question, the reason I showed you the video is because when peer pressure about sex comes up, the two of you will know the difference, and can make your own choices about your bodies. Good night."

Fate walked out of that living room leaving the two of them alone. Six and Tina lost their virginity together in an act of love and procreation thirty months after Fate showed them that video.

CHAPTER 30

Six and Tina didn't just attend school, they inhaled it. Acquiring new skills or knowledge, Fate told them, by itself is nothing without application. He enrolled them both in Anthony Middle School in South Minneapolis.

Fate was like a proud father, every morning watching them leave for school. What they did not or could not learn to satisfy their growing thirst for knowledge because it was not in the school's curriculum, Fate taught them.

Everyday living with Fate was like Christmas. When the big day finally arrived, it was unlike any other. They enjoyed the exchanging of gifts, something neither of them had ever done, but their favorite gifts were their memberships at Bally's Fitness, and the Dojo Fate made for them in the basement of his home.

They would rush home from school every day to learn new Kata's and self-defense from Fate. They had so much fun with him, their classmates were jealous of all the attention he gave them. Truth is, they preferred his company over their friends at school. Fate was their father, brother, teacher and friend. He counseled and instructed them in Philosophy, war, science, history and of course their favorite, self-defense.

By the end of the school year all they wanted to do was spend the entire summer with him. Fate owned two large junkyards, ten tow trucks, and a twenty-five-unit apartment building on Lexington Avenue in St. Paul, they thought he had money to burn. He said he was just comfortable.

On the first day of summer vacation, Six and Tina were cleaning out the wheel when Fate asked them if they liked the country. They assured him that neither of them had ever been to the country to pass judgment.

"Oh well, then the two of you would have no use for a sixty- four-hundred acre farm in Southern Minnesota." They damn near broke their necks packing their bags when he asked, "You two want to spend the summer on our farm?"

Six and Tina left South Minneapolis the summer of 1995, two teenage kids going to spend the summer on the family farm. What they experienced on the farm during those one-hundred days of summer vacation instilled a maturity in them few teenagers, would ever in life get to experience.

They both fell head-over-heels in love with the farm at first sight. It was breathtaking! Mother Nature used just about every earth tone in her palette to paint the farm and the surrounding countryside. Minnesota natives have every right to brag about their farms in the southern region of the state. It's no secret that they grow beautiful farms in Minnesota, and Fate's was fabulous

There were three silos, and an old restored country home that gave the farm a historical feel. Along with the thirty-five-hundred square-foot log cabin home, there were three barns which were homes for horses, cows, goats, chickens and dogs that made the farm swell with the heritage of its old-world Norwegian settlers.

They were greeted by five men Fate said were all decorated combat soldiers, all specialist in their fields. Sergeant B.J. Barella was a weapons expert; Sergeant M. Greedy, was a demolitions expert; Sergeant D, Black, was a communications specialist; and Gunnery Sergeant Peters supervised all. operations. The little Vietnamese man who claimed to be the cook was Kim Pol. He was a Colonel in his country's military.

Fate told them that Kim Pol was a Buddhist Monk who believed so strongly in his countrymen's right to live free, he joined the military to fight for their rights. Kim Pol was an expert in every field of warfare, martial arts, and the kitchen that you could think of.

Sergeant Black gave them a twenty-minute instructional crash course on how to ride and stop a couple of four-wheelers. When he was satisfied that they were a couple of naturals, he showed them the trail and said have fun. It was early morning and the fog had lifted, leaving the meadow grass and the spider webs glistening with the dew that danced with the morning light.

They rode the four-wheelers across rolling hills near a highway that bordered the property. An old man waved at them from a tractor headed down a shiny road, which let them know they weren't the only ones up and about.

It was the beginning of a wonderful day. A hawk glided over the open meadow, and a cottontail rabbit darted up a trail in front of them. A Meadowlark was perched, singing his song to the world while clouds lazily drifted across the blue sky above.

The trail beneath their feet became more than just a place they were standing. They were alive and a part of their surroundings, for this place was now a place their hearts resided. More than that really, it was their piece of God's gift to them.

Tina spotted it first, a fork in the trail. She convinced Six that they should investigate, and the adventure began. They rode the trail for more than a mile until they arrived at what looked like a military base. There were barracks, a chow hall, a building with classrooms, puddle jumps, a place for wire exercises, bridge crossings, a firing range, and Fate and his men were very heavily armed.

CHAPTER 31

It was Tina's voice that brought Six back from his reminiscing.

"Six," she turned in his embrace to face him.

"Yes baby?" He was glad they were talking.

"Has anyone informed you that Mr. and Mrs. Hellman were murdered?"

"No, Tee. Kind of had problems of my own." There was a hint of sarcasm in his voice. Tina took a deep breath and cuddled deeper in his arms.

"The news reports say they were robbed and that the robbers may have gotten away with as much as twenty-thousand dollars."

"I'm sorry to hear that, Tee. I told Mr. Hellman that cashing checks inside the market was a risk because of robbers looking to make themselves a fast buck."

She raised from his body. "Do you realize that in the three years we've known each other, we have never had one single argument?"

"Yes Tee, I'm aware of that fact," he replied calmly.

"Are there any secrets between us, Six?"

"No secrets, Tee. Why do you ask?"

"No skeletons in the closet that will come back to haunt us later in life?"

"Is there a point to all this, or is something wrong?" His

face showed signs of frustration from her questioning.

"Today I've been through an emotional hell that's left me drained and exhausted. I have to ask you something, and I need to know that you are going to tell me the truth."

Six felt a sudden chill run through his body despite the ninety plus degrees in the room. "Sure Tee, ask away. I've never lied to you."

"Not yet!" She threw the four punch combination that Fate had taught her.

"Okay baby, what is your question?" He blocked the last punch and pinned her body to the sofa as he placed his head to her stomach

"Six, what are you doing?"

"I'm listening to our son."

"You damn fool, I'm only three months pregnant. There's not much to listen to. And what makes you think it's a boy?"

"Girl, boy, makes no difference to me as long as it's healthy."

"Stop changing the subject. This is serious. Fate is beside himself with the death of his friends. Plus he won't admit it, but he's lonely in the house since we've left."

"Tina, Fate is a grown man who was living alone comfortably all by himself when we met him. He'll be alright."

"How can you say that? He was against our moving out, and we begged him for this apartment, just in case you've forgotten."

"No I haven't. We wanted to make love, and didn't want to disrespect Fate by doing it under his roof."

"So he gave us this apartment!" Tina leaned into him.

"Rent free!" He countered.

"Your Cadillac?" She raised her voice.

"He co-signed for it!" Six shouted back.

"Your job at the Hellmans'?"

"He got it for me. I know all this, Tee, and I'm grateful to Fate, but what's your point?"

"Are you not bothered by the fact that Fate's friends, your bosses, who by the way loved you like a son, are dead?"

"Tina, I have two concerns of my own right now, and the death of the Hellmans is not either of them."

Six realized the harshness of his tone, but before he could correct his error she turned her back on him. This was a day of firsts for him.

He was about to hug her when she turned to him. "Fate loves you. You know that, don't you?"

"Yeah, he's told me."

"Sorry Six, my hormones are out of control. I'm just worried about you, Fate, our baby, and our future together. What are your concerns?" She kissed him softly on the lips.

"My concerns?"

"Yes, you said you only had two concerns, and the death of the Hellmans was not either of them."

"Damn, that sounded cold. Did I really say it like that?"

"Yes, you did."

"Well Tee, I didn't mean for it to come out like that, but I have selfish reasons. We have a life growing inside of you, which is my first concern, and I'm facing a prison sentence, which is my second. So, if I'm being selfish with my feelings, please forgive me."

She touched his face lovingly. Her nails had been painted with designs. Damn, something he'd failed to recognize. "While you were on lockdown I told Fate that I would be moving back into the house to finish my schooling at Washburn."

"I figured as much, Tee." He caressed her stomach.

"I also let him know that I was going to put my college education on hold to take care of our baby, but he insisted that between the two of us and a decent daycare, there would be no need to postpone my education. So after my senior year I'll be starting as a freshman at the University of Minnesota in the fall."

Hearing her talk about their dream of going to college without him ignited an anger inside of him. His blood started boiling when she remarked "You know Fate has already stashed away enough money for both our college educations?"

"Listen Tina." He paused in thought. "I fucked up! So please stop putting the fucking guilt trip on me, and just say whatever it is you have to say."

"Alright." Calmly she stood to face him. The softness of

her eyes had a melting effect over him. "I think you had something to do with the Hellmans robbery and murder."

The casualness of her voice and her probing stare made him feel an odd juvenile shame and a lack of trust for her that she would accuse him of robbery and murder. He couldn't believe she'd say something like that to him and he exploded.

"Bitch! Have you lost yo' rabbit-ass mind?"

Instead of getting angry, Tina started laughing. Then she calmed herself. "Why do I feel so ridiculously grateful that you didn't use a four-letter-word to insult me?"

Her question threw him completely off guard. She began clapping her hands defiantly-as she walked to the bedroom and returned with a bag that she dropped at his feet. "Read this!" She shoved a piece of paper under his nose.

Realizing that he was having his first fight with the woman he loved, Six calmed down, and quietly asked her to read it to him. He even added 'please' as a softener. The please must have worked because she knelt down before him, and again his heart softened under her stare. Damn, he loved this woman.

"After you were arrested, Lynn and I rode in the ambulance with Corey to Children's Hospital. When the doctors had him squared away, we went in search of Shan ... I mean Sazzar. We found him sitting on a bench with his mom at the St. Paul Police Department. He made gestures with his hands like he wanted a pen to write with, and this is what he wrote:

"Tina at the Lyndale Motel in room 157 in the mattress at the head of the bed nearest the window facing the alleyway is nineteen-thousand dollars. You can have it all to use for Six's bail or Attorney fees, half of the money is his."

"After I read the note, Sazzar reached inside his pocket and handed me the thousand dollars he'd slapped Lynn with." She paused, looking in his face, searching for any signs of guilt. Six held his poker face.

Breaking the awkward silence that followed, Six maintained his composure. "Did you use the twenty-thousand dollars to hire Thomas?"

"Are you crazy, Six? How would I explain twenty-grand

that has the smell of blood and death all over it?"

"Did you tell Fate about the money?" He continued his interrogation .

"Six!" Tina looked flabbergasted. "Are you and I having the same fucking conversation?" She picked the black bag off the floor and threw it in his lap. "Here's your blood money!" She snapped through gritted teeth before storming off into their bedroom and slamming the door.

Opening the bag, Six could see that it was the money from the Hellmans robbery. "Damn Sazzar!" Six mumbled under his breath.

Giving Tina a few minutes to calm down, Six walked to the bedroom door and knocked gently before he turned the knob and opened the door. Tina was sitting on the bed blindfolded in the lotus position, taking apart the .380 automatic Fate had given her for her sixteenth birthday as a gift. Tina always said taking apart her weapon blindfolded had a tranquil effect on her.

"Sorry Tee."

"There's nothing to be sorry for, is there?"

"How long are you gonna act this way?"

"Don't know. It's the first time we've ever had a fight, so I think I'll hold out until you tell me the truth."

"Can you handle the truth, Tee?"

"Let's take it for a spin and I'll tell you." She worked rapidly reassembling her weapon.

"Okay. I was working in the market stocking shelves, and overheard these guys talking about this guy named 'G-Man', who was selling crack in South Minneapolis. Both of them claimed that they had personally seen large sums of cash in his spot. I drove to the Southside, and for the price of a five-dollar rock, a crackhead showed me his spot. I did some serious reconnaissance, and G-Man was making some serious paper selling crack. Seeing how weak his security was, I determined that I could pull off the robbery with one additional person, so when you asked me to help Sazzar, I included him because he was game, and together we pulled it off without incident, and made the twenty-grand you found in the motel room."

Tina pulled the blindfold from her eyes and they felt like

heat lamps on his flesh. "You took green-ass Shanally Robinson with you to rob a drug dealer?" the sound of the clip snapping in place and a round being chambered made him talk faster.

"Listen Tee, I had a chance to make a large sum of money for a project I have in mind and I took it. As for Sazzar, it was you who had been selling me the 'somebody done somebody wrong' song.

So, to make, or what I believed would make you happy, I gave him a chance to put some money in his pockets."

"Now I'm really pissed, Six. What if there had been trouble? You could have been killed, dammit!" She screamed. "I can't believe you took inexperienced Shannally to watch your back when you had me!" She emphasized her sincerity by resting the cocked .380 across her breast.

Relief flooded Six's body all at once; Sazzar hadn't said a word. With all the calm he could put in his voice, he responded.

"If I had told you I wanted to rob a drug dealer, would have tried to talk me out of it?"

"You damn right I would've. We have a bright future in front of us. But you're my man, and if it was your decision to do it anyway, regardless of what I thought, I would have been down for you, Six." She made no effort to wipe the tears flowing freely from her eyes.

"Baby," She used her free hand to grab his chin. "Whatever it is you want to do, no matter what it is, I would lay down my life to protect yours. Is this something you are capable of understanding?"

Six gently took her weapon from her hand, and made her a promise that as long as there was a breath in his body, no matter what he was doing, or how he was doing it, she would be by his side doing it. They held each other the rest of the night, and let the pains of the only fight, and the only lie he ever told her flow between them, and pass through their embrace.

C H A P T E R   3 2

Fate, Six, and Tina sat in the conference room at Thomas Shaw and Associates listening to Thomas explain why his strategy was the best route to take.

"Thomas, are you sure this is the best option?" Fate was curious.

"Lafayette, trust me. We stipulate to the findings in the Pre- Sentencing report, and the prosecutor has assured me that his recommendation to the court will be three to ten years of prison confinement."

"Three to ten," Fate repeated more to himself than anyone else.

"Jeff, how do you feel about the deal the State has proposed?"

"No man in his right mind wants to volunteer to give up his freedom. But I also understand the burden of putting the State through a jury trial. I'm going to accept the State's offer of thirty-six months."

"Well, Miss Lane, that leaves you?" Brenda, Mr. Shaw's legal assistant felt like Tina's opinion needed to be voiced.

"Brenda, Jeff and I would rather our child be in his terrible twos than an eight year old when his father returns. Plus, the thirty-six months is a given, right Thomas?"

"Provided, Miss Lane, Jeff does nothing to violate any of the institutions rules and loses any of his good time. He will be released after his sentence of thirty-six months has been served. With that said, having heard from all parties, it's decided we enter into the plea agreement with the State. Brenda?"

"Yes, Thomas?"

"Call Beise and tell him we have an agreement, and to prepare the necessary documents."

"Anything else, Thomas?"

"Yes Brenda, I promised my friends lunch. Could you please make reservations for five at that Manhattan-Style Bistro I like so much?"

"Five, Thomas?"

"Yes Brenda, unless you have some objections to joining us for lunch?"

"No objections at all, Thomas. I'd love to."

"Good, that's a wrap. Let's eat, I'm starving." Thomas closed his file folder.

CHAPTER 33

It had been three months since Six had accepted the State's offer, and I was standing at my bedroom window admiring the falling snow. Lynn had agreed to move in with me in the upstairs duplex over Mom's with our son.

I turned my attention from the weather when Corey started to cry. I hesitated for a moment to see if Lynn's motherly instincts would wake her from her sleep to attend to her son's needs -- the bitch laid motionless.

I knew her naked frame lying on the bed was a device she used to keep me under her hypnotic spell. Every part of her body articulated her sexiness, and the damn fool that I was loved every part of it. Lynn's sex was so good that being a sucker was worth every moment of humiliation. I pulled my thoughts from her loveliness and went to check on our son. Sho-nuff, his little butt was wet with a surprise.

Corey had healed from his injuries and was a healthy, happy six-month-old kid, showing signs of being the spitting image of his father. My mother, whose name is Moms, some cruel joke by her parents I always thought, pitched a bitch when I told her I was moving out of her place and into an apartment with Lynn and her grandchild. After a couple of knock-down drag-out fights, Moms finally surrendered and suggested, with her forever gaming ass, that we move into the upstairs duplex for four-hundred dollars a month.

The only thing my dope fiend daddy ever did right with his trifling ass, besides die a junkie's death with a needle in his arm, was to be fully insured on his job. The insurance money helped pay the bills. Since Moms owned the house and the upstairs was empty, we moved in.

At first it seemed like a funky arrangement: Moms, the landlord, Moms the babysitter, but with all the money we thought we'd save on a babysitter it made the arrangement all good. That was until the first month's utility bills came in the mail. Neighbors could hear us screaming at one another clear to the end of the block.

"Boy!" Moms griped "The girl ain't hit the lottery, she just gets a welfare check and some paltry food stamps."

"I can't work a job, Moms." I shot back in my defense.

"Why the hell not, Shanally?"

"Cause I got football practice, remember?"

"Shanally, you damn fool, in thirty days it's going to be below zero and football season will be over. Ooooooh!" She groaned before she added, "Boy, on the soul of your father, may he rest in peace, yo' ass is gonna be a father and not some baby's daddy."

"Moms, I am a responsible father and not some baby's daddy. I change his diapers, feed him, bathe him, love him. What else do I have to do?"

"Support him financially!"

"Support what, Moms? The welfare check pays the rent. I can start eating down here, Lynn and the baby can live on her food stamps and WIC."

"Boy, grow the hell up, and I do mean right this very second. You are not going to shuck your responsibilities and lay around on this poor girl and my grandson. It cost four-hundred dollars a month for rent, and yo' dumb ass keeps the heat on ninety, so the heating bill matches the rent."

"I be cold sometimes and forget to turn down the thermostat."

"Baby, your forgetful, lame, funky ass has to understand that the costs of your foolishness is not coming out of that child's welfare check."

"It would help if you'd pay me the two-hundred dollars a

month you smoke up in weed." I immediately regretted saying it.

Mom's didn't say a word, she just grabbed her purse and coat, and stormed out the front door -- without the joint she had burning in the ashtray. She must really be pissed, I thought.

After a few hours, and a severe cussing out from Six, when Moms calmed down I gave her six-hundred dollars from my stash, and an ounce of Panama Red as a peace offering. I assured her that I was a father and not some baby's daddy. That evening at 5:30PM on the nose I started the job she'd hooked up for me at Big Burger.

Corey was starting to spit bubbles, bringing me back from the past to the present. When he looked at me and laughed, I figured he'd had enough. I burped his lil' ass and played his favorite game of airplane that made this six-month-old kid laugh his head off.

I laid Corey in his mother's arms and headed for the bathroom to shower and get ready for school. Lynn had chosen to drop out of school and scam the welfare for the daycare money. She claimed that Corey needed his mother and she needed the money more than she needed a high school diploma.

Today was going to be a bitch. I had football practice, and I had to work until close at Big Burger. Per my agreement with Moms, I worked full time in the evenings to go along with my weed enterprise and Lynn's check to pay the monthly bills.

The beat down I'd suffered at the hands of Marcus had sat me out half the season. I can't explain what happened to me, but when I returned to the lineup I was unstoppable. In five games I rushed for a thousand yards, averaging two-hundred yards per game.

C H A P T E R   3 4

The Minnesota State high school football championships were starting tomorrow night, I wanted to quit my job and take back my statement that I was a real man ready to do the family thing. The shit was killing me. But Moms seemed so proud of me that I was working without fuss, attending all my classes, maintaining a 'B' average, and single-handedly shattering the rushing records of senior halfbacks around the state. I didn't have the heart to disappoint her, so I just kept on working.

Being that I was a working man, who made more on his weed hustle than the job, I decided to treat myself and my family to a few of life's simple pleasures, while at the same time establishing a line of credit. I dipped into the Hellman money, which had grown to more than twelve grand, and I rented-to-own new living room furniture, a bedroom set, and a big screen television.

When Moms saw the hookup, she didn't want to know any of the details. She sat down in front of us, and said that from this day forward, all we had to do was pay half on the mortgage payment and our utility bills. She even let a tear drop fall from her eyes to show that the gesture was from the heart.

Lynn said that she should have received an Oscar for her performance, but she seemed happy nonetheless for the amount of money she was saving from her welfare check. "Sazzar!" Lynn shouted from the bedroom.

"What? I'm in the shower."

"Moms is on the phone."

"Ask her what she wants. I know she can hear this shower running downstairs."

"She told me to tell you to bring yo' narrow ass to the phone, and stop giving her lip service."

"Sorry." I grabbed the phone from Lynn while standing there butter-ball-ass-naked, dripping water on the floor. "Hello Moms."

"Baby, I have to put my car in the shop. Do you still have Six's car?"

"You know I do, Moms. How many times do I have to tell you he gave it to me. It's mine."

"Yeah, yeah, I remember now. Under the condition that you drive that cute little girlfriend of his to the prison once a week. I keep forgetting."

"You know he goes behind the wall day after tomorrow." Sazzar's disappointment was clearly in his voice.

"That's really sad, honey. I really like Six. Anyway, I need to do some major running around on my day off. So, can you follow me to the repair shop, and I'll drop you at school afterwards?"

"Sure Moms, but you're gonna have to pay for your own gas."

"Boy cut it out! I don't make your hungry ass pay for all the food you come down here and eat."

"Give me a half an hour, Moms, I'll be down."

"Shanally, do you still have any of those dime bags of weed you've been selling?"

"You know I do. You helped me bag 'em up last night."

"Boy, just bring one down when you come." The line went dead in my hand.

I handed Lynn the phone and she grabbed me pulling me towards the bed. "Baby," she cooed. "I want to go shopping today. Corey and I need a few things. Can I have some money?"

"How much do you need?"

"Oooh, about three-hundred." She ran her hand across my phallus.

"If you want the money, I'm gonna have to take a rain check on the fun and games."

"Come on baby, whenever I want to suck on your lollipop you never have time for me." She licked her lips in a show of sensuous élan.

I knew I was in the hands of a master when she made herself appear to be helpless and unthreatening. "Lynn, I don't have time to play, get to my stash spot, and make it to school on time."

"Stash spot? What stash spot? You keeping secrets and holding out on me Sazzar?" She stroked my phallus.

I tried to stay strong. I did. "Look Lynn, I don't have time for this shit."

She dropped to her knees and began sucking and licking. "What were you trying to say?" She took me deep into her throat.

Hell, the pleasure alone scared the shit out of me. Lynn was a porn star without the camera rolling. "The money, Sazzar, where is it?" She took me deep into her throat again.

"The money ... oooooh yes! ... the money. I have to ... oooh baby! ... it's in the basement to the right of the furnace. Yeah girl, that's right ... faster, deeper ... yeah baby, damn! ... It's on a string, you'll see it, pull out the bag, take three-hundred, and leave the rest."

Lynn took my entire length deeper into her throat causing me to quiver and erupt my seed. I tried to pull away from her pleasure but it was like she was sexually possessed. I tried to push her head back, but she walked on her knees until she pinned me against the wall of the bedroom, sucking out every drop of my seed.

"Aaaaaaaaaa!"

After I finally separated myself from Lynn, I went back to my now lukewarm shower and quickly showered again.

CHAPTER 35

Lynn made sure Corey was comfortable in his playpen, and ran to the basement, and pulled the string of dental- floss holding the bag of money behind the wall. Feeling the weight of the pillowcase the string was attached to, she yanked it free from its hiding place, and quickly made her way back up the stairs.

Her heart was racing a hundred miles an hour as she picked up the telephone in the kitchen. Listening carefully to see if Sazzar was still in the shower, she dialed the number she'd dialed every morning for the pasts few months. While the phone was ringing, she dumped the contents of the bag on the table.

"Hello baby!" She cooed enthusiastically into the phone.

"Hey sugar, what's up?" Marcus had been expecting her call. "Today is the day. You ready?"

Lynn could barely contain her excitement as she counted the money. Finding her voice she nearly gagged. "To leave bullshit Minnesota? Hell yeah!"

"Girl, what is up with you and this excited attitude of yours?"

"Marcus, baby, listen." She began whispering into the phone when she heard the shower shut off. "I can't stand another day or night with Sazzar. My hatred for this nigga has distilled into a single burning vibrating spot inside of me that longs for your touch."

"Ooooh! Hatred with a passionate erotic twist," Marcus teased in his Barry White baritone.

"Stop it Marcus. I've been trapped in the sexually depleted hell with this little-dick motherfucker while you've been in the hospital, and I know one of those strip-tease bitches has been playing with big daddy."

"Calm down, baby. You have control over that lame nigga. He's so insecure, lustful and easily manipulated, he doesn't have the mind to tamper with what is inside of your head. Besides, you needed a place to stay."

"And my big daddy?"

"I'm not gonna lie, there were some vulnerable moments when I was getting my sponge baths, and I've spent some time maneuvering my priorities. But don't trip. Big daddy is still on vacation."

"Big daddy better be. You know how I wallow in insecurity when I'm not with you."

"We won't have that problem in a couple of hours. Today it's over, we're leaving. Now tell big daddy something?"

"What's that, daddy?"

"What are you wearing?"

"I'm standing in the kitchen in my robe, almost naked, my hand is between my legs, and I'm thinking about the immense pleasure I'm going to get from the ten inches that's swinging between your legs."

"Don't take off without me." Marcus laughed.

"Not without you ... with you. Listen baby can you get a U-Haul Truck, a big one, and some people to help move at least eight full rooms of furniture?"

"Yeah, it's short notice, but I think I can get a few people. Where do you want to move it?"

"To Indiana, with us. We're going to need furniture, aren't we?"

"Sure baby, but to rent the truck for a long distance haul, gas, hire some of the fellas to drive down, and unload once we're there is gonna cost some paper." Marcus paused doing the math in his head. "I've got a few grand, Lynn, but that's to hold us over until I can get myself established. I don't think so baby, the rental would leave us short."

Lynn finished counting the money. "What if I could get you some conscience money."

"Conscience money?" Marcus questioned.

"Don't worry baby, just be here by 8:30AM as we planned. Hire a few people to help us move to Indiana, and by the time you get here I'll put twelve-thousand-five hundred dollars in your hand, and enough furniture for four rooms, some to sell, a big-screen television, a Pioneer sound system with four Omega speakers, and a cabinet full of antique silver."

"You know you'll be committing theft of Rent-A-Rooms property They'll probably call the police."

"Uh-huh!"

"It doesn't bother you?" Marcus tried to block from his mind the thought of returning to Stillwater Prison in a wheelchair.

"It wouldn't be worth doing if we were just stealing it, Marcus. Look at it this way, it's payback for putting you in that wheelchair, and with the twelve-five, and the furniture, we come out somewhere near eighteen-grand. Now, I know that's nothing compared to our loss, but it's a start at our future."

"Well, since you put it that way, consider my problem with the lame paid in full."

"That's what I'm talking about, Daddy. See you soon. Marcus?

"Yeah, Lynn?"

"I love you."

"Not as much as I love you, you cold-hearted bitch!"

"But I'm your cold-hearted bitch, Marcus." She stuffed the money back in the pillow case."

CHAPTER 36

I was standing in the bathroom drying myself off when Lynn walked in and did the damnedest thing: she helped me dry off, and watched as I got dressed.

Before I could get out the front door she stopped me. There was this strange tick in her neck that I didn't think much of at the time because I was running late for school. She grabbed me and kissed me passionately.

When she pulled away she had a weird look in her eyes. "Remember this always sweetheart. Being away from the one you truly love is mental torture." She kissed me again more passionately than the first time.

"Damn baby, save some of that for when I get home. I gotta run." Hurrying I made my way down the stairs.

"Goodbye Shanally! Wave bye-bye to daddy, Corey." She held his little wrist while waving Corey's little hand in the air.

It wasn't until Moms was getting into the Caddy at the repair shop that the picture of Lynn's face popped up inside my head. She was standing in the doorway, biting her lower lip, with a scared look on her face. During the few months that we lived together, I associated that look with her about to do something stupid.

"What's the matter, baby?" Moms was firing up her first joint of the day.

"Just tripping about the look on Lynn's face when I left the house this morning."

"Child, something is wrong with that girl, besides her being a little freak between the sheets. I hear y'all at night. 'Oh ... oh-oh-oh-oh!" Moms mimicked our sexual noises while she swiveled her hips in the seat. When she finished, her expression turned deadly serious. "She's an evil venomous snake on two feet, and mark my words, she's going to do something to show you just how hateful she can be."

"Moms, that is New Orleans talking. Stop with the voo-doo-he- do-she-do, please!"

She took a serious pull on her joint, and through choke and smoke she managed to speak. "Naw Shanally, it's not New Orleans talking, it's yo' mama speaking from experience."

The look in her eyes told me she was serious. I cracked the window to let out the smoke, and drove the Caddy down University Avenue toward Lexington,- so I could get to my homeroom class on time.

During my first period class a cold chill ran through my body, and for a moment I was completely lost. My instinct told me to go home and check on my son and his mother.

And to this very day I still beat myself upside the head for not following my gut. My damn head was so bombarded with images of Lynn that by fifth period I was so tired my eyes were crossed. Whatever was going on with me had me depressed as hell.

During football practice I ran both sides of the ball to relieve myself of the tension I was feeling. Instead of feeling relief, I felt a strange blend of anguish and defeat, a personal wounding deep within my soul.

I told my coach I wasn't feeling well, and headed for the locker room. At 6:00PM I stood in the parking lot looking for Moms' undependable ass, who was a no-show. I walked the half mile to the midway, giving myself time to think, but when I stepped into the job, all hell broke loose.

This sorry-ass crackhead who worked for food prep didn't show, and the kid working bailed. Nothing in this fucked up day was going right. Punk-ass Raymond, the other cook, called in with the lamest excuse known to man. This chump claimed he couldn't drive in the snow. I stood there dumbfounded when the manager told me this. How in the hell do you live in Minnesota knowing how the weather is on the first day of a good snowfall, and yo' ass can't drive in it?

To top off all the shit I was feeling, this pointdexter, big-eared supervisor was telling me not only did I have to work until close, but I would be the only cook.

"Look, Danny!" That's the lame's name. "I got to get some rest. I've got a football game tomorrow, and I can't be running the whole show, and expect to be rested for the game."

This puss-ass punk shot back. "Look Robinson, you wanna play high school sports, work part time and not full. The boss man of this region's Big Burgers already gives too much leeway because you're some superstar jock. Right now the team you play for needs you in the game in the quarterback slot, and you wanna ride the bench."

I was so damn mad I wanted to kick shit down this whip-crackin' white boy's leg. I made a mental note as I dropped the burgers that when I signed an NFL contract, I was gonna buy up all the Big Burgers in this region just to make this punk's life a living hell.

We closed that night at midnight and it took damn near ninety minutes to clean the place up. I'd been calling and paging Moms since eleven, and she finally hit me back around 1:00AM. She claimed she was at the house of one of the defensive cornerbacks for the Minnesota Vikings. After assuring me she would get me an autographed picture, she said she'd be home by dawn.

My mother was thirty-seven and a fitness freak with a weed habit, go figure. She'd gotten pregnant with me in her second year of college, and she still had the figure of a high school cheerleader, and could pass for twenty five on a bad day.

Truth is, she was fine as hell, but her dabbling in Egbo scared the shit out of men who chased her.

The damn buses in the Twin Cities stopped running at 1:00PM.

Moms was doing her thing and I was stuck. Murphy's law was all up in my ass, and I'd left my wallet in my hall locker at school, so taking a cab home was out of the equation.

I started to get angry and thought, what the hell! It was two miles from the midway to my house, and I could run the mile flat out in just under four minutes, three minutes five seconds, but who's counting? I had on a pair of army boots. There was two inches of freshly fallen snow on the ground and slush beneath my feet, and I was carrying at best five pounds of books in my backpack. I set the timer on my watch for eight minutes – thought it would be a nice test for my endurance – and took off running.

I'd just run two miles in eight minutes under extreme conditions, and one stanking-ass block from my house the timer on my watch goes off. I was elated and pissed at the same time.

Walking the last block I couldn't help but feel like a slave to the system, yet at the same time I was providing sustenance for two people I loved dearly. I couldn't imagine living without Lynn or Corey in my life. Lynn being the first woman I had an orgasm with, I guess you could say she was my first real love.

Closing the gate in front of my house, I thought football season would be over in a week or two, depending if we went all the way to the State Championships. Maybe I could ask Danny's child-labor-law-violating ass for some more hours, and spend all my free time with Lynn and Corey. Things wouldn't be that bad after all.

CHAPTER 37

I walked onto my front porch feeling like I was walking through a tunnel. I unlocked my front door, and walked into the most devastating thing that could ever happen to me in my young life.

My home was empty! Everything in it gone. The only thing left was a box on the floor with some shit-stained underwear in it, and a couple of dirty undershirts, and a note. The note was simple, plain, and to the point. It read. **DEBT PAID IN FULL!**

I ran downstairs to the basement. The string that held the pillowcase containing my money was hanging on the outside of the pole. The bag and my money were gone. I felt like a half-educated hustler who let a bitch trick him out of his pockets. I walked up the stairs damn near in shock. I took out my keys, and unlocked Moms' place to sit at her kitchen table, and collect myself.

Moms' kitchen was empty. Her dining room table, Grandma's antique China and Silver Server were gone. Moms' family pride stolen. Moving about my mother's place, I could see there was nothing left. All of my mother's possessions, even our family photos, were gone. That's when I fell apart, blinded and consumed with pure hate. My amorphous enemy solidified into the form of a woman.

I sat down in the middle of Moms' empty living room

floor, and tried to think of why Lynn would want to humiliate me and my mother this way. The bitch's move was about to steal my dignity, but I closed my eyes, and willed the tears back in their ducts. I tried to regain my composure, but I couldn't think straight without the picture of Lynn's lower lip coming to mind. Completely exhausted, I opened my eyes to clear her image from my head, but her face kept coming back. Her features became more distinct, and then there was this disjointed rambling of my subconscious, and all of her features blacked out but one. The lip she was biting, the lips that used to touch me, always soft, even in passion.

The next time I opened my eyes, Moms was standing over me with a cup of tea in her hand. I could hear voices in the distance that sounded like a party in progress.

"Baby, you've been asleep all day long. You weren't doing drugs, were you?"

"Stop with the jokes, Moms. You know I don't do drugs. What happened? Where am I?"

"You're at your Aunt Jean's place. She's downstairs doing some readings. The place is crowded, too. She's got lots of customers now, white folks and some blacks, too. Besides being the victims of a robbery, you blacked out on the floor, and when I couldn't wake you, I brought you here. Does that answer your question?"

"But why Aunt Jean's place, Moms? You know she scares the mess out of me!"

"Jean is not only family, she's a physician in the tradition of our people. Plus, she the only family member who had room to take both of us in for a couple of days until we can regroup. And as an added bonus, she read your palm."

"I don't need to have my palm read to know my future. Lynn took my son, my money, our furniture, everything we owned. When I find her, I'm going to kill that bitch, and anybody who helped her do this to us."

"Shanally, stop with the crazy talk, the girl was evil just like I said. Now you've got to pick up the pieces of your life and move on."

"Moms, she took our family mementos. We can never replace those things."

"Baby, those trinkets don't make or break us. If you need something to motivate you think about the house you are going to buy me on the Virgin Islands, overlooking my own private lagoon when you graduate from college and sign a twenty-million-dollar contract to play football in the NFL."

"Damn Moms, you think big, don't you?"

"Naw baby, Jean read it in your palm, along with some other things."

"What other things?"

"She said that your rise to fame would start tonight at the football game. Your coach called and said that the game is going to be televised. He's worried sick about you. I explained our situation to him and told him I'd have you at the stadium by 6:30PM."

"What time is it now, Moms?"

"Five o'clock, baby. Now drink this tea, it's special. Take all your troubles away. I drank one myself and I feel fine." She handed me the tea.

"Moms, you once told me your pain is what gave you strength and character."

"Child, the things your father put me through, God rest his soul, prepared me for situations just like this one. Lord, honey, that man was something else." She smiled at her late husband's memory. "Truth be told, I loved his shitty drawers. Problem was he loved the dope more than he loved me, you, or himself. So starting all over from scratch feels like your dad is back."

"If this is what it felt like, this kind of hurt, you should be glad he's dead."

"Shanally, don't speak of the dead that way in this house," Moms cautioned.

"Why, because you want me to drink Aunt Jean's tea?" I changed the subject.

"No baby, just a serious superstition is all. As for the tea." She flashed her beautiful smile, "Drink it."

"I don't want to be under the influence of no spells, Moms. I remember the boy who used to tease her. She put a pie in the window to cool knowing the fool would steal it, and he's still in Anoka County Hospital, crazier than a motha!"

"The power of the Egbo is nothing to play with. Now

drink the tea, Shanally."

I drank the tea, swore halfway through it that I was having visions, cried some, laughed some, and in the end Moms simply hugged me.

"Welcome to the world of grown folks."

C H A P T E R   3 8

"Shanally, telephone, boy! It's dat boy ain't got no mudda or fadda!" Aunt Jean yelled from the kitchen.

"What's up, Six? Sorry about Aunt Jean's mouth."

"Jean is one sick puppy. Thought you were scared of her?"

"Not anymore, she's really not that bad to be around. Taught me a couple of spells, better watch out!"

"Sazzar, she could teach you a whole book of spells, and it wouldn't work on me. I'm not that weak minded."

"Just bull-shittin', Six. You need something?"

"Yeah, tomorrow is the big day, and I need my main man with me in that courtroom to help send me off to prison."

"You make it sound like you're going to Camp Granada."

"Naw brother, just want you there with me is all."

"Then I'm yo' boy."

"You're not my boy, you are Sazzar, a king. So what if you let a trifling gold-digging bitch get out on you, and take your possessions and your money. It was a good lesson for you."

"Moms has got a big mouth, I see. And what have I learned, Six?"

"You learned that the bitch had you hypnotized. Her pussy was the instrument she used for the hypnosis. Come on, Sazzar, you knew Lynn was a freak using her pussy, ass, and throat like a whirlpool, sucking in ignorant niggas who were guided by the heads of their dicks."

"I was in love, Six. Don't get it fucked up."

"With the pussy, Sazzar. You were in love with the way she sucked your dick. Her thanks to you was to bite your hand, and sharpen the teeth of your contemporaries."

"My contemporaries? What the fuck does that mean?"

"Marcus!"

"Marcus? What the fuck does Marcus have to do with anything?"

"Sazzar, the world of extremes is not flat. It wraps itself around and into itself. If you open your eyes you'll see that you are at the joining point."

"Stop with the riddles and parables, Six. Just say whatever it is you have to say."

"Alright Sazzar. You've been hustled, conned, played, call it whatever you want."

"You knew this bitch was going to do something like this to me and you didn't warn me?"

"Let me tell you a story. One sunny August morning, I warned a guy to do something, he didn't do what I told him to do, and it cost two people their lives. Today him and I are like brothers. Do you think he would listen to me when his little head was doing all the thinking?"

"Man, that was some cold shit to say to me, Six."

"Cold how? Many a great man throughout history has been one tricked out of his life or his fortune cause he lived on the head of his dick, and not his intellect. The lesson you are so eager to understand about women, yet can't seem to comprehend is don't let the little head outthink the big head. If there's no money involved, kick the bitch to the curb, and find you some bedroom freaks: white, black, Hispanic, oriental, or Indian. Hell, mix an' match 'em if will satisfy your sexual appetite." Six paused to allow his message to sink in.

"Sounds to me like you're worried about my mental health, maybe wondering if I'm going to find Jesus, Buddha, or Confucius, and break down and confess my deepest sins while you're gone."

"I'm usually pretty close-mouthed about someone else's business, but you're my main man, and I need you strong. Sorry for my condescension ."

"No apologies necessary. I'm gonna miss you while you're

in that prison."

"No you're not, cause I'm going to see you once a week. Or have you forgotten?"

"How could I forget? It's the reason you gave me the Caddy. By the way, thanks."

"You always wanted one, thought I'd give you mine. But it's not for free. There's something you have to do for me."

"Consider it done."

"Tomorrow, when I go to prison, Tina will give you a list with five names on it. I want you to find the five people on the list, and when the time is right, bring them to Tina."

"That's it?"

"Not quite. I want you to match the five I've picked with three of your own."

"What's this for?"

"Tina will tell you. I don't want to discuss any of the details over the telephone."

"Does race matter?"

"For right now, I want all African Americans, and they need to have three qualifications: they must be intelligent, they must be athletic, and they must be able to go missing in action for a full three months without a family member putting out an APB."

"What happens when I get all eight?"

"Ten, Sazzar. You and Tina will make ten. When you all come together, something wonderful will happen."

"Do I have a time limit?"

"You have a seven-month window. Your three picks, and my five must be ready the day after the last day of school. After that we'll have to wait a whole year before the window opens again."

"I'll take care of it, Six."

"I know you will, Sazzar. Oh yeah, I made a bet with an associate of mine that in tonight's game you'll score at least three touchdowns."

"Your money is as good as won."

"I know that. I only bet on a sure thing."

The phone went dead and Sazzar placed it back in the cradle. Aunt Jean said there would be ten men and two women that would change my life forever. Must be something different because Six's count is ten.

C H A P T E R   3 9

"Tina, do you think you should be doing Yoga poses at six months pregnant?" Six began the routine with the opening to the Sun Salutation of Surya Namaskara.

"Six, you and I have been posing together every morning for the past two years, ever since Master Kim Pol instructed us on the farm."

"I know Tee, but you weren't this pregnant." He broke his pose, and attentively caressed her swollen belly.

"Boy, stop that! You act like I'm fat and out of shape." She playfully pushed him away.

"Well, you have to admit, you're not the buck-fifteen I remember."

"This extra weight is all baby. I'm not fat, you fool!" She kept her voice low, careful not to make too much noise and wake Fate. "Just pregnant." She held the Utthita Padangusthasana A Pose for a count of eight breaths before changing poses.

"Fate warned me about pregnant women and their hormones. He said I should be careful what I say and do around you. Say the wrong thing and watch the emotions go ballistic."

"Obviously, you didn't take heed to his warning. But I love you anyway. Now come on, this is the last time for three years I get to pose with my man, and I want every single second of my quality time before you go away." She kissed him lightly on the lips before the two of them fell into a rhythmical cadence: synchronizing their breath and movements through concentrating and maintaining uninterrupted rhythm.

Thirteen poses in, during the Warrior Pose, Tina's curiosity piqued, "Six, do you really think that I'm fat and sensitive?"

He cut his pose and pulled her close to his chest, "The comment about your weight was a bad choice of words, and for the forgiveness record, you are the most beautiful pregnant woman in the world, who is neither fat nor sensitive. However, who is pregnant, so I recommend that until our baby is born, his mother should stick to the beginner's poses, and leave the more complicated ones to the professionals."

"Now I know yo' stiff robotic ass did not just have me stand through that speech for you to end it by insulting me."

"Girl, you cannot hang with me!"

"Six, I will pose you inside and out, even at six-months pregnant, and you know this, man!" She punctuated this with a head shake and a finger snap.

"I don't want to take advantage of your disadvantage, so I'll leave you alone."

"Disadvantage? What disadvantage?"

"Your belly, Tee!"

"What about my belly?"

"Besides throwing you off balance, it's just in the way." He laughed and pointed at her swollen belly.

"Oh! just a minute ago I was the most beautiful pregnant woman in the world, and now my belly is in the way. And on top of all that, the shit is funny to you, huh?"

"See, Fate was right. Yo' ass is sensitive. Wait until I tell him about this."

"You're so sweet." She gave him a sardonic smile.

"Don't change the subject, woman. All I'm saying is, in your delicate condition leave the more complicated poses to *moi*!" He slapped himself in the chest matching her sarcasm.

"Ha! check this out, Mr. Complicated pose man." She sat contumaciously on the floor spreading her legs, palms flat on the floor in front of her belly. With the ease and grace of a circus contortionist, she folded in her left leg placing it over her left arm then locking her left foot behind her right forearm. After doing the same with her right leg, to the opposite side she locked them in place, and lifted her body off the floor, supporting her weight with the strength of her arms.

"Ta da! Complicated, hell. Kukkutasana 3rd. Eye. The hard way, No hands!"

"But you still have to get five breaths." Six snickered.

As she began to breathe, she cried out. "Oh no!"

"What's wrong? Can't figure out how to get loose?" Six teased.

"No baby, this is serious." She lowered herself to the floor.

Seeing the serious look on her face, Six became more concerned. "What's wrong, Tee?"

Calmly she looked up into his eyes. Six blinked to clear his vision because he thought he was seeing fear in her eyes. Kneeling down beside her, his heart raced. "What's wrong, Tee?"

"My water broke!"

"Tee, that's not supposed to happen for another three months. Must be something else." He felt the relief as his heart returned to a normal rate. "Alright, don't move. I'm going to get Fate. I'm sure he'll have something to say. He may even be upset with you for a change, posing at six months pregnant."

"No Six, please don't do that. It's only four in the morning, and it very well may be nothing. Please Six, I know what just happened, but we can call him from the hospital? If it's nothing, you guys can tease me forever. But if it is serious, I want to be where our baby can be saved."

"Alright, I'll warm up the Jeep. Do you need me to help you get dressed?

"Just help me off the floor. I can handle it from there."

CHAPTER 40

"Okay, dammit!" Fate shouted into the phone. "Let me get this straight. You and Tina are at St. John's Hospital, and her doctors are saying that she is in labor?"

"That is exactly what I'm saying, Fate."

"How, Six? She's only six months pregnant." He said, his voice becoming a bit louder.

"I don't know, Fate, you're going to have to ask the Creator that one when you stand before him on the Day of Judgment, because her doctors don't have a clue."

"Dammit boy, you got mad jokes this morning, don't ya?"

"I wish I was trying to be funny. Her doctors say she's already four-and-a-half centimeters, and because of the baby's size he may just make his appearance when she reaches eight centimeters or better."

"Six, why didn't you wake me?" Fate's voice clearly expressed his disappointment.

"Sorry Fate, sometimes a man's got to be responsible for his own actions.

"Boy, don't quote me, and yes it's true. But goddammit, Six, having a baby is not what I'm talking about and you know it."

Six put the phone to Tina's ear and they both shared a smile at his grumbling.

"Fate, you are a big part of us. As a matter of fact, you are at the center of us, and we would never leave you out of any part of our lives. Please don't be mad at us." Fate melted at the sound of her voice.

"I could never be angry with you, Miss Tee, but Six!"

She interrupted him before he could get started. "Fate, you are going to be a Grandpa." Fate could hear the joy in her voice.

"How does it feel?" Six shouted.

"About as good as the day the two of you came into my life.

Now let's stop all this sentimental crap. How am I going to get to the hospital and witness the birth of my grandchild when my Jeep is at the Hospital?"

"Already taken care of. Sazzar and his mother are on their way to pick you up. They should be there any minute now."

"That must be his damn fool ass blowing the horn now. Six, I didn't know Sazzar had a mother?"

"Six laughed. "How did you think he got here, miraculous birth?"

"Funny. I assumed he was an orphan like the two of you."

"Naw Fate, Sazzar's got mad family around the twins. His mom is in her late thirties and fine as she wants to be."

"I ain't got time for a woman, Six. All the demons that come back with me from Nam. No good! Negative! You did say she was good to look at, though, right?"

"You'll see."

"I'll be there in a minute, son. Get back to Tina."

"I've never left her side, Grandpa."

***

"Aaaaaaaaaah! Damn that hurts!" Tina screamed when the contraction subsided. "Nurse, Why am I in so much pain? Why is this happening to me? My baby is only six months along."

"Honey listen," the nurse began, "The ultrasound revealed a placental abruption. It's a complication wherein your placental lining has separated from your uterus. Placental abruption, I'm sorry to say, is a significant contributor to maternal mortality. However, because of your quick thinking, and your getting to the hospital to receive medical intervention, you and your baby will be fine."

"So I could have died?" Tina mumbled under her breath just as the next contraction started.

November 3, 1994 at 10:55PM Tina Lane delivered a three-month early premature baby boy with all of his fingers and toes, weighing in at two-pounds six ounces. To everyone present his name by unanimous decision was J.T., initialed after his parents, Jeffery and Tina.

Six wanted a picture of himself holding his son, so, dressed in hospital scrubs he stood over the incubator, careful not to disturb the heart-rate monitor, pulse, and respirator device attached to his son's body. As instructed by the nurse and under her close supervision he placed his left hand under J.T.'s head, and with his right hand he scooped him into his palm.

Mixed emotions overwhelmed him as the flash bulbs popped. A tear of joy formed and fell from the corner of his eye. He vowed it would be his first and his last.

Speaking to his son he imparted. "Your children are not your children. They are lives longing for itself." A man named Kahil Gibran wrote that in his book called 'The Prophet'. I say that all that is good and pure in my life is in the palm of my hands and a hospital bed. Me, I'm your father, and I'm pleased that you could not wait to meet me."

C H A P T E R   4 1

"Sazzar, thanks for coming to court with me."

"I wouldn't've missed it for the world, Six."

"Yeah, I know. That was one hell of a performance you put on last night at the football game. You played like a man possessed. I only needed three touchdowns and you scored five. They say nearly a million Minnesota viewers watched that televised game."

"I made a bet of my own, and mine was for five."

"Who was crazy enough to make a bet like that with you?"

"A scout from U.S.C."

"U.S.C.! University of Southern California?"

"Yep. He said that if I keep running like that in my senior year, I'll have a paid scholarship to play ball at U.S.C."

"You keep running like that, I want tickets on the fifty-yard line."

"College and the pros, you got that, Six." I was thrilled that my friend was admiring me.

"All rise! This court is in session, The Honorable Judge Clyde Davison presiding." The same WWF wannabe Sheriff's deputy brought the courtroom to order.

"Mr. Beise?" Judge Davison took his seat on the bench.

"Good afternoon, Your Honor. For the record, Eric Beise representing the Great State of Minnesota. This is the State versus Jeffery Alexander Lane, SIP number 00033943, County Attorney file 94-3607. Your Honor, Mr. Lane was indicted by a grand jury to Count 1 for Attempted First Degree Murder; Count 2, Assault 1 Great Bodily Harm; and Count 3, Carrying a Firearm Without a Permit.

"The case was referred to Your Honor for trial on October 9th. We held a Rasmussen Hearing, there were plea discussions, and Mr. Lane pled guilty before this Court. His Plea Petition calls for 36 months actual time in prison for Assault 1st Degree. With his acceptance of the plea, the State has agreed to dismiss the remaining charges. At this time, the State of Minnesota is prepared to go forward with the sentencing."

Mr. Beise, it's my understanding that the victim and family members wanted to address the court?"

"Yes Your Honor. However, they had to leave town on urgent family business, and left in their wake sworn Victim Impact Statements which the State omits from these proceedings."

"All right. Is there anything else from anyone with regards to sentencing in this matter?" Judge Davison scanned the faces of those present in the courtroom before he continued. "Okay Mr. Lane, is there anything you would like to say before this court imposes sentence?"

"No, Your Honor."

"Mr. Shaw, we have not heard from you this morning."

"Well Your Honor, this Court has ruled that the bases for the sentencing are the plea negotiations which were given to the court in writing last month, on the tenth. I would add that before Your Honor stands a young man who does not have a violent past. He has complied completely with all of the court's orders, and the Probation Officer's evaluations. For the first time in my career I speak for a client, not from my professional viewpoint, but from a personal level because I have had the pleasure to speak and interact extensively with Mr. Lane on several occasions. Your Honor, I must say that this young man has many messages, tones and sincere ways in which he has expressed his remorse for the unfortunate tragedy that has brought him before this court. I say for the record that the real tragedy is that the system, rather than create programs that would help youthful offenders who commit acts of violence, would rather place sixteen-year-olds in prison with long prison sentences where they may very well become victims themselves. With that said, I submit my client for sentencing before this Court."

"For the record, Mr. Shaw, the court concurs. Youthful offenders who are first-time offenders should receive help instead of presumptive commitment to State imprisonment. However, I am bound by the Sentencing Guidelines Grid that denotes the range within which I may sentence without the sentence being deemed a departure.

"In that vein, Jeffery Alexander Lane, having pled guilty to the offense of Assault 1st Degree in violation of Minnesota statute 609.19, which was negotiated by and through your attorney with your active participation, this Court hereby sentences you to ninety-one months based on the Pre-Sentencing report. You will be committed to the custody of the Commissioner of Corrections for the State of Minnesota until the aforementioned sentence has expired. Thirty-six months of the sentence is the minimum imprisonment, and fifty-five months will be supervised release.

"Now, Mr. Lane, I want to make one thing perfectly clear. Your days of carrying a gun are over in the State of Minnesota. When you are released from St. Cloud Reformatory, there will be a standing order to all law enforcement agencies that if they suspect you have a gun on your person, or in your home or vehicle, you will be taken into custody and directly to Stillwater Prison. Mind you, I am also placing in this order that a dispatcher get a hold of me day or night, regardless of the time, and I will fax the lockup order myself to the Prison Administrator. This Court is in recess for ten minutes. Bailiff, take Mr. Lane into custody."

* * *

"Whooooa, Colonel! You scared the shit out of me, sir. Did you mean what you were saying?" Captain James closed the door to the Judge's chambers.

"Captain James, that was tough love for your young man. Besides, have you ever known me not to be serious?"

"I stand corrected, sir."

"James?"

"Yes sir."

"I can have your boy placed in one of our rehabilitation programs; get him out of the gladiator arena."

"No thanks, sir. It will be good training for him. He has to understand the value of his freedom. If it were up to me, sir, he would spend the entire thirty-six month sentence in the Reformatory.

"I understand Captain. James, listen, don't be a stranger. We truly enjoyed your company the other evening."

"Thank you, sir."

"When the time comes, James, bring that grandson of yours over for some Davison family spoiling."

"Wouldn't miss it for the world, Sir."

The two men walked side by side to the judge's private entrance to his courtroom. Fate heard "All rise" as his friend entered his arena.

CHAPTER 42

"This is it, Lane. Your new home away from home for the next thirty-six months." The Sheriff's Deputy slowed to make the turn into St. Cloud Reformatory.

"Hey Smitty?"

"Yeah, kid?"

"I noticed when I got in this vehicle it smelled like cheap booze. Could that be the reason why on the ride up you kept having moments of bitterness that were accompanied by moments of profound self-pity? Or was it that your drunk ass needs a drink? And by the way thanks for the Wendy's chicken sandwich."

"After riding sixty miles with your smart-mouthed ass, you little shit, I think I will stop and have myself a drink just as soon as I drop yo' jailbird ass off. And you're welcome, kid. Lane?"

"Yeah, Smitty?"

"Watch yourself in here. These people are serious assholes. You hear?"

"Sure Smitty. For an overweight black pig, you ain't no bad dude."

"That's 'Mr. Black-Pig' to you, you juvenile delinquent. And off the record, I don't make the uniform I'm wearing or the gun I tote more important in my life than a kind word or a gesture. Just watch your ass, Lane."

Six turned and looked out the window and there it was.

St. Cloud Reformatory.

Smitty pulled the wagon to a stop just inside the barbwire fence and killed the engine.

"Remember what I said about these people, Lane." Smitty opened the sliding door on what he called his paddy wagon, and Six stepped out to face the two guards whose faces and bodies were indistinct in the blinding sun behind their heads.

"Jeffery Alexander Lane, here's his file." Smitty handed the yellow file folder to the guard, and then turned to Six. "Take care of yourself, kid."

Smitty returned to his wagon and Six didn't speak. From the looks on the guards' faces, he didn't know if it was allowed or forbidden to speak.

"This way." The guards stepped forward. Six noticed that one of them carried a pump shotgun and the other a nightstick. Without another word, their weapons at the ready to show there would be no discussion on the matter, Six began to move his chained feet.

He willed himself to show no reaction, but his stomach was doing back flips from curiosity and the guards' suspicious nature.

Six had made it about five feet when the guard with the nightstick tripped him, and he fell face-first into the dirt. The guard squatted and grinned at him.

"Welcome to St. Cloud, nigger!" Six willed himself to remain quiet when the guard stood, kicked dirt in his face, and returned to his squatting position inches from Six's face. "What, you don't like that, boy?" He asked with a pouty face.

Six blew the dirt from his mouth, and cleared his throat, then spit right in the racist bastard's face. The guard leapt to his feet with a curse and swung his boot back to kick Six.

"I wouldn't do that if I were you." Smitty walked toward the guards as he unstrapped his .357 Magnum. The guard lowered his boot, looking over at the fat Sheriff's Deputy, then back at his prisoner on the ground.

"This little motherfucker fell, and I was trying to help him up, and the bastard spit in my face." He wiped the spittle from his face.

"I'll tell you what!" Smitty was angry. "I'm gonna have the

judge call the Warden, and I guarantee you if one hair on this kids head is harmed, I will be back personally to put the cuffs on the both of you. Am I understood?" Smitty eyed the two prison guards.

"Do whatever makes you happy, Deputy." The Correctional Officers stood there face fighting with Smitty.

Smitty helped Six up off the ground, and watched intently as he was escorted inside the reformatory.

Entering the reformatory, Six was assaulted by the smell of sweat, and the scent of fear that rushed his nostrils. The two guards walked him to the holding cell and placed him inside.

An hour later, still black-boxed and shackled, Six faced the wall, and focused on a peaceful place in his mind. Remembering his training with Master Kim Pol, he smiled at the thought of him, and concentrated on focusing his power. **'The secret is to be more superior in strength of mind to the one who threatens a shackled man'.** Just as he was hearing Master Kim Pol's words, a voice interrupted his thoughts.

"Well-well-well, what do we have here, Luke?"

Six turned around, and standing in front of the holding cell was a cocky, impatient-looking white man dressed in one of those Seersucker suits. He could see the gray patches in the hairline over his temples. He looked to be in his late fifties, lean and tough. Six sized him up to be two-hundred-and-twenty-five pounds of bundled up white fool, on the verge of a breakdown at any minute.

"Are you talking to me?" Six eyed his new arrival.

The man took a step back. He had seen the body language and facial mannerisms in a thousand young punks who thought they were tough mothas, but once on lockdown cried like the little bitches they were.

"It's only you and me, boy, and just who the fuck do you think you're talking to?"

"Who is this belligerent son-of-a-bitch?" Six mumbled to himself.

What's that? you say somethin', boy?" Without waiting for a response he turned. "Baker, get your ass over here!"

"What can I do for you, sir?"

"Why is this boy all fucking dirty about the face and still black-boxed?"

"Don't know, sir. This is the first time I've seen him, sir."

"Who brought him in here?"

"Best guess, Stuckley, sir."

"Tell Stuckley to get his ass in here."

"Yes sir."

"Excuse me, sir. Who are you?" Six was curious.

"Dog-gone-it, this punk has some upbringing but his manners suck. Boy, has anyone ever told you not to interrupt grown folks when they're talking? So shut up unless you're spoken to. And for your FYI, boy, I'm what's called a Warden. You are not in one of those kiddies camps. You're in prison, and your ass belongs to me."

"Warden Conners, you wanted to see me, sir?"

"Yeah Stuckley. What the fuck happened to this kid? Why is he so damn dirty and still wearing shackles?"

"Well sir, when we were bringing him in he stumbled and fell, sir,"

"Stumbled and fell my ass." The Warden turned toward Six, his nostrils flaring. "Kid, how the hell did you get so filthy?"

Six looked at Stuckley and sent him a silent message as their eyes met. "I'm clumsy, Warden. I fell ... just like he said."

"The both of you are full of shit! Get out of my face, Stuckley." Six studied the Warden's face. There was something about his nondescript features, and the cold glint in his eyes that grew colder with every second of Six's silence.

"You eyefucking me, boy?"

Six's eye contact remained steady. "I'm not gay, Warden. Only a homosexual would find something attractive enough about another man to 'eye fuck him'."

"Then what the fuck are you looking at?"

"Not so much what I was looking at, but more what I was thinking."

"Oh, you're one of those smart-mouthed niggers. Baker!" He summoned the turnkey.

"Yes, Warden Conners."

"Give this punk twenty days in lockdown, pending review

by me personally before he is released to population."

"Yes sir."

"Warden?"

"Boy, what did I tell you about talking without permission?"

"Don't you want to know what I was thinking?"

"Not really, smartass, but for the hell of it why don't you tell me."

"The commitment in your eyes, sir."

"The what?"

"A very wise man taught me to always look a man in his eyes. He said that in them you could see his strengths, weaknesses, motives, and potential actions."

"What did you see in my eyes, boy?"

"I saw no hope for a young black man like myself. You even called me a nigger because of your need to be master over me. You believe to the core of your being that it's your God-given right and endowment to feel superior in thought and ability over me. This is so, even if it would mean the sacrificing of my life, or the breaking of my soul."

"Officer Baker?"

"Yes, Warden Conners?"

"I like this young man. What's your name, son."

"Jeffery Alexander Lane, sir."

"Reward Mr. Lane with ten more days lockup for his speech."

"Yes sir."

Warden Conners walked away laughing, and Officer Baker stepped to the cell door.

"Lane, that's a record. You are officially the first inmate in the ten years I've worked in receiving to get a thirty-day lockup order by the warden, of all people, and you haven't even been processed in the joint yet." Baker added, "If you want to make it in here, you're going to have to get with the program."

"Baker, as long as I'm here you will never hear me piss and moan about my fate or hardships. Would you like to know why?"

"Why, Lane?"

"Because nothing matters except my existence, survival,

and release on my terms."

Officer Baker processed St. Cloud's newest arrival, 06657041 Jeffery Alexander Lane, and took him straight to lock up. Unshackled and alone in a narrow cell, Six sat in the lotus position on the concrete floor and free meditated on J.T. and Tina.

CHAPTER 43

The past thirty days had been long and hard, and Tina felt the effects of them deep down in her bones. Since her release from the hospital, she was a full-time student at Washburn High School, and to spend time with J.T. she volunteered as a candy-striper at St. John's Hospital.

The staff at St. John's adored her and her son. Some days during her break, she gladly shared her time with her son with all the other candy-stripers and nurses on duty. Although tests ran on J.T. showed that, his organs were small, they were well developed. Nurse Shelly, a small framed white woman of average looks and the heart of Mother Teresa, assured her daily that with his appetite, in three months he would be six pounds; enough weight to be released to his mother's care.

Unlocking the door to Fate's house, Tina stepped inside, and entered the security code on the key pad to shut off the alarm, and closed the door behind her. She hated being so damn cautious. The stupid alarm was Fate's idea, she told him it was a waste of good money when she was trained by weapons experts and instructed in self-defense, but Fate was not hearing her. The next door neighbor's home had been broken into and robbed by crackheads who freely roamed the neighborhood, and all of her arguments fell on deaf ears.

Fate dismissed her, saying he intended to protect his grandson and her no matter what the cost. In Minneapolis, like most metropolitan areas, the crime rate escalated with the crack epidemic, and Minneapolis was earning the nickname of Crack Alley.

She searched the mail but still no letter from Six. She kicked off her shoes, allowing the carpet to massage her tired feet. With Snuff, who had become her constant companion and watchdog at her side, she flipped on the stereo and the smooth sounds of LTD's 'Love Ballad' filled the room. She tossed the mail onto the dining room table, and put her thoughts on a hot cup of tea, a hot bath, and eight hours of uninterrupted sleep.

Without bothering to turn on the kitchen light, she went to the cabinet, and pulled her favorite mug from the shelf. Snuff yelped out two crisp barks, sounding the alarm that the kitchen door was being rattled by a friend.

"Damn door!" Fate cussed, coming into the kitchen.

"Fate, you would make some woman very happy with your grumpy, complaining self. Why haven't you found a woman to marry and make happy?"

"First off, Tee, why are you standing in the dark? And second, it's complicated."

Tina switched on the light and nudged Snuff to go be man's best friend. Negative! 'Damn dog', She thought.

"Why is falling in love with a woman so complicated for you?"

"Tee, that's restricted information, and on a need-to-know basis, and since it is my personal business, you don't need to know."

"Fate, don't do that."

"Do what, Tee?"

"Start denying me access to your heart and inner feelings. Who knows? It may start a snowball effect, and every time I ask a question that's personal in nature, here you come with this bogus response."

"Tee, I've been up front and personal with you and Six more than I have been with any other human beings on the face of this planet. And for the record I've never lied to either of you. I may not have told you everything about myself, but what I have told you has been the truth and from my heart."

"Fate, you are my father and more. I love everything you are to me. Is it so bad for me to want to know something personal about the only man I've ever known to be my father?"

"Tee you had me feeling guilty and about to bawl until you started fluttering your eyelashes. How in the hell did you learn how to charm men the way you do?"

"It's called instinct, womanhood."

"And what does your womanhood instinct tell you about my personal business?"

"That I can identify you with an African King and not some man with a beer in his hand and abusive thoughts on his mind, sprawled in his favorite Lay-Z-boy, programmed with false ideals of his artificial manhood."

"You actually listen to me, don't you?"

"Every word. And because you love me so much, you're going to spill your guts. No fabrications and declassified."

"Well, you got the first part right, I do love you. As for the second, make mine a double of whatever it is you are having, and make mine with that special blend that I like so much, and I'll give you the skinny."

Tina fixed the tea, adding rum and a slice of lemon to Fate's mug, then sat down at the kitchen table waiting for him to return. She let out a soft giggle, thinking of what Fate was mumbling on the way to his room. Something to the effect that she was part of some woman's information extraction team, designed by women to learn all about the opposite sex, with the only motivation being to get them to eat out of the palm of their hands.

CHAPTER 44

When Fate returned, he sipped his tea, added a little more rum and smiled. "What is your question, Miss Tee?"

"My question is why is such a wonderful man like yourself - who is handsome, educated, banked up, and funny - without a woman?"

"Thanks for the compliments, but like I said, it's complicated. But I will try and explain it. I don't believe I ever told you that I grew up in Las Vegas, Nevada."

"Las Vegas, Nevada? But I thought-"

"Do you want to hear this or not?"

"Sorry, Fate." Tina made the sign of the zipper across her lips.

"Growing up in Las Vegas I was just like any other teenager,

I had interest in girls and sports, I was in popular demand, and in lots of ways, I was just like Six."

"Is that why you like him so much, because he reminds you of you?"

"I like Six because like me he believes he's unique and his life has a purpose. I could not see myself married with a couple of kids, working in one of the casinos, and living in the Regal Estates. That's not how I pictured my life. I wanted to be all I could be, and Vegas could not provide me with what I needed for growth. I even had a girlfriend who was on the same page as me. Hell, I thought my future was secure."

"What was her name, Fate?"

"Her name was Lori Shannon." He paused and smiled delightfully. "She was beautiful, Tee. A small woman, she was a deceptively delicate, gorgeous redbone whose eyes were wide open to the world. She was so impressive, Tee. She had lips so strong and sensuous she could ..."

"Fate spare me the dirty little sex secrets, please."

"Sorry Tee, I got caught up in the moment. I haven't thought about Lori in years. It's strange because sometimes I can smell the jasmine from the shampoo she washed her hair with. Anyway, for personal reasons I joined the Marine Corps. Our plan was that I would career in the Corps, and Lori would finish high school and go to college. When we were financially stable we'd get married, have some kids, and make a life for ourselves in Southern California.

I went to boot camp in the winter of January 1970. Eight months later I was in Vietnam, stationed in I Corps as a perimeter setter and point man. I felt that if I was gonna die in the Nam, I wanted it to be quick. I turned out to be good at my job. In October of 1972 during the third day of fighting in Quangtri City by the Great Wall of the Buddhist Temple, I was wounded for the second time. A month later I received the second of twelve Purple Hearts that I got during the war." He reached in his pocket, and laid a Corps handkerchief on the table, which contained the Purple Hearts.

"The first one I received was a Purple Heart. The second one and all the rest are Purple Hearts in an Oak Leaf cluster. The then President Richard Milhous Nixon, under the standard operations procedures, rotated me back to the States, and I was assigned to the Sanonafrea Camp, Camp Pendleton California, 3rd Battalion Seventh Marines."

"Dag, Fate," Tina interrupted. "Not once did I hear you say you wrote the poor girl."

"Dog-gone-it, Tee, I'm telling this story. And for your impatient lil' behind, during my first two-year tour in Nam Lori and I wrote each other off and on, and agreed to get married. In October of 1972 my Company Commander, as an incentive for reenlisting for another four years, offered me Officer's Candidate School, plus a twenty-thousand-dollar bonus upon completion, and the rank of Captain. The offer was great, but it would make me an Executive Officer in a line company, and place me smack dab in a combat unit in the Nam, and away from Lori again.

"I had rented a one-bedroom apartment in Oceanside, California, with the intentions of going to Vegas to claim my bride. My rank and pay grade as a Gunnery Sergeant provided me more than enough money to pay the one-hundred-thirty-five dollars-a-month rent, so off to Vegas I went.

"When I arrived in Vegas, a good friend told me that Lori had fallen hard for a local pimp and even harder for his friend, heroin. She told me I could find her on the Strip, between the Stardust and Riviera Hotels and Casinos, and knowing that I should have just walked away, tucked my tail, and accepted my losses, my dumb ass believed that if she saw me in my dress blues, medals and all, man in uniform kind of shit, she'd run into my arms.

"I even saw myself punching out her pimp, and carrying my bride to be away into the sunset, to the applause of onlookers, or at least to the nearest detox center." Fate took a sip of his tea and the room fell completely quiet. To Tina the silence was loud and nerve racking, like fingernails scraping against a chalkboard.

"Fate!" She shouted.

"What?"

"The story." She made motions with her hands for him to continue.

"It was a big mistake, Tee. When I found her she had just finished servicing a trick. I called out her name, and when she came over she smelled of sex, booze, and cheap perfume. She was so high she just told me what she would do for twenty dollars. Not a spark of recognition. To her I was just another G.I. Joe she wanted to trick with, and not the man she'd fallen in love with and promised to marry. I was devastated, Tee. I walked down the Strip, lost in my own mind, and bumped into a gang of white college students from the University of Las Vegas, who called me a mass murderer, a baby killer, and a damn rapist! I was completely baffled at the thought. How could these soft-ass kids think that killing the enemy made you want to rape his women afterwards?

"Anyway, what these chicken-shit long-haired hippies did not, nor could they understand was you have to be one sick-in-the-head bastard to kill the enemy and rape his woman. I'd had twenty-seven confirmed kills in the Nam, and I wanted to pull the knife strapped to my leg and kill each of them, making the total number of lives I'd taken thirty-three. I walked away that night angry, and I was a better man for it.

"I made up my mind before I left the Strip that Lori had a right to her choices in life, and I was not going to punish myself wondering what I'd done wrong. I really didn't think she would wait for me, anyway. I'd just hoped that she would.

"Truth is, I was relieved. Marriage was out of the question. Children a big 'hell no!' I made a vow that night walking down the Strip that I've kept until this day. A child of mine does not deserve to be born into this fucked-up-ass-world. So I gave up on women, not just emotionally, but physically and mentally.

"I reenlisted, completed the twelve weeks of hell, and was given the rank of Captain by General Taffey. I returned to Vietnam, and despite being wounded several times, hence the other ten medals, I stayed in Nam until the fall of Saigon, and the closing of the American Embassy. My friend, who just so happened to be Lori's sister, Yettie, wrote me in the Nam, and told me her sister's body was found near a dumpster on the parking lot of the Frontier Hotel and Casino. She said her panties were stuffed in her mouth, and she'd been shot twice in the head with a small caliber weapon."

Fate closed his eyes, and his lips began to move as if he were saying a silent prayer. Tina respected his private moment and sat back and waited patiently for him to pay his respect to Lori's memory.

C H A P T E R   4 5

Fate opened his eyes, and took a well-deserved sip of his tea. "Where was I?"

"Lori's body had been found."

"Right. My job finished in Vietnam, I returned to the U.S. in 1976. On my way to my assigned duty station in Minnesota at Fort Snelling, I stopped in Las Vegas to visit my parents, and pay my respects to Lori. Her sister had her cremated, so there was no grave site. I went to the Frontier Casino parking lot, and to the dumpster where her body was found, said a silent prayer for her soul, and dropped a single rose on the ground.

"Going back through the casino portion of the Frontier to catch a cab, I had the damnedest thought. In the movie 'It's a Wonderful Life' one of the actors, Jimmy Stewart, was told by his guardian angel that every time a bell rings, and angel gets its wings.

"I had never gambled in my life, but I was drawn to the casino floor, where I purchased twenty-five dollars worth of five dollar slot coins. I walked up to the big machine on the main floor facing the door I'd come through. It had a red handle and it took both hands to pull the lever. It was a five-dollar machine, and to win you had to get all the fruits in the tumblers across in a straight line. This machine was loud with plenty of bells ringing on and around it. I walked up to the machine put the coins in the slot, said, 'Hope you get your wings, Lori,' and pulled the lever.

Fate leaned back and took a few more sips of his tea and fell silent. Knowing this would drive Tina crazy, he waited until she was midway into her grunts of frustrations.

"Tee, oranges came up in all five tumblers. I won five-hundred thousand dollars! The next day, with all my winnings after taxes, I flew to Minnesota to report to my temporary duty station. My love for fishing, and the fact that here in Minnesota there are ten- thousand lakes in the State, is the reason I stayed. This home, the junk yards, and the farm I purchased out of the winnings. The apartment building and the tow trucks came later. That's my story, Tee. You happy?'"

She seemed disturbed, and sat quietly while Fate drank the rest of his tea. Then she finally broke her silence. "I'm sorry about the love of your life, and I'm sorry you felt that way about women and children, before and after her death. What I'd like for you to help me understand is what changed, what caused you to go against your principles and form such a deep, trusting love for me?"

The question jarred him more than he wanted to admit. He thought his answer out carefully.

"In my youth, Miss Tee, my ignorance of innocence provided me with a broken heart. With the war, and deaths I'd caused by my own hand, I believed my heart would never heal. So for years I went without making any kind of commitment with any member of the opposite sex. When you and Six came into my life I realized what I'd been missing. I'd gone far too long without commitment of love, without family, children and grandchildren, without the value of growth, without strength of clarity of another person more than myself, all of this I was lacking in my life. To answer your question, it is because of you that I've overcome one of my deepest struggles. Besides that smile of yours is a light that can heal and release the negativity from any man's heart. Enough about me. Have you heard from Six?"

"It's been thirty days, Fate, and not a word. I know no news is good news, but I'm worried about him."

"No need to worry, Six can take care of himself. And he loves you. Believe me when I say there is nothing that can keep him from you, not even those prison walls."

"Yeah, he is resourceful." She brightened, her smile radiating at the thought.

"Yeah, that's what I'm afraid of. I think I'll have Thomas go see him. An attorney-client visit might be just what the doctor ordered.

"Thank you, Fate. I love you." She wrapped her arms around him.

"Yeah, the feeling is mutual, Tee. Now, if there is nothing more I think I'll go to bed."

"There is one more thing. Only I'm afraid if I ask you, you won't love me as much anymore."

"I'll never stop loving you, no matter what you ask me. Our love is safe. Ask away."

"Six wants you to train nine of his friends that he's hand-picked, the same way you trained us on the farm."

"He wants me to what? Has he lost his god ..."

"Fate!" She placed her hand over his mouth before the profanity spewed out in streams

C H A P T E R 4 6

"Excuse me, Warden Conners. Officer Baker is on the phone. He says he needs to speak to you concerning an inmate Lane."

"Thank you, Sara. Put him through for me, would ya?"

"Baker, what is it? That dang fool boy gone an' hung hisself?"

"No sir, quite the opposite. He's the picture of perfect health. Frankly, sir, I believe he could do his entire sentence in lockup, he seems to like it, but that's not why I called you, sir. Actually there are a few reasons. The first is Lane's thirty-day hole time is up, and I can't release him to population without your approval. Second, I can't send him to the compound because he has not fulfilled his A&O requirements; and last but not least, he's engraved written sayings all over his cell, sir."

'What? Gang symbols, graffiti, what?"

"Quotes, sir."

"Quotes of what, Baker?"

"Philosophers he says, sir."

"I'll be right down, Baker. I have a tour of ten future prosecutors and defense attorneys with me from the Criminal Justice program at the University of Minnesota. I think I'll bring them along, maybe get a laugh. Let them see firsthand the kind of shit we have to put up with around here." The line went dead in Baker's hand.

"You're the boss. Problem is, there is nothing wrong or funny about this kid." Baker looked at the phone before returning it to its cradle.

"If you can be cool I can get you out of here and into population, Lane. You can get visits, outdoor recreation, that kind of shit."

"Don't trip, Baker. I'm cool where I am."

"Lane, you're not like some of these other assholes around here. Why are you acting so hard?"

"Who says I'm acting, Baker?"

"Dammit Lane, I'm trying to help you. Just keep your mouth shut for a few minutes, and I'll get you out of here. Oh shit! Here he comes. It's show time."

"Warden Conners."

"Officer Baker. Okay, where's our artist?"

"Cuffed and ready, sir."

"Well, let's get him out here, Baker, and see how much damage he's done to the State's property." Officer Baker opened the door and Six stepped out, facing the wall without exchanging eye contact with Warden Conners or the crowd behind him.

"Lane?" The warden spoke as he walked by Six and into the cell. "Goddammit, Lane! Boy what have you done to my cell?"

"I wasn't allowed pencil or paper per your order, so I used a piece of the chipped wall to write down a few thoughts. Got to stay ahead of my peers."

"This damage may cost you some more time in the hole."

Six smiled at the thought of the solitude, and fell quiet, as the warden and his guest rotated one-by-one in and out of the cell.

"How old is this inmate, Warden? " One of the law students was curious.

"I believe Lane is sixteen, maybe seventeen. Why do you ask?"

"He's remarkable." Another student joined the conversation. "These writings are acquired knowledge, not innate."

"Yeah, no kidding, Helen." A male student pointed and

read aloud one of the quotes. 'Recognize the fortunate so you may choose their company, and the unfortunate so that you may avoid them. Misfortune is usually the crime of folly, and among those who suffer from it there is no malady more contagious: Never open you door to the least of misfortune, for if you do, many others will follow in its train ... Do not die another's misery' Who is this kid who quotes Gracian?"

"Not only Gracian, Michael, but also Fredrich Nietzsche, Niccolo Machiavelli, Jean de la Bruyere, Johann Von Goethe, Carl Von Clausewitz, and if I'm not mistaken, here is a breakdown. Well as much as the space would allow of a DNA strand. Here he has the cell nucleus with X-chromosomes, Y-chromosomes and the hereditary DNA mutations, all of which are fairly new discovery in the world of science. Warden Conners, I have the same questions as my students. Who is this kid?" Professor Riley seemed intrigued.

Warden Conners was staring at a quote he had on the wall in his office: 'There's nothing harder to stop than a thought about to happen.'

"I assure you Professor Riley, I intend to get to the bottom of this matter. Baker?"

"Yes Warden."

"Have Lane in my office in one hour."

"Yes, sir."

"Ladies and gentleman, I believe we can move on to other areas of our tour. Thank you, Baker."

"You're welcome, sir."

"Well Lane looks like you got some splainin' to do." Baker did a poor Ricky Ricardo impersonation.

"Looks like it."

"Well, let's get you out of that jumpsuit and into some institution clothing. At least you can look like an inmate when you step into his office."

"Baker?"

"Yeah Lane."

"What's an inmate?"

"Good question."

C H A P T E R   4 7

While being escorted to the Warden's office, Six looked across the roof to the high walls. Damn this is prison! he thought. Floodlights illuminated the wires across the second highest prison wall in the U.S. prison system. There were cameras at each corner, and Six imagined that at that very moment a Duty Officer was lackadaisically monitoring consoles and electronic equipment.

It would be an insult to his training, while being held in captivity, to not make mental notes of the cameras positions. Fate had given him a direct order that he could observe and calculate, but no matter what the circumstances, nor what opportunity presented itself, he was to remain in the institution until his release date. He could formulate a plan of escape, but to execute was out of the question.

Nearing what he perceived to be a security checkpoint, a telephone rang on a security desk. He watched the guard pick up the phone, and swivel around in his chair toward him. "Open two!"

Six and his escort brushed pass two guards as they entered the security gate. "Close two!" The two guards looked back at them, staring blankly, almost puzzled as the gate closed. "Open one!"

Six walked through the secured gate with Baker, who directed him down a long corridor.

He noticed that he was the focal point of resentful looks

from hacks walking by. He heard murmurs of conversations behind him and looked to Baker for an explanation.

"Relax Lane, my colleagues are just curious as to why I'm escorting a cuffed inmate around the administrative offices."

"Another first?"

"You bet your ass it's a first." Baker had an astonished look on his face.

Inside the Warden's outer office stood a woman by her desk who just pointed at the open door when they walked in. Her smiling eyes made Six reconsider his actions. Had he made a serious mistake engraving those quotes into the walls? He thought.

Entering the Warden's office, he saw several pictures of hunting and fishing trips surrounding mounted animal heads and skins. From the look of it, Warden Conners was a serious Huntsman. On the wall behind his desk was a picture of an old man dressed in his Army uniform saluting an American flag. Underneath it was a Legion of Merit Award.

On his desk were several pictures of two boys in different stages of their lives, standing proudly with their father. To the right of the desk was an antique chess set setting atop an antique table with a game in progress. Six quickly memorized the set-up and began playing the game in his head for a solution and a quick checkmate .

Warden Conners was sitting behind his desk, his whole demeanor emitting impatience. An angry aura filling the room with tension.

"Lane, you piece of shit! Your presence in my prison is becoming a major pain in my ass. Do you know why?"

"Not even a hello," Six mumbled. "I don't have a clue, sir."

"Well let me enlighten you. Minutes after you arrived on my compound, a Judge Davison calls me, and informs me that one of his Sheriff's witnessed an assault by two of my officers on inmate Jeffery Alexander Lane. He threatened, better yet, he promised to have a team of Ombudsmen investigate and interview every single inmate who has ever filed a complaint, and then to send the findings to a special prosecutor if one hair on your head was out of place.

Of course I assured him your safety was my utmost concern, and I would place you in administrative detention until I could perform a full investigation. And right now, goddammit, He slammed his fist into his desk, "Waiting in the visiting area is one of the most powerful' attorney's in the State of Minnesota. Do you know why he's here?"

"Sorry sir, I'm not gifted in the art of mind reading."

"You lil' son-of-a-bitch, he's here to see you. In his hand is an order from the same judge who wants to clean my clock, requiring me to produce you, in the flesh, for an attorney-client visit. On top of all that shit, you've gone and damaged State property by engraving quotes of dead phrase mongers on my walls. What the fuck do you think I should do with you, Lane?"

"Warden Conners, you are this institution's Chief Machiavelli. If you, sir, decline to impose a disciplinary sanction upon me, or at least a threat of future intentions to do so, then my response to your question is I'll bury my thoughts by the hut and wait until you decide what should be done with me, sir."

Warden Conners sat down shaking his head from side to side in disbelief. "Lane, I've read your files." He eyed him briefly. "On your preliminary S.A.T.'s you score 800 on all three tests, making your score 2400, which is unheard of since the tests are designed to make you miss at least a few questions. At first I thought it was a typo. So I called the high school you attended, and spoke to a Mrs. Cook, who assured me the score was legit and you were the genuine article. She says you have an I.Q. that exceeds 150 or better, so you can stop the smart mouth bullshit. I'm not the enemy. I'm trying to help you."

"If you are trying to help me, Warden Conners, then I suggest that you fold up your Scales of Justice, and put them away, and don't make judgment calls against me, sir."

"Are you speaking academically, or from the heart, Lane?"

"Strictly from the ticker, sir. I just want to do my time and go home to my family, sir."

"Officer Baker."

"Yes, Warden Conners?"

"The following is to be given to inmate Lane immediately.

First, he is to be taken directly from my office to the visiting room to visit with Mr. Shaw. Second, he is to be released to population and given a job as an Inmate Instructor of a GED class. Third, set up visiting for family members and give him some time on the landline."

"Will that be all, sir?" Baker smirked.

"Unless you want to give him the keys to the front door, Baker"

"No sir, I don't think that will be necessary, sir.

"Good. Lane, do you have anything you'd like to say?" Warden Conners stared at Six.

"Just an observation, sir, for which I would like some clarification on, sir."

"Observation?" Warden Conners sat back in his chair and removed his pipe from its holder. After packing it with tobacco, he calmly looked towards Six before lighting his pipe. "Shoot your shot, Lane.'

"Well sir, I see that you study complex chess puzzles and end games from Masters' play?"

"Good observation, Lane. Not many people would know it was a game between two master players. I'm impressed. I love the game, but not many people play at my level. So I challenge myself to a good puzzle or end game. Do you play, Lane?"

"I don't just play the game, sir, I live it."

"Interesting. What do you see on my chess board?"

"Without looking at the board, and maintaining direct eye contact with Warden Conners, Six began.

"White has no idea of the threatened disaster or he would have played pawn to king-knight-three. Even then, however, Black has a better position, which allows Black to bring the queen down for a defense at knight-two, sir."

"Aaaaaah, I see." The Warden glanced at his chess board. "Go on, Lane, please finish your analysis."

"Well sir, there are a number of charming combinations hidden within Black's position, but by placing the queen at knight-two ..."

"Like this?" The Warden moved toward his chess set.

"Yes sir. Now as you can see, nothing can be done against the threatening rook-to-king-three, or bishop-three, or rook-three. A move from queen-two forces White to resign." Six was still facing forward.

"Baker?"

"Yes, Warden Conners?"

"Get inmate Lane settled. And Lane?"

"Yes Warden?"

"On Wednesdays I eat lunch in the prison library after my rounds in the hole; I find it quite relaxing. There's a chest set collecting dust up there. If you're free, stop on by and we'll play a game."

"Is that an order, sir?"

"No Lane, it's a request, an invitation."

"In that case, if I can cut away from my teaching responsibility, I'll be more than happy to, sir." Six faced the Warden, check-and-mating his opponent.

"Whoa! Was that good for you too, Lane?" Baker seemed surprised while escorting Six to the visiting area.

"You are one sick puppy, Baker."

"Sick my sweet ass. I've never seen the big guy cower before an inmate. You must have some powerful friends. Who'd a thought a judge got all up in his ass. Now I know what he was doing in R&D."

"No, I'm just lucky, Baker."

"Lucky my ass, Lane."

"Baker, why do you keep saying, 'my ass' all the time?"

"What's wrong with saying, 'my ass?'

"What, are you offering it, or making a suggestion for an offer?"

Baker stopped walking, and for a moment stood completely dumbfounded. Six saw the confused look on his face and started to laugh.

Catching on, Baker flushed red. "Fuck you, you motherfucker. I ain't no freaking fag! You wanna go to the hole?"

"What, and risk you having to bend over and offer your ass to the Warden for disobeying a direct order?"

"You got a point there, Lane."

C H A P T E R   4 8

Thomas Shaw loved his work and had a good team beside him at Thomas Shaw and Associates. He believed in providing his clients superior counseling in all matters of criminal and civil law. Most important to Thomas was that he remain happy with himself. No more bowing and kissing the asses of Minnesota bureaucrats like he'd done when he was a prosecutor for the State. It wasn't until after he'd given them his resignation, and started his own law firm that he found peace in his sleep at night.

When Six entered the visiting room, Thomas knew he had the respect of the people that mattered, like Lafayette James and his young client, Jeffery Lane.

"Hello Jeff." Thomas stood to shake his client's hand. "You look rested, healthy, and in one piece. Not at all what I expected to find."

"Thanks, Thomas ... I think. You look fit and tan yourself. Did you expect to find me badly beaten and four-pointered to a bed?"

"Actually Jeff, I did."

"You did?" Six looked completely bewildered.

"Let me explain. I get a call from Lafayette because he has not heard from you in a month. He also tells me his friend Judge Davison, had to call the prison on your behalf due to one of his Sheriff's being upset because he witnessed an assault by correctional officers against yourself. Then I call the prison personally to set up this visit, and some mealy-mouthed person tells me I am not a part of the court records, and therefore I am not on your visiting list. Well, I call Judge Davison, who angrily tells me to stop by his clerk's office to pick up an Order for the Warden of this institution to produce you in the person. So here I am."

"As you can see, Thomas, I'm in one piece."

"Lafayette will be pleased to hear it. I also have a message from Tina. The baby is doing fine and growing, and the school project the two of you were working on is nearly completed."

"Thanks Thomas, that's great news."

"Jeff, is there something I can do for you, anything you need?"

"There is something I could use, Thomas."

"What is it, Jeff?"

"A copy of the Federal Rules of Criminal Procedure."

"I'll send you copies of the Criminal and Civil Rules, along with the rules of court for the State of Minnesota. Do I need to know why you need these books?"

"Research, Thomas."

"Research. Jeff, what are you up to?"

Six placed his finger to his temple. "Knowledge, Thomas. Knowledge."

CHAPTER 49

During the   months that followed Tina's initial visit, she had become a welcomed visitor at St. Cloud Reformatory. Fate had commented that ever since she'd been going to the reformatory, her personality had brightened. There was a definite spring in her step, and a smile that appeared more frequently, and she even laughed more.

For the past week she had been training in the House of Bags to acquire power in her kicks and punches, this morning was no different. At exactly 5:00AM the alarm sounded the bell for the start of the morning's edifications. She quickly dressed, stretched, and ran the five miles she'd run every morning for the past few months. She ran the last eighth of the last mile flat-out, pushing herself to her limits and beyond. Stopping before the double doors of the two car garage, she refused to lean against it to catch her breath. She stepped to the rear of the garage and opened the door to the House of Bags. The garage itself was twenty-four by twenty- eight feet, and the heavy bags were suspended from reinforced beams from the overlays. The individual bags were set in a bowling pin formation four feet apart. At the rear of the garage were two padded body dummies.

She began, as she had every morning before assaulting the bags, by meditating in a full-lotus position with her palms face up, resting comfortably on her knees. She closed her eyes, relaxed, and cleared her mind. As she began to meditate, she could hear the voice of Master Kim Pol.

"You are one with the Universe, a part of our Divine Creator's plan. Your mind's eye sees a light. There is a comforting warmth that flows from it. You allow its warmth inside of you."

For the next ten minutes, Tina focused her concentration on the warmth that moved slowly toward the center of her body. She could feel it's warm, soothing, healing power moving down her face, throat, neck, and chest, resting briefly in her abdomen.

The warmth began to ascend from her abdomen, retracing its steps through her chest, throat, neck, face, and finally coming to the light that reappeared allowing the warmth its leave. She free meditated for another ten minutes on J.T. and Six before rising from her lotus position.

She donned the padded gloves on her hands and bowed before the still bags. Giving the command, "Ha-shi-me!", She exploded into the first bag with a right front-snap kick. Stepping right she assaulted bag two with a double-punch followed by a series of jabs, hooks, and straight right hands, ending with a spinning roundhouse kick. Before bag one could come back to its set position, she stuck it with a back kick.

Arrow stepping into bag three with an elbow, she paused only for a millisecond before thrusting a sidekick into bag four that left it vibrating. Putting her weight on her right leg, she stepped, and executed a spinning heel kick on bag five that would have made Bruce Lee proud. She followed by launching a jumping front snap kick into bag six. When she landed on her feet she crouched to strike bag seven in the lower portion of the bag, to simulate a groin strike.

Executing a shoulder roll toward bag eight, and coming up in the Tiger style raking the face of the bag, she delivered several knee strikes before she circle stepped into bag nine, allowing the bag to go by her, opening her way to bag ten.

When she was clear, she delivered a roundhouse to the head of the bag that sounded like a whip cracking. Feeling the power of her strikes, she stepped to her left, as if escaping a would-be assailant, and executed a right-spinning-hook kick, the blade of her foot connecting with the bag with such force it jumped from the hook and crashed to the floor.

As she stepped to the padded body dummies, she did several sidekicks low to high then high to low with each leg, before she finished with three high kicks to the head of the dummy.

"Ninety seconds. That was superb, Tee." The voice startled her. She turned to find Fate tapping his watch.

"How long have you been standing there?" Her chest rose and fell with each breath.

"Since you hit bag one. You work those bags like you're preparing for war."

"Not preparing for war, Fate, exercising the relatively simple way through practice to achieve success." Fate smiled because he knew what she was going to say next. "Work harder than anyone else, and never give up, no matter what is before you."

"Well, it looks like Master Kim Pol has another one ready for a black belt."

"Really, Fate?"

"Absolutely Tee, you've trained your body and your mind with regularity to maintain both physical and mental well-being. I think you are ready for it."

"Is that why you're here, to tell me I'm ready?"

"No smartass. I'm here to tell you that you have a phone call from the hospital. One of the nurses."

"Is there something wrong with J.T.?" The fear clearly mounted in her voice.

"Relax Tee, I've already traveled that road. J.T. Is fine, but whatever she has to say, she only wants to say it to you."

Tina picked up the kitchen phone, and the cheerful brisk voice answered her greeting from the other end. "Tina how are you, sweetheart?"

"I'm fine, Nurse Shelly. Is there something wrong?"

"Heavens no, child. I just finished having breakfast with the Director of Pediatrics and tomorrow morning J.T. will be released. Sorry dear, that sounded so criminal. Discharged to your tender loving care. Congratulations!"

Tina felt a wave of relief pass through her and then an enormous sense of joy. When she finally found her voice she spoke between her tears of joy.

"I can't believe it, Nurse Shelly. It's been nearly five months, and I was beginning to think with all the additional testing being ordered that there may have been some sort of problem."

"Honey, stop that! If there were any complications or problems I would have told you. Besides, our special little one is the healthiest five-month-old baby I've seen. The only problem that child was having was not being with his mother, and that problem has been solved."

"Nurse Shelly?"

"Yes, honey?"

"You're an angel."

"I've been called worse."

"Bye, Nurse Shelly." Tina hung up the phone, and was so excited she barely noticed the blood on her knuckles.

CHAPTER 50

I pulled the Caddy to a halt in front of Fate's house, and tapped the horn three times and waited patiently for Tina. I had never looked at Tina other than like a sister, but when she stepped out the front door in a V-neck black dress with a white silk jacket that clung criminally to her curves, I couldn't help myself, my eyes were glued to her figure.

"What the hell is up with the girly clothes, Miss Tee? Where are the army boots, fatigues, ponytail and wrist wraps?"

"I feel good today. I thought, wouldn't it be great if I gave my man's mind, you know that part that activates his pleasure center, a treat."

"Being eye candy is not your style, Miss Tee." She had in fact refused to think of herself in those terms. She reminded me as well as herself, on a regular basis, that she would never follow the pathways of what one's false or abstract perceptions of love may be, nor its manifestations of lust, romance and attachments.

"I understand your point Sazzar, but I could never disrespect my body by using unconscious body language to lure in the notorious connoisseurs of beautiful women." Her lips curled ever so slightly.

I laughed. "Why don't you just call us what we are, Miss Tee?"

"And what might that be, Sazzar?"

"Pimps, Tee."

"Sazzar, no offense, but you don't have the intellect to begin to understand the concept of a real pimp's game."

"Bullshit, Tee. I've got these local bitches dropping their drawers."

"For money, Sazzar?"

"For me." I slapped my chest as I maneuvered the Caddy into freeway traffic.

"The game you perpetrate, Sazzar, the ritual of courtship, you know, talk first, then slobber all over her in hopes of moving together in perfect rhythm between the sheets, is not a pimp's game."

She waved her hand dismissively.

"Then why don't you school me, Miss Tee? I'm stuck with you for a while."

"You got jokes, huh? Okay. The game you play, Sazzar, is merely a game of lust. You're being used, as a boy toy. Women use you for an orgasm to decide whether or not they want to jump the broom with you. But if so and so is a little thicker or a bit longer then, my dear brother, you are set aside. You self-proclaimed pimps are actually being exposed for the frauds that you are."

"Damn, Tee! So what does that make a guy like me who can have any woman he wants, if I'm not a pimp?"

"You are what you are, Sazzar: a male whore, a sperm donor, and a guinea pig."

"Okay, Miss 'I-know-everything-about-the-pimp-game'. What is a real pimp?"

"Something you'll never be if you keep your head between those girl's legs."

"So hook yo' boy up with the secret of becoming a real pimp. That is, if you know?"

"Alright, Sazzar. First, a real pimp has verbal skills, he's a man, who with his words alone, can wrap a female who's either mentally strong, or psychologically weak up in his web work of ties that bind; he simply asks, and she'll turn her body into a business with little or no investment, and she will support the only stockholder with one-thousand-percent profit. He'll make her so proficient in her game she need only throw one leg over the other, clink the ice in her glass, and a trick will offer to buy her another.

"Now, don't get this misunderstood. If you're dropping money into a strippers G-string, you are being manipulated with the illusion of look but don't touch. If she speaks with you frankly about the price of her sex, and you pay the cost, you are a trick. Regardless of whether you break the headboards with her screaming your name, or you're too impatient and rough in bed, and she receives no pleasure from the sexual act, a real pimp, that is the genuine article, collects every penny of her proceeds."

"So that's how the real pimp game works?"

"If that's pimping, Sazzar, what are you doing?"

"Damn Tee, that was cold."

"You're the one who brought it up. I was just breaking down why I'm dressed the way that I am. Sazzar, I'm not one of these backwards teenage bitches who is unconsciously deciding what man she wants by the strength of the orgasm he gives her, or the size of his dick. I'm dressed this way for the sole pleasure of pleasing my man, and that's because of the deep concern and commitment we have for one another."

"Miss Tee, everyone who has eyes can see that you and Six are madly in love with each other."

"You look at us and call our relationship love, but what is your definition of love? Most people's perception of love amounts to nothing more than an overrated obsessive compulsive disorder.

Six and I have something better than that; we share a genuine and real love, the kind that just is. There is no desire for us to change each other in any way. Our love doesn't exist out of the want for material gain. We accept each other as is, advantages and disadvantages. All I desire is him, and all he desires is me, and together our love conquers and provides the sustenance of our union. We grow and improve, becoming better as one, we are committed to each other for life."

"Commitment, love, whatever you want to call it, Tee, it wouldn't matter what label you put on it anyway."

"Why do you say that, Sazzar?"

"God wouldn't've decreed any other man than Six for you, Tee. You wouldn't know what to do with a weak-minded man.

That's why God gave you Six. He's the only man I know that can handle all of your strength and endurance, both mental and physical.

"Sazzar, that is the first sensible thing you've said all morning."

Tina pushed the button on her seat and it reclined. She sat back quietly while I drove. By her silence I felt she wanted some space, so I pushed in the old school tape by Enchantment she liked so much, and set the cruise at 55 mph. I knew I'd done the right thing when she closed her eyes and softly began to sing the words to Enchantments, It's You That I Need.

Tina melted into the soulful sounds of Enchantment, and the events of the morning. Her instantaneous actions and reactions in the house of bags, and Fate's comment had her soaring, but the image of her rocking and singing a lullaby to her infant son sent her into orbit.

Another image drifted into her mind, and she wondered how she would juggle motherhood, school, and a soon-to-be military-trained group of young commandos. She was so happy and wanted to share it with Six that she dismissed the thought, thinking what happens tomorrow will take care of itself.

C H A P T E R   5 1

Six stood when she entered the visiting room, embracing her as she ran into his arms.

"Tomorrow morning I get to be a mommy to our son. We're a family, Six!"

"A family? What family? I don't see J.T. anywhere." Six playfully looked around the visiting room.

"Stop it, you silly fool. Tomorrow the hospital is discharging J.T., and I'm bringing him home, Six."

"You're serious aren't you, Tee."

"Very."

His voice softened as the realization washed over his face. "Baby, this is wonderful, I can't believe I finally get to hold my first born son in my arms."

Tina put a finger to his lips to slow the flow of words. Looking into his eyes she softly caressed his face. "I'll tell you everything later. Right now I just want to hold you. We are officially a family, Six, and I never thought that I could happier than the day I fell in love with you." She laid her head on his chest.

Six let his lips brush against her ear as he whispered. "I'm experiencing sensations myself, several actually."

"Could it be a rise in your testosterone level due to the fact that you've been working out? She could feel the hardness of his body.

"Not quite, baby. There's no guess work in this

demonstration. My heart has been slamming against my chest for the past few minutes because of that dress you're wearing."

"Now Six, you know you have to control your animalistic urges in the visiting room."

"Baby, the Pope himself would not be above temptation if he saw you in that dress."

"Do you think he would give up his mortal soul for a taste of my love?"

"That's exactly what it would cost him if I'm around." His mouth touched hers, tasted hers, making her arch her hips toward his in silent need.

C H A P T E R   5 2

The next morning Tina and Fate sat, quietly watching the play of emotions crossing Six's face as though he were seriously debating the blanket-swaddled bundle cradled in his arms. With bright eyes, and fingers in his mouth, J.T. lay motionless looking up at his father.

"You did good, Tee. He's beautiful." Six barely took a moment to look away from his son.

"I didn't do it all by myself. You and the Creator helped in his creation." Her heart began to do flips as the smile transformed his face

"Enough with the Hallmark moments, you two. We all know that my grandson is our greatest joy, especially mine. What I want to hear from one of you is one good reason why in the Sam Hill I should train nine knuckleheads in the art of war?"

Tina looked at Six and nodded her head for him to speak up. There was a short moment of silence as Six gathered his thoughts.

"Fate, you taught Tina and I to value ourselves. You are always reminding us that we are in times of deep change, and how we can move through these changes more easily if we are able to see the road upon which we travel more clearly.

"We want you to help a select group of others, like ourselves, to move in the world as gracefully as you've shown us, so we can open a window to our futures through which we can visualize a real and meaningful life. I'm asking you to trust my judgment, and open a window for nine young men of the same caliber as myself, and not nine knuckleheads. I only ask that the gift of sharing your perceptions be given to them as it was given to us -- freely."

"Six that was a seemingly good reason, you have a knack for persuasion. I'll grant you that ... your ability to bring people around to your viewpoint despite all logic is uncanny, to say the least ... but still, a lot of good my training has done for you. I believe it was the lack of grace that landed you in your current predicament. Now that said, training these young men would be a hard lesson in the art of war, it's a longing for itself that requires discipline. You can't lead these young men astray as you've done yourself. Righteous leadership is necessary to sustain life's proper balance. I hope these young chosen few possess the necessary character to harness what will be gifted them."

"So, does that mean you'll do it, Fate?" Tina eyed him pensively .

"Of course I'll do it. 'Oooooh rah' is always an invigorating way to start one's day. I spoke to the guys on the farm, and they all told me to relay this message: 'It's not enough to just say that you served your country proudly. We need something that will allow us to push ourselves to do better.' So they want to know when does the training begin?"

"Just like you trained us, Fate, for the past two years, during the one-hundred-days of summer vacation. Only it won't just be the nine boys that will be training. I'll be training with them." Tina once again eyed him.

"This is the age of gender opportunity, Tee. Those young men are in for one helluva surprise. They are going to have to pull their weight against a woman of wonder."

J.T. moved with a surprising strength in Six's arms, as if to say, 'Okay, that's settled, move on man. It's time to make a commitment in the name of raising a child.'

C H A P T E R   53

I walked the hallways of Central High School, energized by the impending challenge of having the team ready by the last day of school. It had been three months since I'd been told by Six that Fate and his men had agreed to train us. May 29, 1994 was the starting date of the recruitment, and I had to have the whole team ready to move out on Monday June 5th.

The first name on Six's list was Michael Williams. He was the same age as Six and I, but he looked much younger. Kids around the school called him 'Badboy' because of his knuckle game. When he wasn't knocking folks out, he was pumping iron. The guy was cool as hell, he had this calm about himself. Kids were enthralled by his mysterious ways. There was nothing you could say for sure about him because he was always changing his day-to-day demeanor.

Nothing rattled Badboy's cage. Six said it was because he cleverly cultivated an enigmatic image with no worries at all about seeming inconsistent or contradicting himself. Maybe that's why Six liked him so much.

I found Badboy at 1200 hours the first day of team assembly in the weight room in Central's gym. He was sitting on the bench press with three-hundred pounds on the bar in the rack over his head. Six instructed me that to get his attention just mention his name. Badboy would hear me out, and give me his decision right there on the spot, whether he was in or out, and halfway through my presentation he held up his chalked hand. "Tell Six I'm in."

He laid down on the bench and grabbed the bar. Before I could move into position to spot for him, he lifted the three-hundred pounds out of the rack, placed it on his chest, and repped it ten times, then put it back in the rack. I come to find out later that Badboy had a four-hundred-plus bench press.

Next on Six's list was Ronnie Green. His enemies loved to call him 'Babyface' which pissed him the fuck off. The name stuck because of his smooth hairless features. Born and raised in Kansas City, Missouri, and a graduate of S.W.U. or Sidewalk University with a degree in street psychology, Face was already a legend, at the tender age of sixteen, on 12th. and Woodland. He was one-hundred-eighty pounds of muscle on a five-foot- eleven frame, with dark eyes, attitude, and a close faded haircut. Face considered himself beyond the reach of the law, treating anything that carried a badge with disdain. It's rumored that while he attended Manuel and Percel High, there were some angry shouts heard in the hallway, and something said that was indecipherable to both students and teachers between Face and security guards.

In midsentence of the argument, Face produced an iron pipe from his shirt sleeve. There were a series of loud bangs against lockers and door frames, and then the sickening sound of metal meeting flesh. Several kids and teachers piled into the hallway, and stood transfixed, as a bloodied Face swung the iron pipe at full force hitting the last guard across the forehead, then watching in horror as he collapsed on top of his comrades like a dropped puppet.

Face's father, affectionately known as Paw-Paw, had decided his son was not going to Jefferson City Prison, known as 'The Walls'. So Paw-Paw defied court orders to produce his son, and helped Face flee Kansas City for a fresh start in Minneapolis.

After hearing this from Six, I asked why he wanted such a violent dude on the team.

Six pondered for a moment. "He's every bit the warrior, born for the urban battle and beyond."

I found Face walking out of South High School in Minneapolis at 1500 hours the first day of team assembly. I mentioned that Six had sent me but before I could get another word out of my mouth,

Face cut me off. "Whatever Six has going on, count me in."

I set out to find the next name on the list. His name was Kenneth Wendell. He was a six-foot heavily muscled human machine. A pretty boy, who was as mean as he was handsome, and simply intoxicating to the opposite sex. There was no single female, black or white, who occupied a more delicate and precarious position than to be Wendell's woman. Six called him 'K-Nine' because he was like a vicious dog who kept people in suspended terror. My mission was to find K-Nine, and hand him the note written by Six and walk away. At 1800 hours the first day of team assembly I drove down University Avenue to the Strip Club, and sitting on his Caddy in the parking lot right where Six said he would be was K-Nine. I met K-Nine's eyes, walked up to his car where he was seated, handed him the note, and walked away.

When I questioned Six as to why I was to do it that way, he offered. "K-Nine is a machine of interpretation and explanation. He has to know what you are thinking, and why you are thinking it. The note will carefully control what we are willing to reveal to him."

"What does the note say?" I was curious.

"It reads 'Central High School parking lot 5:00AM Monday, June 5th. Opportunity of a life time. Expect to be gone three months. Pack light. Six.'"

Tuesday, May 30, 1994 at 1800 hours on the second day of team assembly I met with the forth name on the list, Sir Godfrey Frye. Although he was only sixteen, his head was clean shaven, and he sported a full beard trimmed close to his face, a brush of a black mustache, delicate gold-rimmed glasses, and a dark ferocious look in his eyes.

His father was from Great Britain, and his mother was from Washington, D.C. Both parents were well educated and wanted the best for their two sons. Six called him 'Rasheed.' It was rumored that Rasheed's younger brother had been robbed and murdered by two dope fiends for his tennis shoes, his watch, and four-dollars cash. Rasheed and his parents buried his thirteen-year-old brother, then Rasheed took to the streets of D.C. days after the funeral, and located the whereabouts of the two men responsible for his baby brother's death.

Taking his father's .38 snubnose revolver from his closet, Rasheed moved slowly down Martin Luther King Avenue on snow-packed streets. He walked in silence, and could hear the sounds of people shoveling their walks, and cars creeping gingerly as they crawled around corners. On Goodhope Road, he turned in the direction of Minnesota Avenue. As he walked toward his destination he thought his mind would be full of panic. A fifteen-year-old about to commit a double-murder, or the possibility of facing his own death. This was not the case. A brother he loved had been murdered, and he was empty of feelings.

Standing in the shadows on the corner of 18th and Minnesota Avenue, he saw the two men who'd murdered his brother open an iron gate and descend a flight of stairs. He told himself that the only one to fear was God, the two men at the bottom of the stairs had taken his brother's life.

"Do not think, do not speak, do not hesitate. Two shots each in the head." He recited aloud to himself. He opened the iron gate- walked down the stairs, and saw the two men smoking crack from a glass pipe. The larger of the two men had just taken a good hit.

He had a cold, plain face, and, as the door before him opened, he blew out a cloud of smoke. Walking through the smoke was the face of the child that he had brutally murdered days prior. He stared for a long moment, without expression, as the child held out his watch as an offering for his life.

Rasheed stepped forward, pulled the .38 from his pocket, and shot the larger man at point-blank- range in the middle of his forehead. The other man, frightened by the blast from the pocket cannon began to choke violently on the crack he'd just taken, and spun around to face the kid they had murdered, standing there with a smoking gun in his hand.

His head began to bend forward, his eyes shut, and his lips moved silently, as he knelt down on his knees pressing his forehead to the floor. Rasheed placed the revolver to the back of his head, and pulled the trigger twice.

His parents were proud that he stood on their religious belief of a life for a life, an injury equal to the one given, but were devastated their only remaining son could no longer remain in the District.

Their cousin, Cristy, who worked for Control Data, and living in St. Paul, elected to take Rasheed into her two-bedroom home.

His parents insisted on paying half of all the household bills, and personally drove their son to the Twin Cities.

Rasheed was leaning against the back sofa, his hands thrust deeply inside the pockets of his raincoat, a cigarette dangling from the corner of his mouth, the smoke drifting through the light of the window, making his presence hazy and obscure. I waited patiently while Rasheed moved about the room slowly and speculatively, the end of his cigarette glowing, and plumes of smoke flowing from his nostrils.

"Tell me, Sazzar, tell me the truth. Will I be able to smoke my cigarettes on the farm?"

"Absolutely not." I told him the absolute truth.

"Rasheed butted the cigarette, pulled out his pack, crushed it, and threw it in the trash. "Tell Six I'm in."

By 2100 hours Thursday, June 1st, day four of team assembly, I had five confirmed members. My friend Elijah Cole had come aboard when I asked him a few months ago. The Ball brothers, who had just been released from the Juvenile Detention Center, would be in school first thing in the morning. The remaining name on the list was Player Paul Lopez. Unfortunately, he had been shot several times, and was chained to a hospital bed in a coma.

With Tina and myself I'd managed to successfully put together the best of the best available. Tina had a message for all the fellas from Six, and a meeting was set for Friday afternoon after school.

C H A P T E R   5 4

Ice was a wigger -- white nigger - who walked the halls of Central High School with his gang, the Organization: wannabes whose most urgent desire was that people be afraid of them. The self-appointed leader, Ice, the son of a black University hooker, a trick's baby, who desperately wanted to be a part of the black man's world, but he felt cursed with his father's white genes and skin complexion, was a stone-cold coward by nature, and he started the Organization on the reputation of Mac-Dee, a demon for the love of a fight, who lived on the idea of instilling fear in the masses.

Mac-Dee was Ice's right-hand man and enforcer. Ice, who never raised his voice or his fist, built the Organization out of the ruins of several fallen gangs who needed leadership and a cause. He became their leader on a dare from Mac-Dee, encouraging the fallen gangs to ban together.

He offered them a new cause: drugs, money, and weapons. He gave his new disciples tasks to perform to become members, organizing them into hierarchy, and sacrificing some of them for the assassination of rival gang leaders. In the name of strength in numbers, the Organization grew to become the largest gang in the Twin Cities.

* * *

Albert and Alfred Ball were the inheritors of their dead parent's home. Because the boys were underage at the time of their parents demise, guardianship over the boys' property and trust was given to their father's brother. The uncle, whom they called Landlord hated his dead brother's sons, and would kick their asses, in public and send them home crying when they questioned him about money, food, clothing, or their father's home.

Three years later, Albert, now sixteen and a Golden Glove Boxing Champion in the middle-weight division, whom everyone called 'Babyboss', decided it was entirely ridiculous for Landlord to continue to run their lives. Alfred, his older brother by a year, and affectionately called 'Big Al' by his dad, was in his senior year at St. Paul Central. Big Al, a three sport athlete, who was a strong competitor as Central's quarterback on the football team, point guard on the basketball team, and State Champion in the hundred-meters for the track team and nearly a perfect physique, stood with his baby brother to confront Landlord about moving out of their father's house.

Landlord, who was always in the company of his friends, their days and nights consisting of drinking, gambling, and the constant slamming of those fucking Dominoes, sat in defiance when the brothers asked him to leave their parent's home.

Both of the boys' parents had been blue-collar hard-working church-going servants of God all their lives until a head on collision with a semi-truck abruptly ended their lives. The boys' father had always assured his sons, should anything happen to him, or their mother they would benefit from two separate insurance policies.

In the wake of their parents' deaths, the Ball brothers' had inherited the family estate, inclusive of the insurance policies which paid them a quarter-of-a-million dollars.

The attorney followed their parents' instructions, and paid the mortgage off on their home in the 1500 block of Laurel Avenue.

In addition, Landlord was placed as the boys guardian, as well as, trustee of the Ball family estate in a wrongful death civil action which received a windfall of three-and-a-half-million dollars a year and a half later.

Landlord lived like a king on the Ball family fortune: He remodeled and refurnished the entire house. He bought himself expensive jewelry, and a brand new Mercedes Benz.

He took several vacations to exotic locations around the world -- from Hawaii to Tuscany, Italy to the most beautiful locations in Mexico and the Caribbean. A trip to Las Vegas, the last of exotic trips, quickly set work to stripping Landlord of the family fortune.

His drug and gambling habits finally taking their toll, Landlord had squandered away most of the three-and-a-quarter-million dollars, and was now gambling away the monthly income from the social security and public assistance checks.

They took great pride and strength from each other, the Ball brothers' did, as they walked into their parents' home, and into the dining room where Landlord was in the middle of a poker hand. With their parents' portraits looking on in approval, and their new friend Six standing guard with a .45 automatic, the brothers kicked shit down Landlord's leg.

The brothers' kicked his ass so bad they left him with a deformed left eye, without sight. His upper lip had enlarged and curled away from his shattered teeth due to the severe stomping the boys had given him, leaving him with a grotesque smile. Landlord refused to return to the Ball's family home when he was released from the hospital, and young Alfred and Albert were officially on their own.

Checks began to arrive monthly at the house from Social Security and Public Assistance. The boys had no way of cashing the checks, and consulted their new friend, Six, who knew an old hustler that owned a few businesses on Selby Avenue who prided himself on simplicity, and honesty of the game.

The old hustler detested Landlord, and was more than willing to cash the checks for ten percent. The brothers agreed, and Mr. James Smith, aka Kansas City, became the boys' new guardian. Under the direction of K.C., the boys sold the Mercedes, and converted the spacious basement of their home into a weekend after-hours joint, charging at the door, and selling fried chicken dinners, and bootleg liquor. As long as one of the customers was gambling on the crap table, or playing Vegas-style Blackjack, the liquor was free.

With their new found wealth piling in, the brothers' began

indulging themselves in the passions of the mall, and the many young women making themselves available for a moment of passion.

One night, a fight outside the brothers' residence was a bit much for the neighbors, and the police were called. The brothers managed to keep the police from going inside their home, however, some over-zealous pig wanted to speak to the boys' parents.

The boys' called K.C., and for thirty-percent of the house take on the gambling tables, K.C. accepted the ticket for running a disorderly house with a smile. The judge declined to fine the boys' guardian for their presence in the home because they lived there, but placed them in juvenile detention for their frequent outburst in his court room. A weekend in Woodview Detention Center would do the brothers' good, he said, as he slammed his gavel.

C H A P T E R   5 5

I stood there like a fool whooping and hollering, beating on the lockers, as the Ball brothers' cleared the metal detector in the school's security entrance.

Babyboss stopped to tie his shoes in the midst of several Organization members. When he stood, he was face to face with Nutty, a crazy sherm-smoking 'O' member. They eyefucked each other until Big A1 interrupted the staredown. "Leave that shit alone, baby brother." Babyboss stepped around Nutty, and was a few paces from his big brother when Nutty swung at him from his blind side.

Babyboss slipped Nutty's wild swing easily, then threw a blur of punches and the fight was over. Lying against the lockers was Nutty, knocked the fuck out! Ice saw the whole thing go down, I could tell the shit pleased him, and he let us know it. He flashed a victorious smile, whispered something to Mac-Dee, and his people picked their fallen comrade off the floor. Big A1 heard it first, an audible whisper.

"We're going to kick those Ball brothers' asses after school!'

...

Tina had waited patiently on the corner of Lake Street and 4th Avenue for the twenty-one bus that would take her to St. Paul.

I had insisted that I would ditch my fifth-period class and pick her up, but she wanted time to herself, time to reflect on a few personal matters, she ended our conversation with, "The bus ride will do me good. Plus you can't afford, academically, to miss any of your classes." She was enjoying her bus ride when on the corner of Selby and Snelling a young man entered the bus.

The driver addressed him first. "Bangman. How's it going?"

Then several of the passengers did the same.

Bangman had short wavy black hair, a caramel complexion, stood six-one, and had the damnedest green eyes. Tina told me once in confidence that she had never looked at another man, nor had she ever been attracted to a man other than Six. Yet she found him to be very handsome. She quickly dismissed the thought and continued her sightseeing.

Out of all the empty seats on the bus, damn, he had to take the seat next to her. In their moment of eye exchange she could see that he was extremely muscular in the chest, shoulders, arms and legs. He must have been running because he was sweating, and when he used his T-shirt to wipe the sweat from his face, she could see that he had a washboard stomach.

Just as images of Six flashed in her thoughts, he reached inside his backpack and pulled out a book. She recognized it immediately: it was The Iliad by Homer.

Okay, she thought. He's fine, has a great body, and an inquisitive and comprehensive mind. Just when she was about to comment on Homer, the bus driver shouted out Lexington Avenue. He stood when she did and being the gentleman she suspected he was, he allowed her to exit the bus ahead of him.

Tina crossed Selby Avenue heading toward Central High School. The young, man of much curiosity and self-discipline was right behind her, his face buried in Homer. I was sitting on the stairs at the Lexington entrance of Central with Badboy, Face, Elijah, Rasheed, and K-Nine, whose appearance was a shock and a blessing, waiting on Tina as students exited the school after the sounding of the 3:00PM bell.

The Ball brothers' were together in the automotive class, at the gas station purchased by the school on Dunlap and Selby, when one of Ice's stooges entered the shop, and relayed the message that their presence was requested in the alleyway on

Lexington between Dayton and Marshall at 3:00PM. Nutty was calling Babyboss out to a one-on-one, to the winner bragging rights, to the loser a well-whipped ass. To a no-show, the branding of cowardice.

C H A P T E R   5 6

Tina crossed Dayton and Lexington, and watched as a group of boys who looked to be gang affiliated engage two other boys. There were no shouts or commands given, just an instinctive reaction.

Ten of the gangbangers rushed Big Al and he went down under the weight of his assailants. Tina quickly calculated their weight at nearly fifteen-hundred pounds of fury and hatred on top of him.

Seconds later, all but a few of them were going to the aid of their comrades, who were catching hell from Babyboss. Tina smiled as several of the gangbangers struggled to get up from the ground. The kid was displaying exceptional boxing skills. His slip- and-move tactics were poetry in motion, she could hear them screaming and cursing, as every punch he threw someone cried out in pain. Then she heard a cry of desperation. "Get this mothafucka!"

Babyboss howled in pain, someone had hurt him, and he was going down. The sound of his pain cut deeply into Tina's soul. Individually he would have defeated any one of them with his boxing skills, and his courage touched her. She reached inside her oversized shirt, pulled the .380 automatic from its holster, and fired two rounds into the air.

The street froze and there was a dead quiet. Tina ordered the gangbangers to stand the two boys on their feet, and to move away from them. Ice could feel the fear suppressing his boys and gave the order to stand them on their feet. In Ice's world you left your man lying on the curb bloodied, honor satisfied, the victor going off to establish bragging rights. Now this bulldagger dressed in army fatigues was throwing a monkey wrench into his affairs.

"Yo, dyke bitch!" Ice attempted to flex his gangster. "What are you doing interfering in Organization business?"

Tina grinned broadly. "Because a white punk-looking nigger like you ain't got the nuts, nor the comprehension to understand the concept of a fair one. One on one, man to man. But we all know that's not possible, because you and these future penitentiary faggots had to form a gang to protect your tender pussy-shaped asses!" The crowd around the fight burst into laughter.

"Man, fuck this dyke bitch!" Mac-Dee griped as the other 'O' members prodded him on. "Bust yo' head to the fat meat you put that gun down, you pussy eatin' bitch!" Mac-Dee had spittle running down his angry jawline. To the astonishment of everyone present, Tina let the hammer down on the .380, put the safety in place, and holstered the weapon.

The gang, all twenty of them, looked back and forth at one another dumbfounded, shocked and alarmed at her courage. Mac-Dee stepped forward.

"After I knock your never-been-dicked-down ass out, I'm gonna carry you back to the tilt, and fuck you real good." Mac-Dee made his move, and met a crescent kick from Tina's left foot to the right side of his temple that had a vicious arc -- faster than she'd ever kicked in the house of bags. Mac-Dee's body dropped to the ground as if it had no bones. The crowd roared.

Two of the 'O's finest rushed her in a staggered formation. She raised her leg and delivered a side-downward thrust-kick with the blade of her foot to his knee, the knee hyper extending and bending him forward. She cleared him from her path with an elbow strike to the back of his head before catching his partner with a clothesline that had such force she wondered if he saw his feet before he hit the ground.

Bringing her right knee high into her chest, she delivered a downward thrust-kick to his punk-ass ribs with such force, she was sure the people in China felt the vibration. Out of the corner of her eye she saw movement to her rear, and executed a thrusting back kick to the sneaky mothafucka's chest, propelling him backwards. The force from the kick and his body weight combined sent him slamming into several members of his gang, sending them to the ground.

She planted her foot, and turned her head forward, and running directly at her was a six-foot-two, one-hundred-and eighty-pound man, all muscle. His speed and size momentarily startled her. A split second before he made contact with her, she collapsed to her side on the ground, her leg extended, and executed a makeshift takedown. His body crashed hard to the ground.

Rolling over onto his back, with a closed fist, she struck him hard to the back of his neck. After she struck him, he did a push-up that catapulted her off of him, as he barely reacted to the blow. As she landed on her feet, she watched him roll over on his back and kipped up with the agility of a gymnast.

She held her ground but could see that she had really pissed this big mothafucka off with her defiance of his size. He came at her, and swung at her with a right hand surely meant for a man equal to his size. She circle-stepped with her left foot, catching the right cross between the elbow and the bicep before it broke, and simultaneously took her right hand and struck him in the throat with a Panther's Paw. He went down with a strangled gurgling sound.

Another member of the gang grabbed her from behind, and she immediately stiffened her leg, and using it like a club, she brought it straight back toward her body, the steel toe of her boot breaking his nose on contact. Five of them rushed her at once, picked her up, and slammed her to the concrete. Colors exploded in her head from all directions at once. She blinked her eyes repeatedly to clear her vision just in time to see a raised boot about to stomp her face.

I'd heard the gunshots and stood to see what the commotion was about, and saw Tina kick Mac-Dee. I called out her name and took off running in her direction, followed by the rest of the team.

Bangman said he had been memorizing a passage from

Homer when he heard two gunshots. He looked past his book to see the girl from the bus pointing a weapon at a bunch of fools. Her delicate features had made her look vulnerable on the bus. Belying her firm stance and strong words to the gangbangers, Bangman had the impulse to throw his arms around her, and give her whatever assurance he could. Then she did the damnedest thing. She holstered her weapon.

Tina closed her eyes, ready to take the impact of the boot, but instead of feeling pain she heard the crowd.

"Oooooooooh!" She opened her eyes, and instead of the boot she saw the boy who had been reading Homer. To her right, lying motionless on the ground, was the owner of the boots. Two of the 'O' members rushed Bangman, he met their aggression with his own. He reached the first who swung a wild right hand and met the swing with a forearm block. At the moment of contact, he contracted and relaxed using the technique of Hun-Sau, which circles over and under the attacker's arm like a snake coiling around a branch. Just as a snake tightens around its prey, he extended his arm, and put pressure on the elbow, that brought this foolish sucker to the tips of his toes. At that very instant, to his right, he met his other attacker with a double-kick to the groin and head. As his right foot touched the ground, he shifted his weight to his left side, and at the same time brought his right hand around to the nose of the punk in his arm lock with a ridge-hand that broke the bridge of his nose.

Tina watched in amazement as he executed fast snap kicks, roundhouses, and spinning-heel kicks that sent several of the gangbangers to the ground. The boys holding her down tried to get up and defend themselves, but Bangman walked through them like they were practice dummies.

After he cleared a path, he reached down, and in one motion pulled Tina to her feet, and she immediately got back into the battle. She turned to strike at the sound of crashing bodies. It was me and the team punishing the rest of the remaining 'O' members.

Ice, who had been given a forearm to the back of his head and was trying to stand, wobbled to his feet. Tina stepped to him and hit him with a hook that Smoking Joe Frazier would have admired. Ice's bitch made ass dropped to the ground.

Blood dripped from her knuckles as she pulled the knife strapped to her calf. As the team looked on she stood over Ice and, pressing the blade along the side of his nose, she slashed downward through his lips. She kicked him in the head for moving, slammed her knee in his chest, grabbed him by the chin, and placed the blade along the other side of his nose, and again slashed downward, and cut an 'X' through his upper and bottom lips.

She stood over him and spit in his face. "Watch your mouth, cock-sucker. I may be a bitch, but I am nobody's dyke!"

We heard the sirens in the distance, and with me leading the way, ran to Central's parking lot to my sedan, and K-Nine's Fleetwood and fled the scene in the direction of the Ball brothers' home.

Although the fight only lasted ninety seconds, to Tina it felt like a lifetime. Her body trembled lightly, not from fear, but her first fight ever. The laughter and high siding from the fellas relaxed her, and her shaking began to subside.

Paramedics and police appeared out of nowhere. The hundreds of students who witnessed the ass-kicking of the Organization members and their leaders had vanished. It seemed like an eternity to Ice. As several ambulances began to appear, he looked around at his fallen comrades, many of them drenched in their own blood, some with broken bones, shaking violently from pain.

A team of paramedics were working feverishly on Big-T. It was the blow to his throat and the swelling that was hampering his breathing. Paramedics had to perform an emergency tracheotomy to allow a passage of air to flow. All of his people were alive. Ice shook his head in disgust and shame, his mind already racing over a plan of revenge.

CHAPTER 57

The Sedan DeVille and the Fleetwood were parked side by side at the rear entrance of the Ball brothers' Laurel Avenue home.

The three-story white wood trimmed home was complimented by a large rear deck with a built-in Jacuzzi. Ivy crept along the walls of the home, which was surrounded by assorted greenery in the back and front yards.

Tina realized, as she climbed out of the Caddy, and ambled toward the house that she hadn't expected the Ball brothers to be living in a place half as nice as this one. She made a mental note to herself to never assume or pass judgment on a person place or thing before she had a chance to investigate it thoroughly.

Big Al halted everyone at the foyer, had them take off their shoes, and replaced them with house slippers. Entering the kitchen, she could see that it was equipped with top quality appliances. A tour of the house revealed wall-to-wall carpet so white it looked like freshly fallen snow. The dining room came alive when Big Al drew the shades open. A Moroccan rug lay beneath the dining room table, which was set for ten, and offered its diners a view of the deck and garden.

In the living room there was a custom-made raw-silk white sectional sofa. The family room was equipped with a big screen television and two fish aquariums: one salt, the other fresh. The attic looked more like a lounge than an attic with its paneled walls, carpeted floors, chaise lounge and wet bar. The basement looked like a bar. There were several tables for customers' seating, a craps table, and two Blackjack tables.

Big Al insisted that everyone stayed for dinner and moved the party to the deck. A box on the deck was opened, which contained swimsuits of all sizes for male and female. The grill was lit, and red wine was served in crystal glasses.

Tina smiled at Babyboss when he handed her a brand new sundress that appeared to be in her size, and a bag full of ultra-feminine products. She pursed her lips, as if she were debating whether to question who the owner of the dress was, as well as who the feminine products belonged to, but decided not to force the issue.

"My brother told me to give you the royal treatment, Miss Tee."

"No thanks, I'm fine. I just want to use the phone, check on my baby, talk to the fellas, and go home and soak in my tub."

"Negative! Big Al says to put you in the master bedroom. His she-ro deserves to soak her warrior bones in a scented bath. Besides, you'll hurt his feelings and mine if you refuse, Miss Lane."

"Well, in that case, lead the way. By the way, you can call me Tee or Tina. You don't have to call me 'Miss'; we're the same age. And one more thing, which brother are you?"

"My name is Albert Ball. My friends call me Babyboss."

"You seem to know an awful lot about me, Babyboss."

"You and Six are legends among the teens in the neighborhood. Everyone knows who you are. If they didn't, after today what you done to the 'O', all of St. Paul is going to know your name."

She allowed a faint smile of victory to form on her face at the thought.

When Babyboss opened the bathroom door, at first sight the vivid colors overwhelmed her, the gleaming black-lacquered walls with enameled gold trimmings was spotless and sparkling.

She stepped inside the bathroom to find a large tub with the fragrance of large purple flowers floating in the steaming waters with the scent of lavender.

"Take your time, Miss Tee." Babyboss closed the door. "Try the switch on the wall," he yelled from the other side of the door. She turned the lock on the door and began to undress. Checking herself out in the full-length mirror she could see there were bruises on her back, thighs, and feet. She stepped into the bathtub, the mirrored walls reflecting her every move as she immersed herself in the irresistibility intoxicating scented waters.

"Hmmmmmm." She remembered Babyboss said to try the switch on wall. She flipped the switch and the water began circulating. A royal treatment.

C H A P T E R   5 8

"Bernard 'Bangman' Logan, an award-winning athlete who symbolized what the true character and performance of young African- American athletes should be. Isn't that what the Pioneer Press wrote about you, brother?" I stared at him with a cold,, hard look.

"Don't hate the player, Sazzar. Besides, I'm making a change in my position right now." Bangman returned the frosty look.

"What, you finally coming over to the black side?" I asked sardonically.

"In the game of football, never Sazzar! You're too much fun to play against." Bangman took a sip of his wine.

"Because of you, one of my friends suffered a concussion after you hit him during the televised game. You even had the nerve to celebrate with them Academy white boys afterwards."

Bangman's composed features darkened. "Sazzar, I am a black athlete who happens to play on a white football team. We were playing Central's Minutemen in a televised game, on a grand stage, against the steepest odds; just like you, I refused to allow the team I play for to be defeated. You don't hear me making a big deal out of the white boy I fuck with, who you hit low, and tore his anterior cruciate ligament in his right knee, and ruined any chance he had at a college or pro career."

"You put one of mine down, I put one of yours down." My

nostrils flared from anger. "What are you doing here, Bangman?"

"I second that question." Came from K-Nine. "What are you doing here, Bangman?"

"Ooooooooooh! A pissing contest. Who's winning? Can I watch?" Tina standing in the doorway to the deck. She stood there beyond their casual appraisal of her physical attributes. They seemed to be stunned by her beauty. She looked much older than her sixteen years, with her mature, elegant body, wise eyes, and beautiful smile. While the others continued to stare in disbelief, making a concerted effort not to squirm, Bangman broke the ice.

"Miss Tee, you are not only violent, dark and ominous, you are also a very beautiful woman."

"Thanks for the compliment, and for saving me the pain and the money for reconstructive surgery on my face. And I hate to come off like a rude bitch, and believe me I'm apologetic for what I'm about to say, but I have business to discuss with these gentlemen, and it's private. So unless there is some reason why you are here, one of the fellas can take you where you need to go."

She smiled, a smile he thought was perfect.

Bangman nodded, his gaze remaining on Tina. "This morning I received a telephone call from a good friend of mine. Maybe you've heard of him. His name is Jeffery Alexander Lane."

Tina stared curiously as if she were in a state of disbelief, before he continued. "You may know him as Three-Six or Six. He was the best sparring partner that I ever had." He lowered his gaze from hers.

"So you're Bernard Logan, the three-time intermural kickboxing champion Six worked with?" A look of understanding replaced the look of disbelief on Tina's face.

"That would be me. Six extended me an invite to come hear what you had to say, Miss Tee. I accepted whatever was going down when you were damn near martyred on Lexington Avenue."

"Bangman, why didn't you say something when you sat next to me on the bus?"

"I only knew of you, Miss Tee. I had never seen your face."

"Then why help someone you didn't know?"

"I guess for the same reason that you helped the Ball brothers. Plus, when you were fighting I noticed the similarity of the style of Martial Arts you were using. Six fought the same way, only a little more advanced. I put the connection together right before those five guys rushed you. Sorry."

"Thank you, Bangman. Now that we know why he's here, are there any objections to Bangman becoming our tenth member? Your silence will be his ratification. The nine members remained silent.

"Welcome, Bangman."

"Thanks, Miss Tee. You've just made a friend for life." Bangman smiled.

"Sazzar, you incompetent, inarticulate, lazy, sneaky, judgmental sumbitch!" Face splashed water in my face.

I couldn't control my sudden impulse of anger. "What the fuck am I supposed to do, apologize?"

In unison the whole team screamed, "YES!"

The muscles in my face tightened. "Oh, I see, y'all just wanna tongue-lash a brother. What is this, fuck with Sazzar's head day?"

"What part of his brain would we have to take out that is responsible for his stupidity?" Rasheed slapped his hand against his own head.

"It would be a whole lot easier to find a cure for cancer than to cure his ass. We'd have to put his ass back in the womb to fix his problem." Badboy laughed at his own joke.

"Let us all bow our heads in prayer for our brother, Sazzar," Elijah made the sign of the cross in the air. "Lord ... repeat after me, children ... Lord, you strengthened Jesus with the Holy Spirit, so that he doeth speak to the people in infanthood, and in maturity. Lord, humble your servant. I beg of thee to bestow upon our brother, Sazzar, a brain, Lord. By your leave, Lord, you allowed the Strawman a brain, the Cowardly Lion courage, and the Tinman a heart. Lord, we beg of you to allow brother Sazzar to get at least a 400 on his S.A.T.s"

The whole group, including me erupted in laughter. Bangman and I embraced, the music was cranked up, and the celebration began. Introductions were made around the table, and Tina gave the message Six had given her.

"During my last visit with Six," she began, "He assured me that the only part of you guys that could withstand society's bullshit stigma of young black men and black women is through the growing and improving of our minds. He said that it is a rare thing to have ten young black people with I.Q. between 132 and 170 in the same room, who are all voracious readers, brilliant students that have achieved, even under the shitty conditions of public school, goals that most kids in public schools only dream about. 'Education junkies' he called us. How does the saying go? No pain no gain! Well, that applies to learning as well as training for war, be it in the ghetto or oversees. We, as a team, are going to be better and far richer in heart, mind, and pockets than any teenagers in this country could ever imagine. We are going to snatch existing powers, lay down our will of steel, and create for ourselves new dimensions of opportunity that no teenagers, black or white, have ever done before.

"We will fill any holes in our educations in the arts, history, physics, calculus, most anything to do with economics, and become tomorrow's doctors, educators, scientist, lawyers and this country's leaders. After the twelve weeks of training that you are about to undergo, Six and I promise that you will emerge with the blessed emancipation, and readiness for what we have planned for our future." Tina raised her glass. "Let the training begin."

C H A P T E R 59

0500 Monday June 5, 1994, St. Paul Central High School Parking Lot.

"Listen Sazzar, the longest word in the dictionary is not that shit supercalifragilisticexpialidocious from Mary Poppins." Rasheed challenged.

"Then what's a longer word, old smart-ass mothafucka?"

"Try to fix them crusty-ass lips of yours to say this one: Pneumonoultramicroscopicsilicovolcanokoniosis."

"Bullshit! You just made that up, Rasheed." I dismissed his always-got-his-nose-in-a-book ass.

"Actually, it is a word." Badboy decided to add his two cents. "What the fuck does it mean?" I was dumbfounded.

"It's a disease of the lungs caused by the habitual inhalation of irritants, like mineral or metallic particles. I know you've heard of Black Lung, Silicosis?"

"Looks like Badboy got the last word in on that discussion. Heads up y'all. Car coming into the parking lot. Here comes this Captain James." K-Nine stood from leaning on the car, coming to his full height.

"Do we salute him?" Face stood next to him.

"Naw, just be yourself for now." Bangman remained composed.

Captain James pulled the Jeep to a halt in front of the two Cadillac's and killed the engine. Both doors opened, and Tina and Captain James exited the vehicle. In the dim morning light of Central's parking lot, his features appeared molded, chiseled with an extremely sharp instrument. His presence had the assurance of a black man none of us had ever seen in one of our own. A man who we all came to know owned the ground wherever he stood.

"Alright, listen up! My name is Captain Lafayette James. In my hand I hold ten letters of commitment, which are your Oaths of Office, if you prefer, your sworn allegiances to your team. These letters are for us all. Lane will pass them out along with a pen, you will read them and sign them. Any unsigned form will not be coming with us. Once all forms are in my possession, those who have signed their letter will form a line to be sworn in. Understand?"

"Yes sir." They all sounded unsure. Tina passed out the letters and returned the signed forms to Captain James.

"Alright people, repeat after me: I swear to execute all duties and orders given to me by my superiors, and I swear to aid and assist my comrades in the execution of all orders given to my unit. Further, I swear that in the course of carrying out orders, no one is to be left behind. Congratulations and welcome to an experience that you will never forget."

C H A P T E R 60

0530 Monday June 5, 1994

"Training men has not changed much over the years, and that's something you can take comfort in." Sergeant Barella pulled the Jeep to a halt on the concrete parking area they'd poured a week earlier.

"Dammit man, I can't wait. I feel alive again!" Sergeant Black hopped out of the Jeep.

"Black, do you even remember the sound of a new recruit stomping around on the parade deck trying to get into rhythmic lockstep?" Sergeant Barella reminisced out loud.

"Sure he does. He has first-hand knowledge. He was in rhythmic lockstep just last week, slow dancing with that cute lady at the bar. Poor woman, you stepped on her feet at least twenty times before that song ended." Sergeant Greedy laughed at the thought.

"I'm a combat soldier with a Silver Star, a couple of Bronze Stars, and so many Purple Hearts I can't count 'em all. On top of all that shit, I'm still sane, and one of the best Communications Specialists to come out of any branch of the military. I am not some sissy-ass ballroom dancer." Sergeant Black went on a tangent.

"No kidding. Where's a good old TRANSAT on the dance floor when you need one?" Greedy joked. "Oh shit! Here comes Gunny I'"

"Here's the drill," Gunny began. "I just got off the landline with Captain James and his ETA with the new recruits is 0600 hours. He tells me we're in for a big surprise. Our recruits are not like ordinary teenagers. All of them are athletic, educated, and exceptional physical specimens. He wants them broken down to fresh meat within the first week, so let's break the street for 'em. The gloves are off, let's do what we were trained to do. Sergeant Barella and Greedy?"

"Yeah, Gunny?"

"Take these vehicles back to the barracks and wait on the foot prints for us."

"I thought we were going to have them park here and ride down with us, Gunny?" Sergeant Greedy doubled checked his understanding .

"Change of plans. We are going to put our athletes to the test. Be ready by 0630."

"Alright Gunny. Let's go, Barella." Sergeant Greedy corralled his peer.

"You ready for a five mile, Black?"

"Five minute miles?" Black smiled, looking forward to the run.

"You damn right!" Gunny had that gleam of excitement in his eyes.

"Every morning, noon, and night, Gunny."

…

"Atten-hut!"

Captain James returned the salute of his men, and pulled his Jeep into the parking area next to the two Caddies. He killed the engine and turned to face Tina.

"Are you sure you want to do this, Tina?"

"Fate, that is the first time you've called me Tina since I told you my name. What's wrong, Fate? You don't think I can handle the training?"

"Miss Tee, this is not going to be like anything you and Six experienced. This is the real deal from the rooter to the tooter. There'll be no rooting you on, no applause when you finally make it up the rope."

"I can handle it, Fate." She touched his face gently.

"You know all this training you may only get to see J.T. a couple times a week."

"Fate, we talked about this already. I will just have to cherish the time I do spend with him. Besides he's in good hands with his grandpa."

"I can see that your mind is made up." He surrendered in exasperation.

"Yes, Fate."

"Then kiss your baby and join your team, Lane."

"Yes sir, Captain James." She hugged and kissed J.T. so long she nearly had second thoughts.

Sergeant Black watched as Tina grabbed a small bag, and with mixed feelings, exited the Jeep, joining the boys by the cars.

"How am I-gonna carry Tina like a new recruit?" He spoke without thinking.

"By remembering your pride and duty," Gunny corrected him.

"Now, let's do what we came here to do. Everybody out of the fucking car, now!" Shouted Gunny. "Throw those god-forsaken Walkmans, watches, jewelry, and any U.S. currency you have on your person, and throw them into the car you came out of; then lock the door, and give me the keys. You have just had your last drive, your last look at anything from your soft-ass civilian lives until you graduate from my boot camp. My name is Gunnery Sergeant Peters. Am I understood?"

"Yes sir!"

"Yes who?"

"Yes, Gunnery Sergeant Peters!"

"Listen up, you nothing-ass maggots. We are going to run five miles in the quick step. Line up in two columns. You will run in your formations. Do you understand?"

"Yes, Gunnery Sergeant Peters!"

"Quick-step-hut! Pick 'em up, down. You slimy ass maggots can't even run right. I wanna hear one boot hit the ground. This ain't no casual jog in the park, ladies. Do you want to insult me?"

"No, Gunnery Sergeant Peters!"

"Right now you are running as individuals. By the time you finish my boot camp you'll be running as one. Is that understood?"

"Yes, Gunnery Sergeant Peters!"

C H A P T E R 6 1

"Here they come, 0630 on the mark just like Gunny said. You ready, Greedy?" Sergeant Barella asked.

"You damn right I am." He stepped forward as the recruits ran toward him. "You see these yellow footprints on the ground, recruits?"

"Yes sir!"

"I want your tender asses standing on them as they indicate, at a forty-five-degree angle, feet inside the yellow-foot printed lines ladies. When I say 'Atten-hut!' I want your thumbs along the sides of your trousers, your eyes front, head up, shoulders back, chest out. Atten-hut! They're all yours, Gunny."

"Thank you, Sergeant Greedy. We are going to have what is called a 'call to muster'. When I call out your name, you will answer loud and clear. Is this understood?"

"Yes, Gunnery Sergeant Peters!"

"Michael Williams?"

"Here sir!"

"Ronnie Green?"

"Here sir!"

"Kenneth Wendell?"

"Here sir!"

"Sir Godfrey Frye?"

"Here sir!"

"Elijah Cole?"

"Here sir!"

"Bernard Logan?"
"Here sir!"
"Alfred Ball?"
"Here sir!"
"Albert Ball?"
"Here sir!"
"Shanally Robinson?"
"Here sir!"
"Tina Lane?"
"Here sir!"

"As of this moment, and forever more, you are no longer the individuals on this roster. The shit you've called your personalities, your character, throw the bullshit out. Your tender asses are now in the motherfucking raw, as your Creator made you. You and I are now the sculptors who are going to mold this raw material into unit fighting form. When I am done with you, and you have completed my boot camp, you will be a fighting, thinking unit that lives and thinks as one.

"Now I am going to introduce you to the men who are going to teach you to think collectively as one. The man who will train and instruct you in the use and maintenance of every weapon used in the military and civilian world is our Weapons Expert, Sergeant Barella. Sergeant Black is our Communications Specialist. He has a mess of electronic equipment for tracking and communications, short and long range.

"Sergeant Greedy here is our Demolitions Expert. Everything from the making to the use of C-4 to Napalm, this man will teach you. From the moment that you arrived your training began. Your first lesson is a spoken one, learn it, memorize it, and never forget it. The greatest weapon ever invented are your bodies and you minds. Exercise them both. Sergeant Greedy, they're all yours."

"Thank, you Gunny. Listen up! To bring an individual into the fighting form that Gunny indicated, we first have to kill the individual inside of you. It's not about your individuality anymore, it's about totality. Line up single file for haircuts, clothing, bedding, and field issues. Move it!" Sergeant Greedy roared.

"Lane?"

"Yes, Gunnery Sergeant Peters?"

"Front and center!"

"Yes sir?"

"Where are you going, Lane?"

"To get my hair cut, and to get my issues, Gunnery Sergeant Peters, sir."

"Tina, your pursuit of this training is both flattering and damn uncomfortable. Praise worthy because as a woman you were created for this kick-ass intensity of training. Uncomfortable because your uncles and I love you. We all agreed to teach you how to use weapons, and physically protect yourself, but never did we agree to train you in the art of war."

"Uncle Jake, you told me to never fall victim to the role the world had planned for me, that of a woman cooking, cleaning, and being a toilet for men to dump their fluids into. Do you remember that?"

"Yes, I remember, but that was talk to motivate you to set your own limits against a society that would set them for you."

"Uncle Jake, it's too late to break the mold, the die has been cast. Because of you I have strength, skill, pride, bravery, and endurance. I am a mother and a woman, Uncle Jake, one-thousand percent, who loves being a mom, and a woman for my man. This role as a woman I've become indelibly associated with, but there is another side of me, a warrior, who has yet to identify her cause. This training will help me to be the master of my self-image. Please Uncle Jake, don't make me split the desires of my heart."

"I would never ask you to choose my love over your personal desires."

"Then you'll train me with your blessings?"

"Jesus, Tina. Alright! You will get the physical respect of privacy in the barracks for being female. However, that's as far as it goes. You will carry your own weight, no excuses. Do you understand?"

"Yes, Uncle Jake, I mean Gunnery Sergeant Peters." She hugged him tight, then kissed him on the cheek and screamed triumphantly, "Oooooooooorah!" before turning and taking her place in the line.

For the rest of the first day of training, the ten members G.I.'d the barracks. Sergeant Greedy did an inspection and made them start from scratch. He said they would clean until the barracks shined like a dime in a Billy goats ass!

C H A P T E R   6 2

"So, how did the first day of training go, Gunny?" Captain James asked as he changed his grandson's diaper.

"Nothing like I expected, sir."

"What did you expect, Gunny." He had that I told you so smirk on his face.

"Pissing, moaning, crying, bitching ... none of that happened. From the moment I braced those kids, they complied. During the run I damn near blew my damn heart out, running flat-out to beat 'em down. They weren't even out of breath, Cap."

"Gunny, I warned you that they were not ordinary teenagers."

"Never in all my days have I encountered anything like their behavior from the many recruits that I've trained. And Tina!"

"Leave it alone, Gunny. No matter how hard she tries to blend in, she's going to be a distraction to her surrogate uncles."

"You asking me to ignore her, Cap?"

"No Gunny, I'm asking you to not only train her, but refine her into a lethal weapon."

...

"Sazzar, wake up!" Bangman shook me.

"What is it, Bangman?"

"Wake all the fellas and have them come outside."

"Damn Bangman, it's only four o'clock in the morning.

Are you crazy?" I was looking at the clock on the wall.

"Trust me, Sazzar. Just do it."

"Damn!" I grunted, throwing the covers off myself.

The air was unseasonably chilly, Bangman noticed as he walked over to join Tina and the little Oriental cook performing the Sun Salutation of Surya Nomaskara B.

All the fellas were grumbling amongst themselves as they slowly began forming ranks and mimicking the poses. Thirty minutes later they were dripping sweat and wanting to learn more.

"Who'd've thought I'd be doing sissy-ass Yoga poses and loving the shit." K-Nine put his six breaths to Utthita Trikonasana.

     * * *

"You ready, Gunny?" Sergeant Black stood at the ready in front of the barracks door.

"Yeah, let's wake 'em up and get this show on the road. You grab the empty garbage can, and I'll hit the lights."

Sergeant Black began beating on the garbage can, while Gunny flooded the barracks with light. All of the bunks were empty and unmade. Sergeant Black saw them first.

"I'll be damned Gunny, all of our recruits are doing Yoga poses."

"I can see that, Sergeant."

"What do you want to do now?"

"Teach them how to stand at attention, parade rest, and fall out. Let's go, Sergeant Black. Whose mothafucking idea was this?" Gunny stormed out of the barracks.

"It was mine, Gunny."

"Colonel Kim Pol, soldier was in error, sir. I did not know you were here, sir." Gunny apologetically addressed his superior.

"I yus sneak ober befo breakfuss to perform poses with favorite niece and drew crowd. Not get in way of training." Colonel Kim Pol bowed toward his students and walked toward the mess hall.

"Listen up!" Gunny shouted. "The beginning of any battle formation begins with a marching step, a command step. In order to execute a maneuver such as a pincer formation, which

I will teach you, you have to know the call to any given command. I've put together two squads for training purposes. Charlie Unit: Williams, Frye, Lane, Logan, and Robinson. Delta Unit: Green, Wendell, Cole, and the Ball brothers. This is not a reason for competition between the two units. You are a single team. Robinson and Wendell, you are my right guides. Let's kick this shit off!"

C H A P T E R   6 3

Gunnery Sergeant Peters matched his step to theirs during the next four weeks, all the while bellowing his cadence. "Yegeff right yef, yegeff right, square those shoulders, Frye! Other left Green! Keep those ranks straight you pussies. Quit walking like a girl Lane, this ain't no runway for models. I said keep 'em straight. To the rear hut! Squad halt! Right face! At ease.

"They look good, Gunny." Captain James stepped from his Jeep.

"They learn fast, sir. Too damn fast, actually." Gunny appraised the squad.

"How are they doing in the physical training?"

"Besides breaking records, after I've worked them all day they do the damndest thing. They go back to the barracks, face one another and do a modified bend and thrust with a push-up.

Five hundred they do without stopping. Even Tina, sir. Hell, they even start the day at 0400, sir, doing Yoga poses."

"Yoga poses?"

"Yes sir. I don't have to tell you who has them doing the Yoga, sir."

"Is Kim Pol up to his old tricks?"

"That and then some, sir. Last night he was teaching them to spar blindfolded."

"Blindfolded?"

"Yeah Cap. He'd teach them a series of strikes and blocks. Once they had it down, he would blindfold them and attack.

They love him, sir."

"Who wouldn't, Gunny? I suspect he's also teaching them Zen of Strength and Movement as well?"

"Every night at eight, sir."

"Sounds like you have some objections, Gunny?"

"No objections at all, sir. His aid in the House of Bags has elevated their training in self-defense. He's more than qualified to instruct and train, sir."

"How are they doing in the classroom?"

"They are four weeks in and have committed to memory the full twelve courses we had laid out for them. We are now giving them advanced individual training. Cap, they know more than any West Point graduate."

"Really?" Captain James looked astonished.

"See for yourself, sir." Gunny tried to conceal the smile breaking at the corner of his mouth.

"I think I will, Gunny. Wendell?"

"Yes sir, Captain James."

"What does the term 'cover your six' mean?"

"It's military jargon for direction based on the dial of the clock, sir."

"Continue Wendell," urged Captain James.

"Yes sir. Twelve o'clock is straight ahead, sir, three is to the right, nine is to the left, and six is behind or to the rear, sir."

"Very good. Robinson, what is a wide sweep?"

"A wide sweep is a line of men and women who come no closer than eyesight, sir. Since radio channels might be monitored, a standardized series of hand gestures were developed in the 1930's which allowed communication by using field signals. These signals tell the troops when to advance, retreat, proceed, wait, slow down, speed up, and attack, sir."

"So Robinson, if I raise my index finger, that would be?"

"Direction of the attack, sir. Your index finger indicates North, sir."

"My middle finger?"

"South sir."

"My ring and pinky fingers?"

"West and East, sir. Your thumb would be a go, sir."

"Very good. Frye, tell me what is the standard Combat Tactical Maneuver for close quarter urban combat?"

"Using a three-member team, sir. One would take left, one right, and one center upon entering the dwelling. The team would then proceed to clear the dwelling room by room, set a perimeter, and guard all entrances and exits, sir."

"What happens if you encounter a non-friendly?"

"Double-tap burst from my weapon, sir, body-mass kill."

"Excellent. Williams, what is the purpose of Intel?"

"To acquire data useful in defeating opposing forces'."

"How would you use it, Williams?"

"I would market my information to other sources in exchange for cooperation, or to increase data files to make my potential for future trading more productive, and observe personalities, strengths and weaknesses. Would you like for me to sum it up, sir?

"Yes Williams, please do."

"Intelligence gathering helps you to out-think and out-per-form your adversaries, sir."

"I'm impressed. Lane, what is the description of the device hanging from your web belt?"

"It's a Motorola 600, sir. Gives us eyes like binoculars, ears like telephones, and a mouth that whispers. It comes equipped with five plug-in crystals starting at 147.5 megahertz with a frequency hopper. The earpiece and external mic are hand-triggered, activated with on and off switch, or P.T.T. 'push to talk.' Weighs, with the battery pack, two-and-a-half pounds, and is nine inches by one inch and a half. Under optimum conditions, line of sight is three to five miles, sir."

"Well done. Logan, what is the purpose of weapons training?"

"To identify, load, unload, fire the weapon, take apart, clean and make functional, sir."

"Give me a breakdown of the weapon slung across your shoulder."

"Yes sir. AR-15 .223 caliber, gives the police the blues. Shell exits right, three-quarter-inch muzzle depressor. Matty Matel stock, slide push-rod, pistol grip undercarriage with a selector for semiautomatic fire. Magazine feeds ten, twenty, thirty, and hundred round drum magazines, sir."

"Marvelous! Albert Ball, break down the weapon strapped to your hip."

"Yes sir. U.S. Government issue Beretta 9mm. 15-shot staggered-round magazine capacity, one up the pipe. Pistol grip standard aluminum frame with holding groves, sir."

"My God, Gunny! Albert Ball, best sniper weapon?"

"The best sniper weapon is a .300 Winchester Magnum, but it must be built, sir. Is this a trick question?"

"Why do you ask that, son?"

"Because we are training with the M-l Gerand, sir."

"No son, you've answered my question. Gunny, dismiss the squads. I need to speak with you privately."

"Yes sir. Squads ... dismissed!"

"That was damn impressive, Gunny. What don't they know?"

"To be honest, sir, they probably knew all of this when they came out of the womb, or all of them have photographic memories.

The things that we are teaching them seem damn near elementary to them. Yesterday, with Sergeant Greedy looking over their shoulder after showing the whole class only once, they disassembled a claymore mine, extracted the clay base, cooked golf ball-sized charges of C-4, and set to charge."

"That good, huh?"

"That good and better, sir. I'm so damn excited about these young people that I want to contact some of our people in the Corps, and have them take a look at them."

"If you believe in them that strongly, let's take their training up a few notches, give them the works."

"I knew you would say that, sir. We start first thing in the morning. Would you like to be in on the training, sir?"

"Wouldn't miss it for the world, Gunny."

"I knew you would say that too, sir."

CHAPTER 64

Sergeants Black and Greedy moved quietly around the barracks, securing the windows and doors. Without any exchange of words, they placed the gas masks over their faces, and from their belts removed several gas grenades containers, and pulled the pins.

After rolling them under the beds of the sleeping recruits, they secured their only exit.

For two solid minutes they listened to vomiting and retching, as each of them crawled around on the floor to find a breath of fresh air. The pounding on the doors and walls alerted them that it was imperative they wanted out, as the door came off its hinges.

Staggering and falling over one another, all ten of them found the open doorway, and collapsed on the ground gasping for breath, their eyes, noses, and throats burning from the gas. As they struggled to suck in the fresh air, several concussion grenades exploded near them, and the screaming began.

"This way, dammit! Move! Get yo' asses in gear! Get up! Now, goddammit! Now!" Sergeant Greedy's voice roared.

"Get in the motherfucking truck now! Now motherfuckers now!" Sergeant Black growled.

To the great credit of our mental training and toughness, despite the fact that we had been bested, caught in our underwear and barefoot, we all sat ramrod straight in the back of that truck. For several miles, we rode in complete silence before the truck came to a screeching halt. The back door of the truck opened and Gunnery Sergeant Peters' form filled the opening.

"Out!" He barked. "Everybody out of the fucking truck ... now! His authoritative demand was enforced by our bodies being roughly heaved off the truck.

"Dress-right-dress!" Ten arms stretched into the air touching the person next to them. "Ready, front!" Arms snapped down, heads swiveled straight. "Atten-hut!"

From the blinding headlights of the vehicles in front of us, Captain James stepped forward. "Gentlemen and lady," he began. "There is a figurative expression to the story in the second and third chapters of Genesis in the Bible. In the garden of Eden stood two trees of particular significance, the tree of knowledge of good and evil and the tree of life. About face!" Captain James commanded

"You are now standing in the garden of pain and exhaustion. The two trees before you are twelve-inch-thick, thirty-foot-high pine trees. The one on the right is Pain. The one on the left is Exhaustion. Take note people. The trees in the Garden of Eden were probably a variety of evergreens, maybe even pines like these standing before you.

"Today I'm going to teach you things you did not know about teamwork and pain. Pain and Exhaustion are basic parts of a combat soldier's daily life, and today is your turn to experience it. The bags being thrown at your feet contain your clothing, boots, and ten hatchets. Your mission is to chop down Pain and Exhaustion, make them twenty feet in length, clear them of their branches and bark, leave no handles for carrying, and carry them fifteen clicks back to the barracks. Although I have faith that you will accomplish this task in fifteen hours or less, you have twenty hours to complete your task. I suggest you get started."

"Charlie unit, you have Pain. Delta unit, you have Exhaustion Dismissed!" Gunny ordered.

Both teams took off quickly, found their clothing, boots, some k-rations, and the hatchets inside the duffle bags. With our issues in hand we ran toward Pain and Exhaustion.

C H A P T E R   6 5

Gunny sat next to Captain James in the Jeep and slapped his knee. "Kiss my entire ass! They're working together to bring down those trees!"

"What did you expect, Gunny?"

"Just what they've done, the unexpected." He chuckled.

Our combined efforts took nearly two hours to cut down and strip both trees of their branches, bark, and handles. With splintered hands, both Charlie and Delta units lifted our logs and set a pace. Three miles in Tina groaned at the pain in her arms and shoulders, and Charlie unit opted to stop. Delta, seeing a break in the action sat their log down, welcoming the break.

"You alright, Miss Tee?" Bangman checked on Tina.

"My height is causing us problems. Delta is moving smoothly because their log is balance on their shoulders. I'm using mostly arm strength, and it's faltering fast. Plus, this damn log is banging against my collar bone when my arms tire."

Both units began to gather grass, filling Bangman's shirt until it made a suitable cushion for Tina. Minutes later, we lifted the painful logs to our shoulders and began to move. By 1200 hours the sky was cloudless, offering no shade against the strong effects of the sun.

We were all soaking wet, our shirts plastered to our chest, and pants chafing our legs. The sticky sap from the pines brought out the winged things that feasted on us like fried yard bird thrown to the homeless. The syrupy stench was beginning to clog our noses, not to mention the mosquitoes buzzing inside our ears.

Fatigue, crossed with pain from our shoulders being rubbed raw, and the soft ground, slowed our pace after the seventh mile. The previous night's rain in some spots sank our feet three inches into the ground, making our load increasingly heavier with each step. In spite of our steely resolve our steps grew slower, causing us to sit down several times to rest, precious time being lost. Slowly under the heat of the sun, we made our way over the fields which wound along the hillside.

Big Al was the lead man on the log for Delta. He blinked and rubbed his eyes with his fist. They felt hot and dry in their sockets, he watched the fields for so long that his eyes were fixed, unthinking on the path that led to the barracks. The sudden slope of the ground sent Delta crashing hard to the ground, and Big A1 felt a sharp pain as the corner of Exhaustion slammed into his back.

Delta scrambled to their feet. Big Al managed to sit upright, but the darkness hovered at the edge of his eyes, making him dizzy enough to stay down.

Trembling from exhaustion, her eyes on the silent figure on the ground, Tina hurried to where Big Al was sitting. Her feet seemed to make no noise in the dust and grass, she thought, as she and the others closed in on their injured comrade.

"Are you alright, Big Al?" She kneeled beside him.

"Just a little dazed, Miss Tee. Other than a fresh case of humiliation, I feel fine." He moved to stand up.

"You've been hit harder than that on the football field, big bro. Get yo' ass off the ground!" Babyboss reached down to help his brother, but Big Al made a gesture with his hand.

"Leave me be, baby brother. Don't touch me."

There was a strange silence while everyone waited. Without warning, Big Al's form straightened and stiffened, and began to shake with involuntary muscle contractions. The tremors in his legs caused him to do a sort of hideous dance. A continuous muscle contractions caused his head to start turning toward the ground, and Tina and Babyboss held it in place to keep it from turning completely around.

"Get some help!" Tina commanded.

Bangman was acting like a man caught in a dream, as his wide hungry eyes devoured the scene. Across the field of corn he saw something familiar and took off running. When the rest of the excited group caught up to him, he was leaning on a rough rail fence, his hands under his chin gazing at a CH-53 A/D, which his father had flown in the Navy.

"What the hell is this?" I asked.

"It's a helicopter, stupid." Rasheed chimed in.

"I can see that, but whose is it?" I asked.

"It's on the Captain's property, so it's probably his." K-Nine offered.

"Naw K-Nine, cost too much money. The main transmission gearbox in the helicopter was inspected earlier this year, and the bull gears were mandated to be replaced after inspection revealed excessive wear. The entire fleet around the country was grounded until replacements could be made. Captain James probably uses it to move all of this heavy equipment around this ten square miles of farm as a form of training for him and his men."

"How do you know that, Bangman?" K-Nine asked.

"Look right there under the fuselage. There's a single-point cargo hook below it. You can carry 18 U.S. tons, 16.5 metric tons on a sling load. That's how he's moving this combine around all these miles of corn fields."

"Damn, that's all fine and dandy, but how in the hell is standing here looking at this thing gonna help Big Al?" Elijah asked.

"He's right. Captain James is nearly eight miles away, and none of us knows how to fly this thing." Face spoke with urgency.

"I do." Bangman began to climb the fence.

"Bullshit, bullshit, bullshit! Stop with the Tom-foolery and Jack-assery, Bangman. We need to run the damn eight miles and get some help." Badboy was ready to get moving.

"By the time you finish the second mile we'll be back at the barracks. Pay attention!" Bangman opened the helicopter and climbed inside. "There's some first-aid equipment here.

Look for a stretcher neck brace, shit like that, and double it back to Big Al, and bring him here."

"Bangman, you actually think I'm getting into that thing with you, you're out of your fucking mind." Badboy was adamant in his refusal.

"Suit yourself." Bangman dismissed Badboy's lack of confidence in him.

"You really know how to fly this thing?" Badboy asked, angry with himself for doubting Bangman.

"A few years ago when my dad was alive, he taught me how to fly in an Osage H-55. It was a single design two-seat training helicopter."

"A training helicopter is not this monster in front of us!" Badboy shouted.

"Before my father died, he flew one of these babies. Being the spoiled military brat that I was, he sometimes let me be his co-pilot. Trust me, I can fly this thing like K-Nine drives that Fleetwood."

"Oh shit! We in trouble now, cause K-Nine can't drive worth a fuck." Badboy shook his head from side to side.

"Badboy?"

"Yeah, Bangman?"

"When you bring Big Al, don't forget Pain and Exhaustion."

CHAPTER 66

Carrying Big Al, and Pain and Exhaustion, Charlie and Delta units moved with slow noiseless steps up the ramp of the Super Stallion. All eyes were on Bangman, following his every move, wondering if he really knew what he was doing.

"Lady and gentlemen." Bangman spoke as if he were our flight attendant or pilot. "I don't have time to give you a guided tour, but I will offer you and explanation as to why this engine-powered, heavier-than-aircraft, bolted together piece of metal can be lifted and sustained in the air by rotating wings or blades turning on vertical axes." Bangman took his seat in the pilot's chair and strapped himself in.

"Just in case you're wondering if I know what I'm doing, don't trip, it's a piece of cake." He began flipping switches. We all watched as the control panel came to life, and Bangman shouted out his narration of the flight.

"First of all, the flight control is maintained by a Hamilton Standard FCC-105 Autopilot and Digital Computer. The difference between the helo's I learned to fly and this one is, instead of two engines this one has a third T64 Turbo-Shaft engine fitted behind the main rotor mast." He pressed a button and the engines turned over.

"This thing that I'm now pulling is called the collective. It changes the pitch of the main rotor blades. What I'm doing now is raising the collective. The greater the pitch on the blades, the more lift. The more lift is what makes this machine go up and down." Bangman raised the pitch on the blades to a steeper pitch, and maneuvered the foot pedal, and the helicopter raised smoothly off the ground.

"Now!" He shouted over the roar of the blades. "This thing between my legs is a joystick or a cyclic. The cyclic changes the pitch on the blades, but you don't need to know all this shit." Bangman moved the cyclic forward, climbed to seven-thousand feet, adjusted the airspeed, and shouted over his shoulder. "Piece of cake!"

C H A P T E R   67

"Gunny, would you like to make a small wager as to what time they'll show?" Captain James removed his money clip from his pocket .

"Well sir, we took them out at 0330, and by 0600 they were on their way, so considering the terrain is flat, muddy in some places from last night's rain, and the only hills they're going to encounter are midway, and, they're nine hours in," he checked his watch. "I'll bet you a fifty spot that they'll show by 1930."

"1930 is your bet?"

"1930 is my bet, sir."

"Lock it in." Captain James extended his fist. "Tell me something, Gunny?"

"What do you want to know, Cap?" Gunny took a swig of his beer.

"Is Kim Pol joyriding in the Stallion again?"

"No sir, I just left him in the mess hall when I got the beers. He was frying chicken wings and making fried rice for the recruits.

"Look at the horizon, Gunny. Either that is our helo coming this way, or it's one hell of a big-ass bird."

Gunny moved quickly to his office and retrieved his binoculars

"Yes sir, it's ours ... and kiss my natural ass! Pardon me , sir. Logan is flying it, sir." He passed the binoculars.

"I'll be damned!" Captain James eyes grew wide with

astonishment, as the Stallion banked expertly, slowed, and descended to the ground one-hundred-and-thirty yards from where they were standing.

Bangman went about the business of shutting down the engine while the rest of us carried Big Al, and Pain and Exhaustion off the Stallion. We stood at attention before Captain James and saluted him. He returned our salute.

"Permission to speak, sir?" K-Nine stepped forward.

"Permission granted, Wendell."

"Pain and Exhaustion, sir, and true to our oaths, no man left behind, sir."

Captain James looked at our faces, and beneath the perspiration and soiled clothing he saw the faces of children: stern, hard, with no reflection of fear in our eyes.

"Today you have become not men and a woman, but members of an elite team. You've welded your common personalities into one dominant force, and created a single desire to perform as a team. I salute your efforts."

Captain James snapped to attention, and saluted both Charlie and Delta units. He walked over to where Big Al was lying on the stretcher, and on his face he could detect a mixture of merriment and agony.

"Do you need a doctor, son?"

"Only if he has a cure for embarrassment, sir." Big Al sat up even thought his body was in pain.

"I'm going to have you checked out from head to toe, and have you X-rayed to make sure nothing is damaged or broken."

"I can assure you Captain James, the only thing wounded is my pride."

"Gunny?"

"Yes sir?"

"Make sure Ball gets the VIP treatment down at the local hospital."

"You got it, Cap."

"Wait a minute!" Kim Pol interjected. "Dis wha wong wit you Amerikans. You know, know how to fix injury. Jus know how to inflick injury. Bring young warrior to my quarters. Me fix."

"Captain?" Gunny waited for further instructions.

"He's a ranking officer, Gunny. Plus we'll never hear the end of it. One hour, Kim Pol, and the kid gets X-rayed."

"In one hour he doing back flip. Dis why Vietnamese people such a great people, we no need X-ray, just human touch." Kim Pol helped Babyboss carry Big Al to his quarters.

Captain James stood retardant for a moment, his eyes holding an awestruck expression, as he looked at the young man climbing down from the Stallion, and walking toward him.

"Permission to speak, Captain James?" Bangman saluted his commanding officer.

"Permission granted, Logan." He returned the salute.

"Other than a few twisted wires, she's all there, sir."

"I can see that. What I want to know is, how in the hell do you know how to fly that helo?"

"My father, sir."

Captain James looked puzzled for a moment before he spoke. "I'm sorry Logan, I thought you were an orphan like the others."

"Kinda sorta, sir. My father is dead, died nine months ago. He held the rank of Lieutenant Commander in the Navy."

"Did he die in the service of his country?"

"No sir. After my mom died in 1987 my dad was assigned to Sikorsky Aircraft in California to assist in the development of the Pavehawk SOF MH-60."

"The Pavehawk, I'm familiar with both its development and it's use in active service."

"My pops loved his new assignment, sir. He told me the Pavehawk would be used for special missions, like search and rescue and transporting of covert and reconnaissance teams behind enemy lines. At the age of thirty-seven, my dad was shot dead by an unknown assailant in a grocery store parking lot near our home in Pomona California."

"Did the authorities ever find the people responsible?"

"No sir, no suspects, no witnesses, and no clues. Police said it was an attempted robbery, and gave the stupidest reason that I've ever heard. They said that because all the money and identification was left in the wallet, it was a foiled robbery attempt."

"I'm sorry for your loss, son."

"Thank you, sir. My dad would have liked you, sir. He told me his comrades in the battle brotherhood were more important to him than the cause they were fighting for."

"I'm sure I would have liked him as well, and he's right, there is a mysterious camaraderie born on the battlefield of danger and death. So how long have you been flying?"

"Since I was thirteen, sir."

"Really?"

"My dad was preparing me for Annapolis and wanted me to have some aviation experience. So I started training in the Osage H-55 training helicopter. By the time I was sixteen, as a birthday gift, for two weeks I was taught to fly a Super Stallion just like the one you have here."

"You are truly a remarkable young man, Logan. If you like, I have friends in all the right places that can help you get into Annapolis."

"Annapolis was my father's vision for me, sir. I've since developed my own dreams. I'm going into the medical profession." "Good for you, Logan."

"Yeah, my dad's sister says the same thing, sir."

"You hungry, son?"

"Starving, sir."

"Let's go and get some of Kim Pol's chicken wings and fried rice.

"Does he have that sweet and sour sauce to go with it, sir?"

"Kim Pol wouldn't put the plates on the table if he didn't."

…

Kim Pol walked into the mess hall an hour later. "Ta-da!"

Big Al jumped through the door, did a few jumping jacks, bends and thrusts, all to the applause of his team.

"Acupuncture and acupressure is the greatest medical treatment ever discovered!" He looked as if he had never been injured.

"This ancient medical miracle is great, people. But over the next few weeks we are going to do it all over again with a twist. I suggest you get plenty of rest." Gunnery Sergeant Peters chuckled.

"Gunny?"

"Yes sir, Captain James?"

"You owe me fifty dollars."

"Sir, I can say this is the best fifty-dollar loss I've ever experienced. Glad to pay it, sir." He handed over the money.

"Would you like to go double or nothing?"

"What do you have in mind, Cap?"

"A little contest on the firing range between Charlie and Delta."

"It would be close, Cap. They're nearly equal in marksmanship. "You promised them a twist, did you not?"

"That I did, sir. What do you have in mind?" Captain James leaned over and whispered in Gunny's ear.

"I'll get right on it, Cap, first thing in the morning. And Cap?"

"Yeah Gunny."

"Lock it in, sir." He extended his fist.

C H A P T E R   6 8

"Atten-hut!" Ordered Gunnery Sergeant Peters. All bodies present snapped to attention when Captain James stepped forward holding his grandson, who was dressed from head to toe in Army fatigues.

"At ease, everyone. It saddens me, and the men that have been training you that in three days this training session will come to an end." He hesitated and then added proudly. "Until next year." He held up his hand to calm the applause.

"For the past two weeks you've been building a make-shift Hogan's Alley. Sergeant Black tells me that you geniuses have the pop-ups and turn targets all set up on electronics. I'm going to tell you for confusion and judgment calls, we've added friendly and hostile targets, some with mothers holding babies. Some of the mothers are carrying weapons. Others are using their babies as shields. You will have a split second to decide.

"Now for the treat that I promised you in the parking lot that first morning three months ago. 99.9 percent of all law enforcement officers and agents in the field have never been shot at with live ammo. Their ability to function as a team is practiced shock and awe, designed to overwhelm you because they are the authority. Your qualification over the next few days will be under live gunfire on the course, unlike the police, who, if you shoot at them, their practiced plan goes to hell in a hand basket, and all you'll see is heels and assholes." He paused until the laughter subsided.

"Also, pyrotechnic special effects have been added to the

course to scare the shit out of you. Your score will be based on a combat-situation score. Kill or no kill. Gunny has told me that the course can be completed in three minutes. As a word of caution, when you move between targets, run. Do not hesitate, as live rounds will be a full five feet behind you. If you do not want to participate in this exercise you will not be branded a coward. I promised you all an experience you would never forget, and I'm here to close on the deal. Anyone wishing to join me and my grandson in the shade behind the glass is more than welcome. That will be all. Gunny?"

"Just as I thought, none of you hardhead son of a guns would back out, so here's my deal. For safe measures you will be fitted with FBA or full-body armor. These flack vests that are being issued to you were built for combat soldiers. The bulletproof vests worn by civilians are not as well made. Each day you will shed pieces of the body armor to help speed you through the course. Talk it over amongst yourselves as to who will go first. You have two minutes to decide."

I have to say, it was the best day of my life to date. Maybe all of our lives, because all ten of us stood before that obstacle course with choked voices and happy emotions. We'd done it. We were about to complete a military training only the elite of soldiers would be granted the privilege to participate in, and each and every one of us was eagerly anticipating what stirred in the deepest depths of our hearts and souls: Six's plan for our future.

Elijah, with an outpouring that moved everyone present, made a fervid pleading and moving prayer in a beautiful language. The burden of his supplication was simple: that an ever merciful and compassionate Father in heaven watch over us and shield us from any fatal live round.
"Ooooooooooooorah!"

CHAPTER 69

We grumbled amongst ourselves about who would go first, and in the end it was 'lady first'. Tina elected, over the protest of Gunny, not to wear the full-body armor because of its bulkiness, and only wore the vest. She stood at the ready with the AR-15 and a twenty round clip and awaited the starting signal.

Two concussion grenades exploded simultaneously on both sides of her to take her focus off the target that was twenty-five feet away. The thunderous sound and the shock of the grenade blast threw her body to the ground automatically. She rose, adjusted her eyesight, and as she walked toward the target, she emptied her clip. She heard the report of the M-16 and took off running. As she ran she could feel the live rounds at her heels as chunks of dirt behind her were flying shoulder high. The experience for her was both exhilarating and frightening at the same time. She kept running.

She reached the barbed wire, laid on her back with the AR-15 across her chest, and crawled beneath it under the controlled gunfire from Sergeant Greedy's M-16. As every well-placed round penetrated the wooden target, it splintered wood and buried itself in the twenty-foot berms above her head.

She nearly pissed on herself when several rounds hit inches above her face, showering her with wood chips. She scooted faster.

Her heart was pounding so hard she could hear it behind

her ears.

She stood, a bit shaken from the experience, discarded her AR-15, and drew the 9mm Beretta, released the safety, and stepped into Hogan's Alley.

Gunfire erupted around her, and she began to run through the makeshift town. A pop-up bandit shot up in front of her, and without a second thought, she double-tapped into the upper torso of the target. Still running toward it, she placed a third round through the head of the target for a perfect kill.

She stopped ten feet past the target when concussion grenades exploded to her right and left, again the shock of the blasts automatically throwing her body to the ground.

"Damn!" She hear three turn-targets hit back to back. She quickly jumped to her feet, and through the smoke she fired at what she believed in that split-second to be hostiles. Straight kill shots on all three targets.

Moving between the structures, it became extremely quiet. An uneasy feeling fell over her like a sheet had been thrown over her head. The pop-ups came seconds behind one another. Her fourth target in was a lady with a baby in her arms. In a millisecond she deduced that the woman was carrying a weapon. Her weapon, already sighted on the target, dropped slightly, as she saw the woman held a baby rattle in her hand. Her indecision caused her to miss two turn-targets just as the three minute horn sounded.

Striding exhaustedly back through the course, her ears ringing, she saw figures standing in a staggered formation applauding her. While the others hurried off to reset the course, Captain James stood holding her son, who with his ear protection and sun shades, put a smile on her face.

Wrapping his arms around her, Fate smiled. "You done good, Miss Tee, I'm proud of you."

"Fate, those grenades going off scared the living mess out of me. I don't know how you guys dealt with that during the war."

"Miss Tee, you've done better than some soldiers I know. But I'll tell you the secret that every combat soldier knows within the first day of battle, if you like."

"Please do."

"You know you're still alive when you hear the explosion."

She smiled and watched as her team assaulted the course. The first day no one shot a perfect score. There were points lost for upholstering weapons, chambering rounds, and recovering from live gunfire, and explosions. On the third and final day all ten of us not only graduated Gunny's boot camp, we mastered the course and scored perfect scores of **20/16 X RING DEAD HITS.**

C H A P T E R   7 0

"This is an incredible story up to now, Sazzar. Let's talk about this Six, this Jeffery Alexander Lane. What were his plans? Who were his contacts, his connections?" U.S. Attorney Hughes threw his cards on the table.

"No one really knew who his contacts or connections were." Sazzar reached for his bottled water.

"You mean to tell me you were never curious who he was working with?" Special Agent McMurtry had a look of disbelief on his face.

"I'm human, I had my suspicions, Agent McMurtry."

"We'll, let's see if we can put a positive spin on those suspicions, and fill up the gaps in the reasonable doubt areas." United Stated Attorney Hughes' appetite for useful information was seemingly insatiable.

"Alright, there was this guy I always thought was Six's man. He played chess with the guy through the mail, on landlines, and on the Internet."

"His connection was a chess geek?" agent McMurtry looked dumbfounded .

"I don't know, unless you consider a Master Gunnery Sergeant of the United States Marine Corps a geek?" Sazzar didn't wait for a response. "What I am about to tell you is purely speculation from my viewpoint. There is absolutely no truth to it, only what I believe happened from bits and pieces of conversations Six and I had over the years. As my friend Ronnie Green would say, 'it's not even good hearsay'."

"You let this old spider spin the web, you just tell the story, Sazzar." U.S. Attorney Hughes had cunning look in his eyes.

"I always believed Six's man was Master Gunnery Sergeant Andre Miller. This is a man of incredible resources, and entrepreneur of the black market on a global level. Born in Salt Lake City, Utah, the oldest son of an open-pit mine worker, Andre joined the Corps, not to fight for his country, but to get away from Utah.

"Andre, as he liked to be called, was a hard man who served several tours in Vietnam. A warrior not a patriot, Andre was eight months from retirement as a twenty year soldier when Six met him.

"A born operator of the con-game and the hustle, Andre amassed a small fortune while in charge of the U.S. Marine Corps Armory.

"He began after his last tour in Nam, selling cigarettes, M-16's, K-bar knives, and military uniforms to Army and Navy surplus stores On his return to the states he stepped up his game using military transport planes to ship his goods around the globe. Jeeps were sold to lumber companies, auto parts to auto-supply houses, helicopter parts, and land clearing equipment to oil and construction companies.

"The real money rolled in when the military switched from an abundance of the Colt .45 model 1911 to the Beretta 92F. On a routine trip to identify firearms, and electronic communication parts at the Minnesota Armory, Andre decided to drop in on his old friend Captain Lafayette James.

"Captain James introduced him to an extraordinary thirteen-year old boy that he called Six. Six's love for chess made them instant friends. Andre, a chess addict, who considered himself a learned player worthy of international competition, was fascinated by Six's ability to recognize, develop, and evaluate positions on the chess board.

"For three years they played through the mail and over land- lines. On Six's sixteenth birthday, Andre prepaid a first-class- round-trip ticket on United Airlines for Six to fly to Huntsville, Utah to spend a week on Andre's ranch. During that week, Andre tutored Six not only in how to systematically recognize themes that occur in chess play, but also how to gain advantages through means of domestic and counter intelligence.

"He gave Six a mission that week of collecting information, some of it secretly, some obtained by conducting surveillance operations, and analyzing the data received into detailed plans.

"He also taught Six how to conduct clandestine conversations. Control your inner restrains and listen carefully to the details of a conversation, he taught Six. Conceal or reveal your deepest purpose with body language: a date, a name, a place, 'bits and pieces of the craft' he called them. In the end, it was up to the one listening to spell out the message."

C H A P T E R 7 1

Andre, who was of medium height, but powerfully built with chiseled features, sat smiling in the visiting room at the St. Cloud Reformatory, as he recalled Six's visit to his ranch.

Dressed as a priest, Father Bishop -- his cover name, a true saint he thought himself to be -- was motivated by amusing himself, and guided only by his sense of self-preservation.

Andre knew from the letter he'd received from Six that he was an indispensable link, and the holder of information, to a young man's dream. He had to admit, the kid always came with something exciting and challenging.

Six was stumped when the guard called his name for a visit. Everyone he knew and loved was a hundred miles away, kicking up serious dust. He was even more dumbfounded when the guard strip- searching him told him that it was a priest waiting to see him.

Six walked into the visiting room and was relieved and delighted to see Andre.

"Father!" He warmly engaged his friend knowing they would not be able to speak their hearts and minds in their present company, Andre set the stage.

"Yes it is I, my son, Father Bishop in the flesh."

"It's nice to see you again, Father Bishop." He quickly got into character with Andre.

"Every church school wants only the honor students who are well-mannered and tote Bibles to be a part of their flock, but I say what about the wayward youths? Do we really want or know them?"

Staying in character Six answered him. "I'm not a desperate teenager crossing the threshold of the church without an offering, Father. Much is at stake, and how I am treated will determine whether I remain a member of the church."

"My son, a man should never greet his friend with man-made restrictions or prejudices. He should want to treat his friend with dignity and affection, regardless of their appearance. Today's young people." Andre sighed as he made the sign of the cross over his chest. "Now, come give old Father Bishop a hug! He stood with outstretched arms. Six hugged Andre and the two of them sat down and began their visit.

"I received your letters, Jeff. How can old Father Bishop help with your transition back into society after being released from prison?"

"By counseling and mentoring a project I have in the making, Father."

"Would this be faith-based ministry work, or work that would later be administered by a task force of federal prosecutors?" The Father stared with an arched eyebrow.

"If I don't receive the proper guidance from the church and correct some of the flaws in my faith, the impact may become more marginalized and reflect my current situation as a lifetime of prison culture."

"Oh, I see. The Bible teaches those who understand its message are men who will always be intrigued by Jesus' teaching when he ministered to those faithful few on earth. They always want to hear more. You have my ear, son."

Six leaned in closer to Father Bishop. "How well do you remember my visit to your ranch in Utah?"

"Besides the fact that you embarrassed me and defeated me by two-and-a-half points during our chess tournament. I thought you had a wonderful time."

"Do you remember taking me to the open-pit mines in Bingham Canyon?"

"Sure, I was being the tour guide. You know, Jeff, when one goes meandering down memory lane, they eventually reach the tough subject."

Six took a deep breath, squared his shoulders and began.

"On that day, Father Bishop, you showed me a conveyor belt, which was twenty-four-feet wide and twenty to thirty miles long that ended on the outskirts of Magna."

"Yes Jeff, Utah is particularly dependent on its copper and other nonferrous metal industries. Is there a point to all this?"

"There were two armored trucks that left the smelter that day that you told me were headed for the gold reserve in Salt Lake City Do you remember the trucks?"

"Sure, they run from a couple of different locations every Tuesday and Friday. Some of those trucks carry as much as a hundred and-fifty-million dollars or more in gold. A dagger in the heart to a man in my position. Why do you ask?"

"Perhaps, Father Bishop, you may wake up one morning, and find yourself part of an elite group of professionals that will remove the dagger from your heart, and not smudge your reputation."

"Oh my, dear boy!" Father Bishop laughed. Six could see it was more for show as the other visitors smiled and waved at the Father. "Listen Jeff," he leaned closer until they were inches from each other. "As much as I would like to defend that chosen profession, there are several disturbing factors that would have to be eliminated at the mercy of human handling. Twenty-four souls in all. In God's sight, my son, these thoughts you think constitute a covenant with Hades, or an agreement with death himself."

"I take it you mean the quartet that accompanies the trucks?"

"Absolutely, my son. Besides, your intelligence would have to be flawless to be able to defuse them before they could threaten your very existence."

"This is why I need your help, Father Bishop, in my scenario planning. I don't want to be forced to rely on guess work and put my people in jeopardy."

"Listen Jeff, I'm not saying yes, nor am I saying no. Let's just say that without the benefit of intelligence and opinions, even an uncomfortable opinion can get sidetracked in arguments that don't matter, and fog things up. If it can be done, I will do what a faithful servant was meant to do."

"Thank you, Father Bishop. You know I work in the

education department here in the institution. Maybe the church could donate some educational materials?"

"I'm sure, should things pan out, the church could donate the necessary educational materials. When do you need them?"

"Within ninety days, Father."

"Father Bishop leaned in even closer. "It would take that long just to put a decent team together, Jeff."

"What if I told you there is already a team in place?"

"Lamebrains, misfits, unprincipled thugs, killers, and wannabe gangsters could never be a part of anything of this magnitude. You would need a team of professionals to handle such a job."

"I have a team being trained as we speak, Father, and the momentum is starting to roll. Most of the minor details I've taken care of. What I need from you, Father, is intel ... and what is on this piece of paper." Six pulled a piece of plastic from his mouth and passed it to Father Bishop.

Father Bishop gave him a noncommittal shrug and pulled the strip of paper from the plastic. After reading it, he balled it in his napkin, and placed it in his inside jacket pocket.

"Can they be trusted to act with discretion and judgment?"

"Stony looks and sealed lips, Father." There was a long pause.

"You want the merchandise to go to the address on that date?"

"Yes, Father."

"And the one-hundred-thousand dollar donation to the church will be sent by these charitable donors?"

"Three weeks after delivery."

"The team you speak of, Jeff, it's obvious that it does not include you due to your current situation. Am I correct?"

"Yes, Father Bishop, you are."

"Disciples of yours?"

"Well-trained chosen successors who will help you retire in the comfort and style of the extremely rich and famous, Father."

"Talk about ambitious undertakings, Jeff. Do you really think you can pull this off from a penitentiary cell?"

"The real question, Father, is can you get rid of the prize?"

Father Bishop was quiet for a moment before he cleared his throat. "I'm a field rep for the King of Kings. If you were to measure honesty, ethical integrity, and the ability to find a buyer for a product among twenty of those in my profession, you, my dear friend, would find that my name is at the top of the list.

"Noted and honored, Father Bishop. Now, how about a game of chess?"

"I thought you'd never ask, Jeff."

CHAPTER 72

"Sazzar, you are going to be the perfect witness. You are one hell of a believable sumbitch! Damn if I didn't believe every word you said!" U.S. Attorney Hughes rose from his seat.

"It was fabrication, Mr. Hughes. I don't know if that is what really happened."

"Bullshit! McMurtry, wasn't there a robbery of two armored cars Nineteen years ago in Utah?"

"Yes sir, one that still has the agency baffled. Why do you ask?"

"Correct me if I'm wrong, Sazzar, but did we just solve the crime of the century?" U.S. Attorney Hughes was definitely going to take the credit for this one.

"Do you want to hear the story in the sequences in which they happened, or do you want me to jump around?"

"Hot damn!" U.S. Attorney Hughes became excited.

"Calm down, Mr. Prosecutor. He did not admit to his or anyone else's involvement in that crime." Miss Corning interjected.

"The hell he didn't!"

"He said it was a fabrication, Mr. Hughes. The entire contents of the statement are false, no good, a lie, bull-fucking-shit!" She banged on the table to emphasize her point.

Ignoring her, U.S. Attorney Hughes turned to Agent McMurtry.

"I want to know every man, woman, and cockroach Six spoke to in that damn reformatory. I don't give a fuck if you have to put a hundred agents on the case working day and night. I want the 302's of those interviews on my desk in one week."

"U.S. Attorney Hughes?"

"Yeah Sazzar, what is it?"

"I can save you the trouble. Six only had one friend and one enemy in St. Cloud."

"You have a name, Sazzar?" Agent McMurtry asked.

"Better than that. Six's only friend, who was his next door neighbor and workout partner in St. Cloud, was Abdullah bin Sa'ad. Born Ulysses Sutton, U.S. to his friends and family, he married his childhood sweetheart, Marie Jones, and together they pledged their Shahaadas, or testimonies of faith, a combination of negation and affirmation that there is no true God except Allah alone.

"Imam Abdur Rahman Hameed gave them their attributes of Abdullah bin Sa'ad and Ayesha. They graciously accepted, legally changed their names, and began living their lives as Muslims.

"Two years later, Abdullah moved his wife and newborn son into their home on Colfax Avenue in North Minneapolis. On the eve of their second wedding anniversary, Ayesha went shopping at the local Islamic market to prepare a special meal for her husband. On the drive back, she momentarily took her eyes off the road to attend to her infant son, and rear ended the car in front of her, causing minor damage.

"The driver, a young black man, pants sagging, rag wrapped around his head, sprang from his car, and shouted obscenities at Ayesha. Unable to arouse her anger, he went back to his car, pulled a crowbar from beneath the car seat, and began smashing her windows and beating the hood of her car.

"Fearing for the safety of her child she stepped on the gas, ramming her car into the young asshole's car, sending it across the intersection, jumping the curb. It rolled to a stop on the lawn of an old man, who was now shouting his own obscenities. Ayesha accelerated away, leaving the asshole and his passengers, cursing and screaming.

"Badly shaken and in tears, she parked in front of her house, lifted her son from his safety-seat, and began to run to her house. Midway to her front door, the car with the young assholes in it turned the corner on her block, and a hailstorm of bullets assaulted her home. Despite her own desire to run, to throw herself to the ground, with a pure heart and the armor of obedience to her Lord, Ayesha stood perfectly still. Bullets whistled pass her ears, and shattered the windows on her home. When the gunfire stopped, she heard the young assholes scream. "Get the hell out of our neighborhood, you rag wearing bitch!"

"Abdullah returned home to thirty-five bullet holes in his house and a swarm of Minneapolis Police, and crime scene investigators standing around talking to his trembling wife. Unable to control himself after the police had gone, Abdullah with pistol in hand, and a description of the men and the car that Ayesha had withheld from the police, drove his car down on Plymouth Avenue to the local youth center. There in front of the center was a Buick Electra 225 with a dent in the bumper. The two men responsible for the assault on his wife, son, and property were leaning against the wall of the center, sharing a forty-ounce.

"Dressed in all black the epitome of death, Abdullah walked swiftly to where the men were standing. Without a word, he shot both men in the head at point-blank range, reaping their souls instantly.

"The African-American community of North Minneapolis applauded Abdullah's self-served justice, and together with the Mosque raised thousands of dollars for his defense fund. At the sentencing phase of the trial, the judge found his actions to be of noble character and sentenced him to twenty to life with parole eligibility." The Judge admonished, "After serving twenty straight calendar years."

C H A P T E R 73

Abdullah stood in the doorway of Six's cell shaking his head from side to side.

"What's wrong, Abdullah?" Six closed the book he was reading.

"Just marveling at how a young black man with an I.Q. of 150 or better, who knows for certain the true value of his intellect, can sit around reading crap like that." Abdullah pointed at the closed book in Six's hand.

Six seemed taken aback by Abdullah's comment. "What could possibly be wrong with reading Robert H. Decoy's 'The Niggers Bible?'"

"Several reasons. The first of which is that he claims to be an acknowledge nigger, writing about the experiences of niggers ... addressed exclusively to his nigger people!"

Six laughed. "Don't start, Abdullah. This is merely a true classic of the American black experience."

Before Abdullah could respond, there was a thunderous applause in the cell block. Abdullah and Six stepped out onto the range to see what the commotion was about.

Entering the block was Punchy, a high-ranking Organization member. Punchy was tall in stature, six-three or four with a round face, and an expression on it that seemed to have been sculpted imperfectly with the dull edge of the blade. His blue-black skin made him look like a shadow in broad daylight. He had glittering eyes, small but keen, and looked to weigh in at 235 pounds.

"Punchy!" Abdullah hissed with disdain.

"Sounds like there's some bad blood between you two?" Six was concerned as he watched Punchy twist a cap backward that was placed on his head. Six noticed that he walked in a self-contained way, as if there was nothing or no one in the reformatory that could garner, or was even worthy of his attention.

Punchy stopped, looked up at Abdullah, and smiled. His teeth were bright white, yet his smile appeared mechanical.

"What's the deal with you and the big fella, Abdullah?"

"No deal. Punchy is an extremely dangerous homosexual. He went to the hole six months before you got here for having sexual relations with an unwilling inmate."

"So he's a fag?" Six had a baffled look on his face.

"Yes he is. But like I said, a very dangerous fag, and I want no part of his trifling ass."

"And I had you pegged as a man who fears nothing!" Six teased.

"Growing up I had two giant-sized fears. One of them is that I fear Allah, and would rather face ten hells than hear Him speak negatively against me on the Day of Judgment."

"And the other?"

"The other is having sex with an ugly woman."

Six threw his head back and roared with laughter. "Why would having sex with an ugly woman scare you?"

"I'd be scared because she might have the best sex in the world. Rockets would be bursting and I'd be seeing stars and fireworks. My dumb self would fall hopelessly and madly in love with her, wouldn't be able to go anywhere without this ugly woman on my arm."

Six was laughing so hard, tears were streaming down his face. When he finally got himself under control he became serious. "Well, you don't have that problem. Ayesha is beautiful."

"Thanks, Six. Allah has been good to me. All praises due."

"Okay, so what is the story with Punchy? He seems so popular." Abdullah took a deep breath. ,

"Punchy, and the ignorant dude walking with him, Daddy Rat, were suppose to send a message to all the Twin City pimps and hustlers who were holding down corners that the

Organization either wanted their cut, or they pay protection money to work their ho's on the corner.

"Anyway, there was this particular piece of real estate on the corner of Lake and Portland in South Minneapolis, it was a hot spot for drugs, women, and gambling. The 'O' wanted the site for their drug distribution, so they sent Punchy and Daddy Rat to deliver the message.

"Well, when they got to the spot, sitting on the stoop in front of the house was this very beautiful five-foot-seven, tightly built hooker with features hinting at blended Spanish and European ancestry. Tricks and homeboys alike were fascinated by her beauty because she had inherited the best features of both races: with the thick straight hair, and voluptuous curves that Spanish women are so blessed with.

"After a short, whispered conversation with Daddy Rat, whom Punchy had sent to retrieve her, her lips parted, and she murmured something to Daddy Rat, and pointed in Punchy's direction. Now Punchy, who from the age of eleven had always been attracted to men, smiled when she rose to her feet and began making her way toward him. Punchy became disturbingly aware of the scent of her flowery perfume, as she came closer to him. For the first time in his pathetic life he felt the thickening inside his trousers start to ache, not from the thought of a man, but from this woman in front of him.

"When she walked up to him, she stared blatantly at the rise in his crotch, and felt both turned on and uneasy. Punchy, the fool that he is, thought the simple gesture of her staring at his crotch gave her some kind of edge over him mentally. Although he was going to rob her and kick her ass, her seductive manner began to piss him off, but not so much as the betrayal going on between his legs which was burning him up inside.

"Her lips parted again and she whispered something that Punchy couldn't hear. He moved closer. She said it again, whispering it in his ear. This time he heard it loud and clear.

"'You want to fuck me, Papi?'"

"She made no moves, letting him know that the ball was in his court exclusively. When he didn't answer right away she began to smile at him like she knew what he was thinking.

Punchy threw her a cruising glance from head to toe. 'How much?'

"Without answering, she grabbed his hand, leading him up the stairs and into the whorehouse. He followed her, knowing she was on the losing end of the deal. She angered him with the seductive swing of her hips like her fucking body was butter dripping off a hot biscuit." Abdullah paused, as Punchy and his entourage began climbing the tiers.

Before Six could say anything he continued. "She deposited Punchy on her bed in a sparsely furnished room, and brought him a shot of whiskey without even asking him if he wanted one. She knew. She sat and watched, as he downed the drink in one long gulp. Punchy studied her unabashedly, his face devoid of any emotion.

"In a warped kind of playful manner she got down on her knees between his legs, and unzipped his trousers, and removed his manhood. Holding his engorged phallus in her hands, any fear of him quickly vanished, she was once again in control. She trusted him.

"'You pay me what you think I'm worth.' She licked him.

"'You look just like a pretty little boy I raped.' He pulled the .45 automatic from his waistband and placed it to her temple.

Her pleas were, spontaneous, and she began sucking and stroking his phallus.

"'Tell me what you want me to do, Papi?' She inhaled him. 'How can I please you? I'll do anything, Papi. Please don't hurt me,' she cried.

"I guess her pleas made the heartless bastard feel in control, because he slapped her hard across the face, and asked her where the money was stashed. On reflex she cringed, the thin line between the fantasies she had produced, and the reality of her here and now were a blurred deception being stripped clean away.

"Even as her panic began to settle in, she felt a guttural desire clot in her throat, and began sucking harder and faster. Punchy screamed.

"'You wanna die, bitch!?'

"'No!' Her voice was barely a croak.

"Punchy cocked the hammer back on the .45, pulling her to her feet. She began crying, 'Please Papi, please don't kill me. Me do anything.'

"'Where's the money, bitch?' Punchy turned her around, pulled down her panties, and exposed her bare behind.

"'Me have no dinero, Papi. Please don't hurt me?' She begged as he bent her over, her tears flowing down her face."

Six looked at Abdullah's eyes, followed his gaze, and watched Punchy step on their tier. He turned back to Abdullah, who's eyes never left Punchy. He continued his narration.

"'Shut up!' Punchy told her. She began sobbing loudly, and shaking violently, her heart racing. To her horror and revulsion, her whole body began to throb as Punchy penetrated her anus. Her begging and now screaming grew louder with each stroke Punchy thrust into her.

"Paranoia suddenly gripped Punchy and he believed that someone would hear her cry for help and come to her aid. So he shoved her face into the bed and placed a pillow over her head and put three slugs in the back of her head. The tightening of her anus muscles at death caused him to blow seed inside her.

"Unfortunately, for this sick bastard, there were police from the Vice Squad in the whorehouse getting serviced. They heard the screams and the gunfire. Right after the sick fuck's grand orgasm, the police burst through the door, and arrested his dumb ass."

Six looked into his friends eyes. "How is it that you know so much about this dude?"

"Tell him." A deep voice resonated.

Six turned around and standing directly behind him was Punchy. Abdullah, never took his eyes from Punchy's. "Meet Marc Sutton, my baby brother."

CHAPTER 74

"Obviously there is a reason why you told us that story, Sazzar. What is the significance of these two Sutton boys to the crimes connected to this case?" U.S. Attorney Hughes searched further.

"Absolutely none."

"Then why in the fuck did you tell the story?" U.S. Attorney Hughes became angry.

"Because you were making such a fuss about who Six may have spoken to in St. Cloud. I just saved you hundreds of hours of man power. Besides, only one of the brothers is remotely relevant to this case."

"How is that, Sazzar? Both of them are serving life in prison and not eligible for parole until 2018, according to my calculations." Agent McMurtry was feeling left out of the conversation.

Sazzar laughed. "Abdullah bin Sa'ad has been out of prison for eight years, and is free, thanks to Six."

"How the hell did he manage something like that?" U.S. Attorney Hughes remained the inquisitor.

"Six hired a group of lawyers to work on Abdullah's case after we graduated from college. Investigators uncovered a series of Brady violations by an overzealous prosecutor. The two men Abdullah killed were the suspects in several home invasions, and the rape and torture of an elderly woman, and the drowning of her husband in the bathtub of their home.

"At the time of their deaths, warrants had been issued for their arrests. Fingerprint matches and photographs of the crime scenes were withheld as well as their being the primary suspects in the rape and murder, from Abdullah's defense team. It seemed this particular prosecutor and police investigators had a pattern of this type of behavior.

"Remedies were exhausted at the state level, and the case was finally taken to the federal court. A very young, gifted, and black aspiring Assistant United States Attorney felt strongly that justice should be served for the conduct of the prosecutor and the police, and charges were filed with the Office of Professional Responsibility. To make a long story short, a judge was convinced, and Abdullah's case was overturned."

U. S. Attorney Hughes put his face in his hands, and spoke through them. "Kiss my ass. Early in 2005 Ronnie Green came to me with investigators from the Office of Professional Responsibility, and enough evidence of corruption in the Attorney General's Office to send several prosecutors and police to prison. A serious black eye for the State. I convinced the judge that a terrible wrong had been committed, and the judge overturned the case."

"Bingo!" Sazzar smiled wide.

"What happened to the other brother?" Miss Corning chimed.

"Sorry Counselor, we haven't come to that part yet.'"

"Well, what part are we at, Sazzar? Up to now all we have are a few fist fights, and some training by authorized military personnel on private property. Which I don't know if that is a crime. Nothing you've told us thus far has connected you to a federal crime. The murder of the Hellmans was clearly accidental on your part, and I'm positive if you stop right now, right this second, I can win this case for you, Sazzar."

"Counselor, no offense to your seasoned or experienced hand, but the federal government has a ninety-nine percent conviction rate on all drug related crimes. I would beat the state murder charges, of that even I'm sure. But the drugs found in the warehouse. For the drugs alone I'd receive a life sentence. Can you guarantee a win against those odds?"

"Sazzar, you have nothing to do with the drugs in that warehouse."

"You and I know that, but all the government has to prove for a conspiracy to distribute is my presence in the warehouse.

With all the dead bodies inside the warehouse it can be inferred that it was a drug deal gone bad. Officer Moran's testimony puts me smack dab in the mix and the carnage afterward. Do I want to gamble with my life on a case you can't win? Me thinks not. Besides, the deal I've negotiated can't be rivaled with what I am about to tell you."

Counselor Corning sat back in her seat contemplating what Sazzar had just said. He could see that she was going over the legalities in her head.

She exhaled loudly. "What happened after you graduated from boot camp?"

"Alright Counselor!" Shouted U.S. Attorney Hughes. "Glad to have you on board."

"Let's get something straight, Mr. Hughes. I'm filing complaints against you throughout the entire chain of commands until I receive justice for what you've done to Mr. Robinson. I specifically asked you not to speak to my client without me being present. You can take this to the bank, and deposit it in your account: I'm going all the way with the charges against you until I get your job."

"I knew you were the kind of woman who would go all the way, counselor. I like it rough, wouldn't have it any other way." He sat with a smirk on his face.

"Oooooooooh!" she grunted. "This man is impossible!"

"Sazzar, don't you think it's about time you turn this old hawk loose on federal territory?" U.S. Attorney Hughes probed.

Sazzar took a drink of his bottled water, leaned back in his chair, and thought about what his attorney had just said to him, and the fact that he was about to walk through a door from which there was no return. He breathed deeply and began.

C H A P T E R   7 5

"After we drove back to the city from the farm, I took Tina and J.T. to St. Cloud to visit Six, and to get the instructions for the team.

Six glanced at Tina standing near the soda machine, her hands lost in the Cardigan sweater she was wearing. They caught each other's eyes, and she smiled at her man bouncing their son on his lap.

She looked much younger and innocent with her short, curly hair. If it weren't for the severe curves of her body, and of course the healthy eight-month-old baby boy on his father's lap, you would have laid odds that she was a mature thirteen year old. Then out of nowhere she does the damndest thing. Walking seductively back to our little visiting area, she lets out this soft giggle.

"Six?" She murmured in this excited, but sexy way, walked over to where he was sitting, took his hand in hers, kissed it, knelt down, placed his hand on her breast, and said with such passion, like she was a prize he'd just won in a battle. "The team and I are ready to do whatever it is that you want us to do. Just tell me what you want done and it's done."

Six smiled, and looked down at his hand. "I'm getting a bit aroused her, baby. Aaaa, do you mind?" He nodded his head toward his hand on her breast.

"Of course I do." She flashed her bright light smile. "I wouldn't want you to be suddenly overwhelmed by my sexuality."

"God forbid, you would be the type of woman to lead a

man on." He squeezed gently.

"As hard as it is for you to resist me right now, I want you to know that it gives me great pleasure, and motivation to be your woman and the mother of your first-born son. But do me a favor, baby?" She asked again with the real sexy voice.

"What's that, Tee?"

"Lose the cocktease implication." She seemed imperturbable.

"And you were doing such a great job carrying me through my moment of weakness and shame." Six fired back.

"I'm the one facing the moral dilemma here, Six. Look me in my eyes and tell me that my moral position is still intact."

"Tee, you're the one introducing all the temptation to a brother on lock-down, and you're worried about your moral position?

"Six, you are not that weak."

"Tee, you put too much faith in my willpower. I'm a young black man with strong sexual urges."

"Is that why you haven't moved my hand?"

"There are two reasons why I haven't." He was as a matter-of- fact holding out for a few more moments of pleasure.

"Give me the first?"

"First, you know damn well your body is shielding your wrong doing, so the guard can't see what's going on anyway."

"And the second?"

"Your efforts are being wasted on the officer. Look at him, he doesn't care. His head is buried in that magazine. You want further proof, look around the visiting room. Some of these guys have been down for years, yet they're bouncing toddlers and infants in their laps. Babies are being made in this room, Tee."

"Stop it, Six."

"Stop what? I'm serious."

"Prove it."

"Okay, see the girl sitting on her man's lap?"

"Yeah, they just talking. We've been in that position many times ourselves."

"You need more observation training, Tee. Look at the

position of her dress, the expression on her face."

"That nasty heifer!" She stood up.

"She's not nasty, Tee. He doesn't respect her, and she doesn't respect herself is all. Sex governs so much of our physical life, and so much influence over our emotions that we forget our higher nature." Six stood J.T. in his lap, who immediately grabbed his nose with a tiny thumb and forefinger. He looked at Tee. "In my arms is the importance of making love to you and the future of our family existence."

"Damn! Am I glad you're my man." She minded hers as the raunchy innocence of adolescents continued on behind her.

"Now that we've gotten past that, here is the answer to your question. Listen carefully. You too, Sazzar, and get yo' mind out the gutter."

"Just trippin', Six. They going at it like they the only ones in the room."

"They are. It's called minding one's own business. If you need further explanation, put yourself in his position. He's serving twenty to life, and this maybe the very last time he gets the opportunity to have sex. Now can we get down to business?"

"Sure, Six."

"For thousands of years the white man has created and been involved in secret societies. I think it's time, as black men and women, we start our own."

"Six I thought you were against the programmed alteration of individual consciousness," Tee pressed.

"I am, baby. But I found my equals in you, Badboy, Face, K-Nine, Rasheed, Bangman, Elijah, Sazzar and the Ball brothers. These fellas impress the shit out of me. They're all Princeton and Harvard material. How many black men have the mind to understand the difference between Machiavelli's conception of princely virtues, and Hobbs' arguments regarding absolute sovereignty, and at the same time keep it hood?"

"You got that right." Tee laughed.

"Which part, Tee?"

"All of it. Yesterday we were together, and they were going to copy Locke, and some Federalist papers, but enroute they bumped gangster rap harder than any thug we passed along the way. Truth be told, they are dangerous in the classroom, and on the battlefield, and for the record I wouldn't want to be caught dead without any of them beside me."

"That's good to hear, Tee, because to start this secret society we are going to need some start-up money."

"How much money?" I became intrigued at the talk of money.

"A quarter million, Sazzar."

"Only two places to get that kind of money. Banks or drug dealers, and I do mean serious drug dealers."

"Sazzar, drug dealers have their own problems with 21 U.S.C. §848 and 848 (e)(1). Look at the case that's all over the news of Jeffery Barnes and Kenneth Jones, the government is calling for the death penalty for murder in the furtherance of a criminal enterprise for the crimes alleged against them. Besides, you would have to have Intel that the amount of money we seek is on the premises."

"So that leaves the banks. You want us to rob a bank?"

"You make it sound so criminal, Tee."

"Armed bank robbery has a mandatory sentence of what, Six?" Tee challenged his statement.

"Depends on if you have any prior offenses. If not, twenty-five to life in a federal prison."

"And that's not criminal?" She was careful to keep her voice low."

"Only if you get caught."

" Let's say we get away with the money. What next?" I thought I'd give Miss Tee a break.

"The money is an investment that will net us, for one hour's work, four-hundred-million or more, but you'll have to break your moral code on the second job. You will have to kill."

"The second job?" Sazzar's eyes widened.

"It's the second job where you will lose your souls to the pits of hell."

"Six, people rob banks all the time and don't kill people." Tina's voice was somewhat frustrated.

"I know Tee, that is why we are robbing a bank and not a

drug dealer. The success of the second job can only be accomplished if twenty-four people lose their lives."

"Six do you even believe in a heaven or a hell?" Tee sounded exasperated.

"You can't believe in one without believing in the other."

"So what is your position?" She became inquisitive.

"I neither renounce this world for a religious belief, nor do I allow myself to become engrossed in what society has left for me."

"And what is that, Six?" Miss Tee and I asked at the same time.

"Society's garbage: drug dealers, pimps ho's, intravenous drug users, crack heads, pill poppers, and welfare recipients. You and I deserve happiness for ourselves, for our children, and their children. Success, prosperity, and freedom from anxiety, conflict, or doubt about our futures will only come if we stand up."

"I love it when you get all revolutionary," Tee teased.

"Tee, do you realize we as a black race have been out of slavery for less time than we were in slavery? From 1619-1865 is 246 years in slavery. From 1865 to 1994 is 129 years of so called freedom. With the new federal drug laws Congress has passed, in ten years you'll see federal prisons as the new plantations. When you and the fellas get this money, we will create for our members a society based on the external principles of righteousness and fair dealing, cleanliness and sobriety that were meant for our people. Nothing in this fucked up country," his tone cause Tina to sit upright, "Was built upon without the loss of life, at human handling."

"Does this secret society have a name?" I wanted to know.

"No, it's a secret."

"Six!" Tina raised her voice.

"I spoke to Big Al before you guys got here, and at exactly 8:00PM tomorrow night I'm going to call and reveal my plan, or as much as I can over a landline."

Tee and I both sat quietly while father and son played together.

Knowing that he had just put a load on our minds, he gave us time and space. After ten minutes Miss Tee broke the silence. She stood and knelt between his legs, to where they were eye to eye.

"If you wish to walk in hell, then I'll clear us a path."

C H A P T E R   7 6

The ringing of her private line awakened her. For a moment, she was disoriented by her surroundings, until she realized she was in her bedroom in Fate's home. She fumbled for the phone on the night stand.

"Hello?" Her voice was heavy with sleep.

"Miss Tee, this is a friend of Six's, and a friend of yours. I'm sorry to wake you at this hour, but it is imperative that you personally take possession of the packages sitting in your garage. The dial tone alerted her that the conversation was over.

Andre smiled, hung up the phone, and went back to studying the chess game he and Six had under way. He'd just played a major piece now it was Six's move.

Tina hurriedly made her way to the garage, where she found several crates stacked high on the floor. She grabbed a crowbar and pried open one of the crates. Inside she found military-issued flack vests, brand new. In another, she found electronic equipment. In another, weapons, ammunition, and enough C-4 to level the city.

Finding herself running back to the house, she called K-Nine and less than an hour later all the crates were safely stored away in the Ball brothers' garage. By the first weekend of September 1994, all of us were eager to discuss what Six and Tina had in store for us.

C H A P T E R   7 7

"He wants us to what?" Elijah was truly taken aback.

"Calm down, fool. No need to be doing all that screaming." Rasheed admonished.

"Rob a bank." Badboy spelled out in sign language.

Elijah signed back, "Fuck you!"

"Miss Tee, to get two-hundred-and-fifty-thousand dollars we are going to have to rob the largest bank in the Twin Cities." Elijah thought he would throw the obvious out into the open.

"You're right, Elijah, and we have the perfect bank all lined up." K-Nine gazed at Elijah with a twinkle in his eyes.

"What, the First Bank of Minnesota?" Elijah quipped jokingly.

"This is why you are such a valuable member of this team, Elijah. You're clairvoyant." Bangman teased.

"Alright people, let's get serious. We have fifteen flack vests, ten AK-47's, fifteen forty-five automatics, five AR-15's, fifteen black web belts, each equipped with two live grenades, and enough C-4 to bring St. Paul to its knees. And as an added bonus, there are additional magazines with twenty-five-thousand rounds of ammunition for all the weapons. My personal favorite is the 1903 30/06 with a Leopold Scope." Big Al smiled with pride.

"What's our time table, Miss Tee?" K-Nine searched for details.

"Six says we have to have everything in place in two weeks time. The second part of the job depends on the success of the first."

"Second part? You didn't happen to mention a second job." Babyboss didn't miss a beat.

"I was saving the best for last. The quarter million we're going to borrow from the bank is an investment in our futures."

"And how much will this investment pay us down the road?"

Big Al was about as perceptive as his brother.

"Four-hundred million." A collective gasp filled the room when Tina dropped the bomb.

"What are we going to rob next, Fort Knox?" Elijah was beside himself.

"Elijah, I'm going to have to agree with Bangman. You are clairvoyant." She laughed.

"So I'm right, we're robbing Fort Knox?"

"Not quite. We are going to Utah to rob two armored cars filled with gold." I offered from across the room.

"Sazzar, do you have any idea how much that shit weighs? Its six times heavier than rock!" Elijah shouted. Everyone's mouth fell open with his use of profanity. "What?" He looked around the room. "I'm not in the pastoral mode yet. A little profanity is not going to hurt my chances of getting into the church."

"What if I told you, Elijah, that, we were going to have to kill people on the second job."

"How many people, Sazzar?"

"Twenty-four in all, maybe more." The room fell completely silent.

"Let's just concentrate on one thing at a time." Badboy broke up the exchange.

"You're right, Badboy. We need to get through the first job. Once that's accomplished we can figure out the best approach for the second." Rasheed had no reservations it seemed.

"I can go completely unnoticed in my first-period class, so I'm going to do some reconnaissance on the First Bank of Minnesota." K-Nine was all in.

"Me and Babyboss will go with you, Nine. We can get away as well." Big Al offered.

"Let's say we pull this whole thing off. What is the money going to be used for?" Face asked.

"Actually, there are some long-term plans going down with the money. But I'd rather you hear it from Six." Tina had done her part.

"How is he going to do that, Miss Tee?" Face asked.

"Before you get started, Face, we've already solved that problem." Big Al held up a speaker phone. "In exactly five minutes this phone is going to ring, and it's going to be Six. He has assured me that he'll be on a secured line to avoid any of the conversation being overheard or recorded, or he won't call. So, while we wait, I propose a toast." Big Al raised his glass of wine, as did the others. "May we accept whatever comes our way with great coolness, objecting to neither gadzooks nor the grave. To our futures. Salute!"

C H A P T E R   7 8

Exactly five minutes later the phone rang. Big Al pushed the button on the speaker phone, and Six's voice resonated throughout the dining room. After the exchange of greetings, the room fell quiet, and Six began to speak.

"Society has always believed, and warned themselves that one day a phenomenon would occur amongst the blacks that would bring about a strong desire to correct their weak-ass position in this world. The eleven of us are the birth of that phenomenon. Together we will create a secret society of the world's finest black minds, who are academically driven by the same desires for self-improvement as we are. We will be known as the G.H.E.T.T.O.B.O.Y.S. We are not a gang, nor will we ever be. However, what we are is a society of young blacks who will. 'Gather Higher Education To Teach Others Beyond Ordinary Young Suckers.

"We will no longer be a part of the establishments' mind wash, and continue to sing, dance, and hate one another because of a color, a street corner, or a neighborhood. The eleven of us will construct our own culture with great care. A hierarchical structure will be in place. Only the eleven of us will hold those positions. New candidates will be given a set of moral values that stress loyalty to their pledge of membership, and over a course of time advancements within the society.

"No street stumblers will be allowed. This will separate those who are committed from scared suckers looking to belong because of strength in numbers. Like the establishment does us, they will be handpicked and approved by us, and placed in positions only for the windfall they provide by opening doors our skin color is denied entry to. They may become members. However, they will never be allowed into the society's hierarchy. Those that we do select will be only of a dependency state, which we have provided them solely for the purpose of extracting from them useful productions for our businesses and pleasure.

"By now Tina has told you of our plans. Some, maybe all of you, may be crucified in the public spectrum or taking a trip to the morgue. This is nothing because it's exactly the problem we face daily just growing up, and living in the hood. As American blacks, our futures are unseen and out of control if we remain in the present state that we are in. We have been raised by the Establishment and our own people to be mentally weak and dependent on the man, but physically strong. In the many conversations we've had collectively and in private, we have all yearned for some sense of authority over our lives so that we could control our destiny.

"You can try your hand at the Establishment's get-rich-on-the- nigger dope game and help destroy our people, making them richer, while we kill one another and serve Buck Rogers prison sentences; or you can earn in two weeks time, in less than two minutes, a quarter million dollars, which invested wisely, will yield four- hundred million and bear witness to the GHETTOBOYS.

"I can say proudly that you will be successful in both missions." There was a momentary pause before he continued. "I want you all to look around the room into the eyes of those seated. Each one of you is responsible for the lives of the others. There are no drugged-out, uneducated street stumblers watching your backs on these missions, but nine men and one woman who have defied all boundaries: mental, physical, social, and economic that this country has portrayed American teenaged blacks to be encapsulated within.

"I promise you all that by the end of this school year you'll be able to pick any Ivy League College of your choosing to attend, paying your tuitions to the degree of your choice. In ten years time, the net worth of our society will be in the billions, and by 2016 one of our own members will be in control of the

Oval Office. Brother Elijah?"

"Yeah Six?"

"We've only met in passing, and Tina tells me you are a very religious person."

"Miss Tee is to kind to say such a thing. To answer your question, I do have a strong desire to pursue a position in the church."

"I can respect that. Our goal is simple, brother Elijah. After the completion of our mission, and some serious repentance and apologies for our sins, the GHETTBOYS will be a bright and shining example for others who eschew wrong. In the end you'll have the power, if it is your calling, to speak to the masses about experiencing God. The Bible says, 'To count the cost of what it will take to build the house of God."

Elijah finished the verse. "Lest haply after he hath laid the foundation and is not able to finish it all, that behold it began to mock him saying. This man began to build and was not able to finish.' Luke 14-28."

"I see that you're well read as well, brother Elijah. Are you with us, my brother?"

"Through success, misery, penalty, punishment, or death in this life and in the next, I'm down Six." Elijah raised his glass. "I propose a toast. To the birth and growth of the GETTOBOYS."

Six heard the glasses coming together and smiled. The primary building block of his plan had just been laid.

C H A P T E R   7 9

"Tell me again why we're robbing the biggest bank in downtown St. Paul?" Rasheed had become inquisitive.

"Because no one expects us to." Badboy replied.

K-Nine unfolded a diagram of the bank onto the table and they all gathered around. "Pay attention! There are fifteen tellers in this bank. Every teller has a camera panning their area, there are eight cameras in all, five of which are on the tellers. There are single cameras on each exit, entry, and lobby. Big Al tells me he and Babyboss have worked out something special for the surveillance systems. "I'll let them explain."

"What we've done," Big Al placed a briefcase on top of the table and opened it. "Is taken an Omni-Directional Transceiver, paired it with a 50-watt transmitter with a power source of two motorcycle batteries to boost its range. Once it is powered up and turned on, it transmits a signal just like the one it receives, thereby canceling out or looping the outgoing signal from the bank's security system."

"So what you're saying is this thing disrupts audio and video surveillance?" Badboy offered.

"Absolutely," Big Al replied.

"Does it work?" I asked.

"Listen Sazzar, me and big brother tested it in a department store with a gang of boosters. They had a field day. I wish you could have seen all the confusion of the security personnel." Babyboss donned a huge Kool-Aid smile.

"As a dry run, we also tested it in the First bank of Minnesota. It took them twenty minutes to start us a new account, and for those twenty minutes they were going crazy. Before we left the new account section, the Diebold Security System techs showed up, and looked completely dumbfounded as to what the problem was." Big Al bragged proudly.

"So, the answer to my question is?"

"You bet your shit-stained draws it works." Babyboss left no doubt.

"The good news, Sazzar, is the bank has two exits." Big Al pointed out the two locations on the diagram.

"Why is having two exits such a good thing?" Elijah inquired.

"Because you never want to go out the same door you came in. Don't want some pain-in-the-ass Joe citizen pointing out what direction you fled the scene." Bangman emphasized the point for them all.

"We also learned that this bank has what is called an Automatic- Teller Box, or a cow which services all the tellers. It's on wheels, and contains anywhere from two-to-five-hundred-thousand dollars," K-Nine informed everyone making them aware.

"So we could just get by knocking off the cow, and getting the hell out of dodge." Elijah commented without expectation.

"We could, but what if our estimates are incorrect, and we come up short on the quarter million?" I queried.

"That's why we knock off the tellers as well. Each teller has three drawers. The first is hard cash and coins. The second and third are where the large amounts of cash are kept. However, there's a trip alarm in the drawer. Go past a certain amount of cash and a silent alarm is sounded." K-Nine cautioned, as he looked each one of us in the eye to make sure we understood his instructions.

"What about those exploding things the banks put in the money. What are they called?" I didn't want to miss those.

"Dye packs, Sazzar, easy to spot. Two banned together money packs, they have a knot in them. You can't miss them." Big Al was all business.

"Here's how we solve that problem. We handle all cash that goes into our sacks. No bank employees handle any part of the money." Face instructed.

"What about guards?" Tina asked.

"There are two of them, Miss Tee. Old men, early to mid-fifties. One on the floor, and the other in the control center, both of them armed with old school .357 revolvers." K-Nine was very informative.

"What about escape routes?" Rasheed prompted.

"As your driver, I've driven the escape routes at least ten times. I know every crack and crevice of the routes we've chosen.

No problem." Badboy assured them that he was on top of his assignment .

"What about vehicles?" Tina asked.

"Again Miss Tee, your friendly neighborhood Badboy has acquired two brand new Chevy Suburban's."

"Will we have time to go for the vault?" Bangman asked.

"I can give you a full five minutes in the bank with my diversion. But my recommendation is, in and out in two minutes or less." Babyboss cautioned the team.

"I knew someone would ask about the vault, so I have photographs of the three people who can open it." K-Nine tossed the photos on the table. "This gentleman here, with the white hair, is the bank manager. The blond is the head teller, and the woman with the dark hair is the supervisor. This particular bank has a Diebold Safe with an electronic combination vault. I was told by a very attractive bank employee that the bank manager, supervisor, and head teller all know the security code to open the vault." K-Nine pointed out.

Tina studied the faces for a moment, burning them into her memory. "If the opportunity presents itself, we'll go for the vault."

"Sounds good, Miss Tee, but we have another lick that can be done if we don't go inside the vault. Tell 'em K-Nine." Babyboss prompted.

"While we were watching the bank, we noticed an armored car that arrived at the bank at the same time every morning. One morning we decided to follow it. It stopped at nothing but Check Express Check Cashing and Distribution Services. At each stop large amounts of cash were taken inside." K-Nine allowed Big Al to pick up the story.

"We did our homework by pretending to be a business in need of their services. A very friendly young lady explained how, as new clients of Check Express, our accounting department would wire to Check Express's bank account the amount of money that corresponds to our payroll payday. Check Express would then provide, via the armored car, to its onsite services the cash necessary to cash our employees' checks." Big Al finished

"Those check cashing places are all over the Twin Cities." I commented.

"How much do you think they're carrying?" Tina asked.

"Considering the fact that Check Express contracts with the majority of the larger corporations in the Twin Cities, I'd say near a million dollars or better." K-Nine equivocated.

"How many of us would you need to take down the armored car?" Badboy elicited the important information.

"Three of us could pull it off." K-Nine was confident in his assessment.

"I say we take down both jobs at the same time." Face recommended.

"K-Nine, Elijah, and Face can deal with the armored car, the rest of us can handle the bank." Bangman suggested.

"I'm game." K-Nine was out front on the idea.

"Everyone agree?" Tina asked.

"Agreed!" Everyone replied in unison.

"Well, let's get to work. We have one week." She finalized the plan.

C H A P T E R   8 0

"Always the motherfucking unexpected, no matter how well you plan, or how much attention you pay to details, always count on the unexpected." Face drove the garbage truck onto the expressway.

"What is the problem, Face?" Elijah asked.

"We watered down the curare to take down a man of normal height and weight. This new guard that we saw yesterday is six foot three, two-hundred-thirty pounds easy."

"Let's ask our resident expert." Elijah raised his hand to his face. "K-Nine?"

"What's up, Elijah?"

"Face is worried about the mixture of curare you put together. He thinks we need a stronger dosage to bring the new guy down."

"Face, don't trip. This shit will take down an elephant in fifteen seconds. Even watered down for humans, his big ass will fall faster than the smaller one will."

"You're probably more right than wrong, K-Nine." Face adjusted his uniform, and sped the garbage truck toward the Check Express in South St. Paul, the Chevy Suburban with the tinted windows directly behind him.

C H A P T E R   8 1

Big Al closed the door to the vacant office on the thirteenth floor of downtown St. Paul's tallest building overlooking the First Bank of Minnesota, and spoke into his handmic.

"Check on your earpieces, people. Miss Tee, Bangman and Rasheed.

"Check," came their reply.

"Sazzar and Badboy."

"Loud and clear," they replied.

"Are you in position yet, Babyboss?"

"Give me forty-five seconds and I'll be there," Babyboss replied .

"Roger that. One minute and thirty seconds and counting to entry." Big Al time checked, as he laid the 1903 Springfield on the windowsill.

The street, which was normally a bit crowded during the morning hours of surveillance, was now deserted. The robbery gods must be looking up from hell on us, K-Nine thought, as he sat motionless behind the tinted windows with three unconscious garbage workers sleeping peacefully in the rear of the Suburban.

K-Nine patted the air-tranquilizer gun on his lap, and spoke into his handmic. "They should be coming round the mountain right about now!"

"Like clockwork. Going off the air now!" Face turned on the jammer.

The driver of the armored car pulled alongside of Check

Express just as he'd done every morning. The rear doors opened, and the big guard exited first followed by the older guard. As soon as their feet touched the ground, each carrying two sacks, they both watched, as the black Chevy Suburban with the tinted windows rolled slowly toward them, its passenger window coming down as it approached. The sight of the man pointing a weapon at them caused them to drop the bags they were carrying, and go for their guns. K-Nine shot the big guard with a dart, just as Elijah was firing his dart into the smaller one.

Both guards winced at the pain shooting through their necks, and had collapsed at the rear of the armored car, when the rear entrance of the building opened, and an armed man stepped out of the door, closing it behind him.

Elijah saw the pistol in the man's hand and hollered. "Shout if you love Jesus!" The startled man turned around, and Elijah grabbed his gun hand, twisting rapidly to his right. The pressure against his wrist turned the weapon up just as Elijah swept it from his hand. On reflex he grabbed a dart from his belt and plunged it into the man's chest. Within seconds the man was unconscious and being dragged to the rear of the armored car.

The driver, who was more concerned with the danish he was unwrapping and his coffee, didn't notice the garbage truck pull up next to him blocking off his exit. Dressed as one of his fellow employees, Face walked up to the armored truck, pulled out the Silly Putty he'd molded to look like C-4 equipped with a detonator, and placed it on the windshield. The startled driver, a newlywed, and only on the job six months, watched the man turn his back and walk away, holding the detonator switch high above his head. He thought about dying for some insured shit that didn't belong to him, and fumbled for the door handle. Face heard the door open and did an about face just as K-Nine shot the dart. Before the guard could hit the ground, Face was at his side helping him to the rear of the vehicle.

Throwing the man inside the rear of the armored car, and securing the door, Elijah smiled at Face, as he walked passed him, and climbed into the garbage truck. K-Nine and Elijah pulled off, and Face casually walked toward the front of the vehicle. He waved at some fresh young white girls who waved back, giggling like they'd just seen R. Kelly.

"Minnesotans," Face mumbled to himself, picking the jammer off the ground, and climbing behind the wheel, then pulling the armored car behind the Chevy Suburban.

Face caught the smirk on his face in the reflection of the mirror and lifted his hand to his mouth. "The perfectly executed crime."

CHAPTER 82

"Two minutes, no longer. The clock starts running when I see you walk in the door. I'll see you guys at the extraction point." Badboy dropped his team at the front entrance of the bank.

Carrying the briefcase with the jammer, Rasheed flipped the switch.

"Goddammit! These fucking cameras are going screwy again." Officer Riley cursed himself. Keying his radio, he gave one last disgusted look at the screen. "Bill ... come in, Bill!"

"What is it, John?"

"I'm seeing nothing but herringbone interference. These cameras are going screwy again. You need to get up here."

"I'm on my way, John." Bill Sweeny turned to go to the control center when he saw four armed, masked gunmen enter the bank carrying assault rifles.

Like everyone else, without being told Bill Sweeny laid flat on the floor, hoping the gunmen wouldn't notice him.

"Everyone down on the floor now!" Rasheed commanded. Bangman and I jumped the counter and began shouting directions.

"Bank tellers step backward, turn, and bury your faces in the cracks of the walls. Anyone who does not immediately comply will be shot. Do it now!"

"We are here for the bank's federally insured money. Do as you are told and no one will get hurt. One-minute-fifty seconds!" Rasheed shouted.

Tina never took her eyes off the bank manager or the

woman lying next to him. She walked over and motioned for both of them to stand up. Without warning she pulled the air tranquilizer gun and shot the woman, who stumbled, and fell over a chair unconscious.

"The vault, open it! There won't be a second request." She maintained a calm tone, pointing her AK-47 at the bank manager's head. She nearly had to run to keep up with him. Seconds later she was standing inside the vault. She saw the bricks of hundreds and fifties, and quickly did the math. Twenty-pounds equal one-million dollars, five bricks to a backpack.

She pulled out the backpacks, and screamed at the bank manager, "Face down on the floor, hands over your head!" She quickly filled the backpacks with the hundred-dollar bricks.

Rasheed shouted, "Thirty seconds!"

She filled the third backpack, ordered the bank manager to his feet, handing him two of the bags, and left the vault. Bangman and I snatched the backpacks from the bank manager and Tina, and walked out of the bank. She raised her AK to cover our six.

Badboy produced a big shit-eatin' grin when he saw me and Bangman walk out of the bank with several backpacks, which appeared to be heavy with cash.

Big Al, looking through his sniper scope, slapped the windowsill. "Alright people, we are looking good. Now let's vacate the scene."

Rasheed and Tina dropped several smoke grenades to cover their escape, then walked out the rear entrance of the bank. Special Agents McWilliams and Newberry of the FBI were in the bank investigating an embezzlement scam by some of the bank's employees when the robbery began. They were on their feet, shouting out orders for the bank personnel to call the police and the FBI. With their weapons in hand, and joined by the banks security officers, they went in pursuit of the robbery suspects.

"Walk a little faster, Miss Tee," Big Al mumbled, looking through his scope. "Turn around, Miss Tee!"

Big Al had seen them first. Special Agent McWilliams never raised his weapon completely before the round from Big

Al's 30/06 splattered his brains against the bank's walls.

Rasheed sat down in the Suburban and saw movement at the exit behind Miss Tee. He raised his weapon shouting for Miss Tee to move. He held his fire on the outside chance that he might hit Tina, then he saw the man with the gun knocked from his feet, his brains plastering the walls of the bank.

Tina reacted to Rasheed's body language, spun around to protect herself, and was hit three times in the chest by Agent Newberry's 9mm, and twice by Officer Sweeny's .357 Magnum. The impact from the .357 hitting her in the solar plexus took her breath away, and she dropped to the ground unconscious.

A stream of bullets hit the metal all around the Suburban.

Rasheed fired a sustained burst from the AK-47 that nearly cut Agent Newberry in half. Blood, guts, and chipped masonry covered the ground. Badboy, Bangman, and I took up firing with Rasheed, creating a horizontal wall of gunfire.

Officer Sweeny tried to run and find protective shelter behind a pillar when he was struck hard in the back of the head. A red cloud filled with fragments of gray and ivory-white material exploded into the air, as his body slammed to the ground, his legs twitching.

Officer Riley was frantically trying to load his revolver when Badboy stepped around the pillar he was hiding behind, and emptied his clip into him, watching each successive bullet walk its way from his leg to his chest, until the final round entered his skull.

Badboy ran back to the Suburban and jumped behind the wheel, while Bangman and I picked Miss Tee up as gently as the circumstances allowed, and placed her in the back seat. Rasheed, who was covering our six, slammed the door, and Badboy pulled away from the bank.

"Big Al, you there?"

"I'm here, Rasheed."

"Miss Tee's been hit. I repeat, Miss Tee has been hit!"

"I saw the whole thing go down, and right now there are at least four police cars enroute to your location, and police are piling out of the police station. Get moving, we'll slow 'em down. Baby brother, you copy?"

"Loud and clear, big brother. I heard what happened to Miss Tee, and I'm gonna make these mothafuckas pay. The package has been delivered. I repeat, the package has been delivered!"

"Push the button, baby brother." Big Al's tone is calm as he watched through his sniper scope. He could feel the vibrations from the four explosions of C-4, as one detonated in front of the station, and three in the parking area.

Several police cruisers near the flash point flipped and erupted into flames, as the blast from the C-4 blew out windows, and showered the street with glass and debris.

Big Al could see policemen laying in the burning doorways of their vehicles, their mangled bodies without movement, as their comrades worked frantically to save their lives. Babyboss peddled his bicycle toward the rendezvous with Big Al, as all the fire alarms in the city went off.

CHAPTER 83

Badboy steered the Suburban onto highway 52 and punched the accelerator, with four St. Paul police cruisers in pursuit. Rasheed flipped the switch on the jammer.

"Bangman, have you checked her yet? Is she hit?" Badboy weaved in and out of traffic.

"Drive this mothafucka!" I leaned over the seat, and scanned over Tina, looking for any wounds.

"Tina jerked awake racking breaths, struggling to get her vest off." It's burning," she mumbled. "Get it off, please!" Bangman pulled the vest from her body, running his hand over her bruised chest.

"No holes, no blood, and broken bones!" He smiled wide at the good news.

Lines of pain etched Tina's face. Her chest was stiff and sore and there were massive red welts where the rounds had impacted. Bangman could tell she still had her personality when she winced in pain from his examination and spoke.

"I've just been shot and this fine-ass man thinks he can cop a free feel on my breast." It hurt when she drew in a breath, but she managed a smile for Bangman.

"Can you sit up, Miss Tee?"

"Do I have to?" Her voice sounded weak.

"Right now we are having a slight problem and we all need to be alert." He informed her.

Badboy navigated the Suburban into the far lane where several cars were slowing in front of him. He cut back to the inside lane, passing the slowing vehicles, when a semi-truck swerved to the inside lane blocking his path. He punched the accelerator to go around and the trucker cut him off again. Badboy was trying to figure out a way to get pass this trucker, when a police cruiser slammed into the back of the Suburban.

"Motherfuckers!" Rasheed kicked out the shattered back window, and focused his fire on the imaginary seat belt, then emptied the clip from the AK into the police cruiser.

The driver, reacting to the gunfire, ducked, yanking the wheel of the cruiser hard to the left slamming into the divider, its tires riding the wall, and the cruiser taking flight. The vehicle rolled over the divider ten feet in the air, crashing into the oncoming traffic, and erupted into flames.

The trucker managed to slow their speed to 55mph, and was pumping the brakes, zigzagging to keep them from passing.

Bangman, I've had enough of this bitch-ass trucker. Do something about him when I cut back!" Badboy shouted over his shoulder.

He cut back, driving on the shoulder, and bringing the semi to the inside lane. Bangman leaned out the window, shooting beneath the truck, and shot out the left front tire. Badboy slowed down, and the tracer rounds ripped down the side of the truck, puncturing the fuel tank.

Diesel fuel spewed out onto the highway, as Bangman flipped the clip, and shot out four of the tires on the right side of the semi. The truck swerved on the flat tires, and the sudden weight- shift heaved the fully-loaded truck off balance. With nine tires in the air, and the other nine on the ground, the rig began to fall into the inside lane.

Yanking the steering wheel hard to the left, Badboy accelerated around the semi, and Tina grabbed a grenade off Bangman's belt, pulled the pin and threw it at the truck as it slammed to the ground, and jackknifed across the highway. The grenade exploded causing the gas tank on the truck to explode into a huge fireball across the highway.

The explosion ejected the truck's load of mannequins onto both sides of the highway. Vehicle after vehicle slammed into one another trying to avoid hitting what they believed to be burning human beings.

Rasheed sat looking out the windowless window as the semi, blown to a stop, burst into a fireball twenty-five feet high. There was no police pursuit, only what appeared to be rolls of humans on fire.

Rasheed leaned over the seat to where he was inches from Tina's face. "Kiss my ass, Miss Tee! I think we just killed a truckload of Mexicans."

Badboy pulled into the underground parking garage and we quickly changed vehicles. Rasheed grabbed the can of gasoline from the trunk of the Caddy, jumped inside the Suburban, and drove it to the rear of the building. He doused the interior with gas, and pulled the pins on two grenades, tossing them into the Suburban. Rasheed closed the door on the Caddy, and none of us looked back when the explosion came. I just steered the Caddy in the direction of South Minneapolis.

C H A P T E R   8 4

Six had been watching the morning news for any reports of the robbery. When the reporter had gone to sports, he relaxed.

No news was good news, he thought. Suddenly the Viking footage was interrupted by the live coverage of a robbery in downtown St. Paul. Six sat straight up in his bunk, listening intently as the news report began.

"This is Ryan Sinclair for WCCO News, reporting live from downtown St. Paul in the aftermath of a bank robbery at the First Bank of Minnesota, one of which has gone terribly wrong, and left four dead. I'm standing beyond the police barriers, but as our cameras are now showing, there are numbered markers on the ground indicating the position of the spent shell casings of the gunmen's' weapons, as well as the bank security guards, I'm being told.

"Here with me is one of the hundreds of witnesses to the gun battle between the gunman and the bank security. Is this correct?"

"Yes, Mr. Sinclair!" She responded excitedly.

"You say that you are an eye witness to the gun battle. Can you describe for our viewers what you witnessed?"

"Yes, I can. I was going into the bank through the rear entrance when armed, masked men walked out of the bank. I stood perfectly still as they walked by me. A few seconds later another man, and I'm sure a woman, walked out carrying weapons. They made it to the vehicle and sat down inside, and this FBI Agent comes out screaming ."

"Wait a sec. Did you say an FBI Agent?"

"Yes, Mr. Sinclair, I did."

"How do you know he was an FBI Agent?"

"Because he screamed, 'Freeze, FBI!'"

"What happened next?"

"There was this crack in the distance that sounded like fireworks going off, and the man screaming that he was an FBI Agent, his head literally exploded on his shoulders."

"How horrible! You must have been terrified!"

"Nearly peed my pants."

"Please continue."

"The woman, the gun lady-"

"Please forgive me for interrupting, but how do you know if the gunman was a woman?"

"I'm a woman, Mr. Sinclair. Women know women. Anyway," she waved dismissively, "She was five-foot-seven maybe. She looked menacing in all that black she was wearing, and the weapon she was carrying ..."

"Please, don't stop, continue your narration." Sinclair nearly pleaded when she paused.

"After the agent gets shot, she turns around to defend herself, and is hit by gunfire that dropped her where she stood. I'm sure she was dead before she hit the ground."

Six got lost in the falseness of the report, and for the first time in his life he was afraid. Had he gotten Tina killed?

Her face came into his mind as clear as the picture on the television .

"If you're correct, that would bring the death toll of this robbery to five. Hold on, folks ... I'm sorry, Miss, we would love to continue this interview but we have a disaster that is unfolding at the St. Paul Police Department."

CHAPTER 85

Fully alert now, Six's ears fell on the news reporter's every word.

"This is Julie Graham reporting live from the St. Paul Police Department. Attack, diversion, or both is what is being questioned here, as six separate explosions near the gas tanks in the police parking area, and the front entrance created the craters that you see here.

"Seven officers have been killed as a result of the explosions, and last count forty-six others injured; three of those officers suffering the loss of either an arm or a leg. Witnesses to the blasts say that the explosions flipped cars, and hurled debris into the air which landed nearly a block away. Along with the few prisoners who were being housed in the detention area of the jail, the explosions have forced the evacuation of the entire police department.

As you can see, directly behind me fire fighters are putting out fires they say were nearly volcanic in temperature. One of the officers here, an Officer Dupree, says a blast threw him ten feet into the air after flipping his car over.

"I'm okay." A tear-stained-face Dupree cried into the cameras.

"The most tragic story we are hearing, is of the death of a female officer. Her cruiser was at the flash point of one of the explosions, flipping it end-over-end and trapping her inside with ; the under carriage of her vehicle on fire. While a secondary blast occurred officer's worked frantically to save her life. Unable to get the doors of her cruiser open, they watched in horror as the fire, too intense to continue rescue efforts, consumed her.

"I'm being told that there is breaking news on Highway 52, where there are yet more deaths authorities are now saying are associated with the robbery. Greg McLead is on the scene. I'm Julie Graham reporting live from the St. Paul Police Department. Greg?"

"Yeah Julie, the buzz here is that all of these acts of violence were caused by the bank robbers. Fire fighters from the Twin Cities and surrounding counties are on the scene battling flames from burning wreckage, and assisting in the rescue efforts of what is being called the worst pile up in Minnesota history.

"There are forty or more cars and trucks involved in the tragic event. Going to live footage ... If you look across the highway you can see all the mutilated cars, and victims being pulled from their vehicles by civilians who are working side by side with rescue workers. Twenty-four of the victims have been triaged and taken to area hospitals. So far, the death toll here has risen to five.

"Sorry folks, this is a busy day, and there is something newsworthy about to unfold at the scene of the robbery. I'm Greg McLead, back to you, Ryan."

"Thanks Greg. I'm here with special Agent in Charge Dave Jimson of the FBI. Agent Jimson, can you confirm for our viewers whether federal agents from your division were killed by the gunman?"

"Yes Ryan, at approximately 9:05AM two agents, in an attempt to apprehend the suspects were killed in the line of duty, along with two of the bank's security guards."

"Sources are also reporting that a female gunman was presumed killed during the exchange of gunfire. Could you confirm or deny this for our viewers?"

"We've spoken to several eye witnesses, who have confirmed that one of the gunmen, possibly female, went down under fire. However, there is no physical evidence to support the allegations."

"What are the FBI and the police doing to apprehend these suspects.?"

"Right now a Joint Task Force has been assembled utilizing agents of the FBI, and Investigators from the St. Paul and Minneapolis police departments. Agents are rounding up all the usual perps for these types of crimes, and leads are being followed."

"I would suspect bomb makers are on the list as well, considering the damage at the St. Paul Police Department?"

"I can't answer that, Ryan. Sorry."

"One last question, Agent Jimson. Since the authorities don't have a clue as to who their looking for, do you feel any arrest are likely?"

"Mr. Sinclair, all searches for criminals are complicated by the fact that the investigators from the Bureau don't know who we're looking for. But our record for solving bank robberies in the Twin Cities is nearly perfect. We are confident that we will find the people responsible."

"Thank you, Agent Jimson. Back to you in the studio, Dave. I'm Ryan Sinclair reporting live for WCCO in the aftermath of the bank robbery in downtown St. Paul."

Six quickly searched his feelings. There was always an alternative to the propaganda coming over the airwaves of the media in America. If Tina had been martyred right there on the streets of St. Paul, there would have been some physical evidence. He looked at his watch. In five hours she would home from school. That is, if she made it.

CHAPTER 86

"Miss Lane, you are awfully late getting to school. This is not like you." Principle Rork accosted Tina as she cleared the security entrance at Washburn High School.

"Sorry Principle Rork. It's my period. Really, really bad cramps."

"You don't look so good, Miss Lane. Come with me and we'll go and see the Nurse."

"That won't be necessary, I'll take a couple of aspirins. Really, Principle Rork, I'll be fine."

"Nonsense, Miss Lane, you look terrible. Come with me." He reached for her arm. Tina grimaced at his touch.

"I'm feeling really bad, Mr. Rork. Maybe this one time you can excuse me for the day, and I promise I'll go straight home, and get some rest?" She gently removed her arm from his grasp.

"It's against my better judgment to allow you to leave without first seeing the Nurse. However, you are one of my top honor students, and I'll excuse you under one condition."

"What condition might that be, Principle Rork?"

"That you allow the school security officer to drive you home, Miss Lane."

"That is the best thing you've said, Principle Rork."
***

"Sazzar, you're late man. Thought you were gonna meet me before third period?" Elijah had a concerned look on his face.

"Had to make a couple detours. But all's good."

"Problems ?"

"Nah, just a little war is all."

CHAPTER 87

"Sazzar, I'm an overly pessimistic bitch, who has trained herself to always expect the worst from any given situation, in order to ensure that any surprises that may arise will be pleasant ones. Since I've passed the bar, nothing has surprised me until now. I strongly insist that we stop this debriefing right now, and get the conditions of the deal you've made with the devil here in writing." Miss Corning warned, clearly disturbed by Sazzar's direct involvement in crimes she herself found discountenance with.

"I agree with counsel, Sazzar." Chimed a voice from the back of the room.

"Mr. Grayford, thank God. Maybe you can talk some since into him." She was relieved to see her boss and mentor had entered the madness.

"This decision you've made, Sazzar, is troubling me. I can't think of any justification for it. How much damage have you done to yourself?" Carl Grayford warily eyed his famous client.

"If you're searching for a motive, Carl, you have to look in the direction of Satan over there." Sazzar pointed at U.S. Attorney Hughes.

"Mr. Grayford, your reputation precedes you. However, even if you were Jesus Christ himself, you could not save this sinner. He has already sold his soul to the United States government."

"I'm sorry, who are you?" Mr. Grayford asked, being facetious.

"Excuse me for being the complete asshole that I am. I am

Evan Hughes, the United States Attorney for the State of Minnesota."

"So you're the arm twisting son-of-a bitch who's involved my client in a secret meeting without his counsel present?"

"That would be me, Mr. Grayford. Just call me the man to meet at the crossroads of life. I'm the deal maker." U.S. Attorney Hughes smiled proudly.

"Just wait until O.P.R. gets a hold of your little dick ass. We'll see how long you'll be singing that song." Her tone dripped with contempt.

"Mr. Grayford, I take it that you've taught your student over there to comport with the same professionalism and dignity as yourself?"

"Calm down, Fanny. Filing a complaint against this bastard would be absolutely fruitless."

"But Mr. Grayford, he-"

Carl Grayford silenced her with a raised hand. "This Texas piece of shit was in bed with the country's two top law enforcement officials. I was briefed on the flight here about Mr. Hughes. It seems he was awarded a degree from Harvard Law School the same year as his former boss, Alberto Gonzales, he's done some major covering up for the former FBI Director Mueller, in the case of the terrorist he had an trial a few years back. Now I understand that he's on first name basis with Eric Holder."

"Ouch! I see Rick Dees isn't the only one with sleazy spies," countered U.S. Attorney Hughes.

"I know you think your shit don't stink, Hughes, but I travel in some pretty powerful circles as well, and my idealism gave way to cynicism a long time ago. Right now, it appears from the set up that you and I are allies on this one and not enemies." Mr. Grayford feigned a half smile.

Miss Coming's jaw clenched, and she made no attempt to lower her voice. "Are you serious?"

"Fanny, I thought I taught you to observe the signs. Even bitter adversaries must be willing to put aside their differences for the greater good."

"Way to go, Carl. Delegate your authority, dog-gone-it!" U.S. Attorney Hughes instigated the exchange.

"She was getting her feet wet in your bullshit, Hughes. From what I heard when I walked in, she'd done her best to mete out what justice she could, as expeditiously as she could." Turning toward Miss Corning he pointed at Hughes. "This pathetic piece of shit would probably fall on the sword if Obama or Eric holder told him to. So fuck filing a complaint with the Justice Department, and instead concentrate on damage control." He winked his eye at her and turned back to Hughes. "I need to speak to my client alone for a moment.

"Suit yourself, Mr. Grayford, but it won't do any good."

"Five fucking minutes, Hughes. This is no longer a request!"

He raised his voice, his face twisted like a man with a bad kidney.

"Five minutes." Hughes submitted with a self-satisfied grin on his face, as he turned and walked out the door with his entourage in tow.

The silence between them was like the calm before the storm.

"Sazzar, what the fuck are you doing?" Carl asked.

"I had a decision to make. Otherwise you'd be representing me in a death penalty case. I don't have time to go over the events of the last five hours." Sazzar's tone turned deadly serious when he added. "They have a credible witness who puts me in the warehouse, Carl. Her testimony puts me on a slab with a deadly cocktail running through my veins."

A look of resignation crossed his face. "Oh well." He sighed ran his fingers through his graying hair. "I hope you've gotten a decent deal for yourself. You know hogs get fat and pigs get slaughtered?"

"I'll say," Miss Corning interjected. "He needs to be working for the firm. No jail, no prison, plush hotel suite on the tax payer's tab. Round-the-clock protection from ten FBI agents, and tomorrow morning while you're scraping the burnt edges off your toast, his ass will be eating crepes and omelets, but he must sign the plea agreement now, Mr. Grayford, before he utters another word out of his mouth."

"Why the urgency, Fanny?"

"If he says what I think he's about to say, then we need to

be inside with our noses under the tent because the shit is about to get real deep."

His tone was decidedly skeptical. "I'm listening."

"Mr. Grayford, so far Sazzar has admitted to the robbery and murders of a Mr. and Mrs. Hellman in 1994; the robbery and deaths associated with the robbery of the First Bank of Minnesota, and the bombing of the St. Paul Police Department later in that same year; and if I'm not mistaken, he's about to admit to the crime of the century, the Utah armored-car robbery."

"That's ludicrous, Fanny. He was only sixteen or seventeen- years old."

"The story he's telling, all the crimes were committed before he graduated from high school, Mr. Grayford."

"And you believe him, Fanny?"

"I'm allergic to stupid people, and I haven't had a reaction to him yet. Best guess, I'd say he's the real deal, Mr. Grayford."

"Sounds like a dream to me, and I'm no good at dream interpretation. I need hard evidence, something tangible."

"Carl?"

"Yeah, Sazzar."

"Did you stop by my place and pick up the photograph of my daughter from my bedside table?"

"Have it right here in my briefcase. Why do you ask?"

"I knew when all was said and done no one would believe me, no matter how much detail I put do this nineteen-year-old story of the crimes I committed. So I had you bring the proof."

"A photo of your daughter is proof that you committed these crimes? Sazzar, spare me the bullshit, will ya!"

"Carl, the tangible evidence that you seek is on the back of her picture." Carl Grayford lifted the framed picture from his briefcase and removed the backing, and there staring him in the face were an armed young woman, and nine very heavily armed young men.

"Fanny?"

"Yes Mr. Grayford?"

"Let's draw up the plea agreement before another word is spoken." He passed her the photo.

"Holy shit! He is the real deal!"

"You bet that sweet round ass of yours I'm real." Sazzar reached for the photo of his daughter. "I want my family placed in protective custody, Carl."

"Absolutely, Sazzar. Fanny, tell dipshit we're ready, and use his personal secretary to draft the agreement while we discuss the details of Sazzar's family's protection."

"Right away, Mr. Grayford. Sir, did I say how glad I am that you're here?"

"You just did, Fanny Corning."

C H A P T E R   8 8

"Now that we've taken care of the minor details, let me officially welcome you to the team, Grayford." U.S. Attorney Hughes extended his slim manicured hand.

"Let's you and I get something straight, Hughes. Don't let my ally comment go to your head. My client and I are genuinely relieved that the details of the plea agreement have been taken care of. However, I trust my gut, and right now it's turning from distrust of you. So, until you earn yourself some points with me, I'm not on your team, you're on mine. Understood?"

"I'm insulted, Grayford. Your client, of whom I have no power over whatsoever ... and who by the way, has single-handedly negotiated the greatest plea agreement in the history of the justice system, presented this deal to me. So if you're looking for someone who has deceived you, I suggest that you look on your side of the fence first."

"You are a fucking piece of work, Hughes, playing the loyal and trusted public servant down the line. I liked you better when you were the snake that you are."

"You got that right, Mr. Grayford. He's a noxious creature that creeps, hisses, stings, and whispers."

"Fanny?"

"Sorry, Mr. Grayford, couldn't resist myself. The man is the devil!"

"Enough of the name calling. Who gives a flying fuck how it all began? We are all connected now, and knee deep in the shit, so let's just get on with it." U.S. Attorney Hughes blew out a long exasperated breath of air.

Ignoring Hughes' dramatics, Mr. Grayford turned his attention toward his client. "Sazzar, you and your team, as you refer to them, had just robbed the First Bank of Minnesota, bombed the St. Paul Police Department, and have a body count nearing twenty souls. Now you have the District Attorney's tiny little dick, ..."

"Mr. Grayford!"

"Sorry Fanny, couldn't resist myself." He flashed that smile she loved so much. "His little pig in a blanket," he continued, holding up his thumb and forefinger an inch apart. "Is leaking semen all over the place because he believes that you and your team are responsible for the Utah armored car robbery. Care to tell us how that is possible?"

Sazzar allowed the suspense to linger in the air like the silent passing of odorous wind. He let it hang there until all eyes were on him.

"How should I begin?" He queried more of himself than anyone else.

The look in U.S. Attorney Hughes' face was restrained. His expression was not quite a smile, but more intuitive, as if he'd been reading Sazzar's mind. There was an awkward period of silence that followed as Hughes waited for Sazzar to put the events in sequence. Unable to control himself any longer U.S. Attorney Hughes exploded.

"Spit it out, man. This is not some Alfred Hitchcock suspense thriller! Did you rob the goddamn armored cars or not?"

Sazzar smiled at the lines of stress in the corners of Hughes eyes, which made him look like he'd aged ten years in that moment. Keeping him, and everyone else in the room on edge, Sazzar fired back.

"Isn't this a bit blunt for a prosecutor? What happened to details, details, details?"

With all the power and mystery of the unspoken word, U.S. Attorney Hughes gave Sazzar a look that would make the average witness shit his pants, and wallow in it like a pig in slop.

Taunting Hughes, Sazzar took a drink from his bottled water, screwed the lid on slowly, then looked directly into

Hughes' eyes.

"What do you know about EMP, Mr. Hughes?" His gaze never wavered from the District Attorney's.

Agent McMurtry could see the confused look on his boss's face. "What in God's name does Electro Magnetic Pulse have to do with anything?"

"It was the last thing Six said on the phone before the riot started in the reformatory." Sazzar silenced everyone with a raised hand. "Before any of you get started bombarding me with questions, let me tell the story in the sequence in which it took place."

A blankness set in on their faces, as if they were pondering his request. Miss Corning spoke first.

"Jesus friggin' Christ, Sazzar. Just tell the damn story!"

"Now that is the three-hundred-and-fifty-dollar-an-hour advice I'd expect from you counselor." U.S. Attorney Hughes snickered. Sazzar could see the fury mounting in Miss Coming's face and he began.

C H A P T E R   8 9

After school the fellas and I were worried about Miss Tee, so we drove to Fate's house to check on her. When we walked to the front door we could see through the window that she was sleeping on the sofa. She must have really been tired because we rang that damn doorbell a full two minutes before she answered.

"How are you feeling?" We all asked at once when she finally answered the door, our eyes holding the looks of sincerity.

"I got a few bruises on my chest and y'all are acting like it's a catastrophe or something. The beat goes on, fellas. What happened to those poor bastards that shot me?" She asked as she walked back to the sofa and made herself comfortable. A seriousness crept into her voice. "Did you kill them?"

Rasheed shared the news. "Yeah, Miss Tee, both security guards and two other men. The news is reporting they were FBI Agents."

"Seven police dead, and forty-five injured at the St. Paul Police Department." Babyboss added.

"Two policemen, and three civilian causalities during our getaway. Twenty-four civilians with serious to life-threatening injuries in the pile up. Haven't you been watching the news, Miss Tee?" Badboy asked.

"I haven't heard a damn thing. I just shut down as soon as I walked into the house. No TV, no radio, nothing ... just me, my guard dog, Snuff, this sofa, and sleep."

Face sat on the edge of the coffee table, locking his eyes with hers. "Well, let me be the one to inform you, Miss Tee.

The news is reporting that a female gunman may have been killed during the gun battle."

"I'm not! Those son-of-a-bitches! That means that Six thinks I'm dead!" She barely got over the shock when the phone rang. We all watched as the mixture of dread and delight appeared on her face when she heard Six's voice.

"How was your day, baby?" His voice sounded both sweet and concerned.

"It just got better." She laughed good naturedly. "Are you okay, Six?"

"Besides shouldering the crucifix of my stupidity."

She cut him off before he could get started. "Six, you or no one else could have foreseen the problems we had to face. Nothing that happened is your fault. We all knew the risk we were taking."

"Worrying about you over the past five hours, my mind malfunctioned. I've been sitting here affirming and reaffirming that our love existed, that you existed." She swallowed hard a second later when he continued. "I held your heartbeat in my hands, Tee." Before she could wipe the tears that were forming in the corners of her eyes, Six shouted, "Tell K-Nine to remember our experiences and readings of electricity and EMP!" The line went dead in her hand.

For a moment, she held the look of a woman who had just been informed that her face was on the Ten Most Wanted list of the FBI, as she stared at the phone.

Even after hearing from Six, we all recognized that she was feeling like shit. All we wanted to do was to comfort her, and to show her what two-million-two-hundred-thousand dollars looked like. The bank advanced us a loan on our futures of a million three, and the armored car contributed nine hundred and fifty thousand.

When she finally placed the phone back in the cradle, the only words that came from her mouth were, "Cancel the search party and pack your bags, fellas. We are going to Utah!"

CHAPTER 90

Six slammed down the receiver, and ran to Abdullah's aid, he stopped short of the five white boys attacking him, delivering a ridge hand to the groin of one of them. The kid slumped to the ground in pain. Six stepped left, and with a vertical punch to the jaw, dropped another, momentarily stunning him. Before the kid could regroup, Six put him to sleep with a round house kick witnesses say had so much force on it, they could feel the impact fifteen feet away..

Instantaneously, looking over his shoulder, he saw a blur, but before he could react a right hand connected with his jaw. On impulse, without letting the blow stagger him, he rolled with the momentum of the punch into a spinning back fist. His attacker blocked it with ease and hook kicked him to the back, sending him sprawling to the floor.

Admiring his work, the white boy broke off his attack to taunt what he believed to be his victim. "I'm gonna beat the black off your ass, nigger!"

Six looked up, and into the face of Pig Farmer, a racist redneck cracker with short-cropped yellow hair, a handlebar cavalry- style mustache, a Confederate flag bandana wrapped around his head, and '100% PECKERWOOD' tattooed on the back of his neck.

Six rolled on his back and kipped up, his face expressionless. Pig Farmer attacked with a variety of front snap kicks, roundhouses, and spin kicks. Six defended them with ease just to frustrate this swine breeder.

"You didn't think this ass whuppin' you promised me was gonna be easy, did you ... you white nigger?"

With a scream of aggravation, Pig farmer took a strong stance. Six noticed the fixed position of his feet, and exploded with a roundhouse to his jaw, snapping his head violently to the side. To Six's surprise, this swine breeder spit out some broken teeth, tasted his own blood, and smiled a jagged-tooth grin.

"I like it rough, nigger!" Hissed this bloody-mouth mothafucka.

Six met his gaze with perfect equanimity. However, his discipline was failing quickly, turning to anger by this fuck's arrogance. The faltering of his self-control pissed him off, and he lashed out with a thunderous front snap kick to the solar plexus that had Pig Farmer's bitch-ass sucking gulps of air. The double combination that followed shattered his jaw bone.

Pig Farmer's eyes grew wide with fear, showing the whites around his irises, as Six leaped into the air, and delivered a spinning-heel wheel kick to his head. Pig Farmer wobbled like a duck with a wounded wing before slamming head first into the concrete.

Abdullah screamed for Six to move, the steel chair in his hands wind milled in a wide sweep, smashing into the nearest white boy's head. Six danced out of the way, and caught one of the attackers with a forearm smash to his throat. He went down, gasping for breath.

Abdullah dropped the bent-up chair, grabbed one of the white boys, and smashed his head into the nearest wall. Feeling the weight of a man on his back he backpedaled until he found a wall. Slamming into the bricks made his punk ass submit, and his body hit the ground jerking from the pain. Pissed, Abdullah shattered his knee with a swift kick just for the fuck of it.

Abdullah turned, just in time to deflect a thirteen inch piece of steel with an open-palm block to the inside of his attacker's arm, as he lunged forward, with the precise accuracy that he had developed in the many hours of training with Six. The right hand to the jaw was his own, as was the steel toed boot to the head.

Six ran with the crowd of blacks to meet the whites on the flag, and heard heavy footsteps behind him. He turned to defend himself when Abdullah tackled him. Dragging him to the ground just as the others engaged the whites. Explosion after explosion of concussion grenades, followed by shotgun blasts of rubber bullets, reverberated throughout the housing unit.

Six told us eight weeks later, after he got off lockdown, that he'd been involved in a riot that had started behind Punchy and his crew.

A white boy had agreed to smuggle in some China-white-heroin for the Organization, and one of the twenty balloons in his gut had sprung a leak.

Fearing for his life, the white boy wanted to go to the authorities and get medical attention, but Punchy convinced him that the feeling he was experiencing was normal, just an upset stomach, no need to panic. Drink more hot chocolate to get your bowels to move, he had told him. The dumbass fool agreed, went back to his cell, and stretched out. A half hour later he's deader than a mafucka, foam around his mouth like a white-mouth Georgia mule.

Punchy and Daddy Rat had taken a single-edge razor blade to his gut, and removed their drugs from his stomach, their little stunt caused the riot that in some areas of the prison lasted six hours, leaving hundreds injured and three dead.

An hour later we all sat mesmerized, watching the news coverage of the riot at St. Cloud Reformatory.

Jeffrey L Barnes

C H A P T E R   9 1

We knew that it would be weeks before the reformatory would return to normal operations, and we would hear from Six, so without the layout of the armored cars, the trip to Utah was tentatively on hold until a new window of opportunity presented itself. Then the doorbell rang.

Tina thought the mailman looked a bit uncomfortable in his Army boots, but dismissed the thought, she asked about the regular postman, and signed for the package. When she opened it there was a cell phone, a phone number, and instructions for when the phone was to be used, and then destroyed. There were also maps of Utah with circles around various locations.

Photos of the Kenacock Copper Mines were spread across the table, with overhead shots of the Ophir Mountain Range, and an isolated area of the Bonneville Salt Flats. We sat at the table, and began to conceive what military tacticians call a 'Coup de Maître', or a master stroke, trying to decipher what Six meant by using electricity or electromagnetic pulse.

We began trading ideas while K-Nine sat quietly in the corner of the room, going over maps and diagrams.

"I believe Six wants us to use an electric charge to stop the trucks."

"And how do we do that, Face?" asked Rasheed.

"By creating the force of a lightning strike on the ground, using capacitor systems to hold the desired kilovolt amperes."

"So what you're suggesting is that we create an electric field that the trucks pass through?" Bangman supposed.

"Don't we need a positive and negative field for it to work?" queried Tina.

"Miss Tee, we could use the highway pylons for a positive and negative field. They're made of cast iron." Face turned the idea over in his head.

"Won't work!" K-Nine walked forward from the back of the room.

"Before you knock my idea, at least hear me out, K-Nine."

"Face, before you get started, the plan has one tiny little flaw."

"Besides not working, what?"

"I'll let you fill in the blanks, Face." K-Nine made his way to the table. "Answer this question for me. In an open field, where is the best place to be in a lightning storm?"

"Inside a car," Face mumbled.

"Why?"

"If the vehicle is struck by lightning, its metal body will conduct the electric charge around the outside of the car, leaving the interior unharmed."

"Exactly, Face. These are dual-rear-axle International trucks that are reinforced with three-inch armor plating. At worst, they will ride straight through, and enjoy the light show."

"So what did Six mean when he told us to use electricity?" Babyboss asked.

"Boss he didn't say tell us to use electricity. He said to remember our experiences and readings of electricity and EMP."

"K-Nine are you winging this shit, or do you really know what the fuck you're talking about?"

"Sazzar, if you ask me a pertinent question, I'll provide you with the answer you need, if I know. If I don't know, then I'll research the subject, and give you the answer. I don't have the shit wrote down on paper, if that's what you're asking. I never do. I'm just well-read and criminal minded.

Conceding, Face yielded the floor and posed the right question. "What is the plan, K-Nine?"

"Glad you asked. Keeping it strictly business, he began. "Six and I debated heavily over a book we'd both read, called 'The Curb of Binding Energy' by Ted Taylor. Mr. Taylor was a designer of nuclear weapons, and was employed by the Los

Alamos, New Mexico Research something or other, the name escapes me, but his accepted theories on EMP devices were genius. Six wants us to use electromagnetic pulse to stop the trucks."

"We would have to set off a nuclear bomb to generate that kind of power." Elijah emphasized.

"Stick to memorizing scriptures, Elijah, and leave the gangster stuff to us thugs." Rasheed joked.

"Rasheed, you are a far stretch from a thug. You hide behind that tough persona, but what you really are is a gangster nerd." Elijah blasted back.

"Bullshit!"

"I'll prove my point. Give me the textbook answer to what electromagnetic pulse is."

"Electromagnetic pulse is a high-intensity pulse of electromagnetic radiation generated by a nuclear blast high above the earth's surface, and is used to disrupt electronic and electrical systems."

"Proves my point. What thug, from any hood in America, with a fifth or sixth grade education is going to know something like that?" Elijah gloated triumphantly.

"He's got you there, Rasheed." K-Nine played referee to the friendly dispute.

"Don't you start, too, K-Nine." Rasheed was clearly getting into his feelings.

"I don't have too. I already know that you're a killer with a scholar's brain. Miss Tee?"

"Yeah, K-Nine?"

"I need you to make a call to our benefactor. There are a few supplies we are going to need to pull this off."

"Go." She grabbed the pen and pad from the table.

"We need three EMP rounds configured to be detonated by a cellular mobile phone."

"EMP rounds?" She interrupted him looking baffled.

"Yeah Miss Tee, EMP rounds. You heard me right, if our benefactor is as connected as I think he is, it should be no problem for him. Is there something wrong with my request?"

"No, K-Nine."

"May I continue?"

"Please do."

"Two semis with trailers, and a winch installed in each of them, and two large dump trucks. These trucks have to have conventional ignitions, plugs, points, and vacuum tube electronics, otherwise the EMP will affect them as well. Also the location of a place where we can steal a helicopter."

"Anything else?" She checked.

"Yeah, a forklift, a couple of braided-steel cable, a really large steel-mesh netting capable of holding two truckloads of gold, and last but not least, an isolated area around the Bonneville Salt Flats," he pointed at the map, "So we can test an EMP round for noise factor and distance."

"Done!" She picked up the phone and dialed the number. We all listened to the one-sided conversation, watched Tina nod her head a couple of times, then agree to a dollar amount without negotiations. In the end, our benefactor offered to supply extra men to drive the trucks. The operation was a go!"

C H A P T E R   9 2

This is not the textbook operation we had learned in Gunny's boot camp that consisted of frontal attacks, or sending troops to outflank, envelope, and crush the enemy. This was a robbery, and when it was over there would be nothing left of the crime scene to say that a crime had been committed.

We went over the plan, admonishing one another, over and over, about the slightest mistakes that could be made. This was not an exercise, it was the real thing, and it would be flawless.

Every shred of information Six had provided us was scrutinized until the utmost details were committed to memory. Be flexible thinkers, Six would say. We told Six we could do it, and we intended to deliver on that promise. We wrote him a short note which he would receive while on lockdown. The note simply read: We are deeply moved behind the news of your situation, and promise that nothing will be omitted on our part to fulfill our assignment. We remain dedicated to gathering higher education to teach others beyond ordinary young suckers."

September 25, 1994 at 0800 hours, one-hundred hours before the robbery, due to our classroom schedules, all of us except Rasheed and K-Nine attended our classes that Friday, the 27th day of September.

K-Nine and Rasheed flew out via United Airlines on the 25th and found their way to the safe house in Huntsville, Utah. The evening of the 26th, they made some adjustments to the EMP rounds that would lessen the noise of the explosion, and awaited the arrival of the rest of the team.

A strong spirit was driving our mechanism. Bangman and Face caught a flight to Galveston, Texas, where they would steal a helicopter from Oilfield International Supply. This company, according to our intelligence, leased out helicopters to oil companies that operated in the Gulf of Mexico, and at any given time there were hundreds on the ground at the Galveston Airport.

The remainder of the team traveled on different airlines, placing us in Utah, at the safe house, on the evening of the 28th.

We tested the EMP round at the Bonneville Salt Flats in an isolated area in the Great Salt Lake Desert, with automobiles in a staggered formation over a mile from where the EMP would be tested to gauge its effectiveness for distance. It worked perfectly. Upon detonation, it released a high-intensity electromagnetic pulse that fried every electronic device we had set up, and running inside a mile perimeter.

The robbery would take place on 1-80, Eastbound, near the entrance of the Kenacock Copper Mines, where construction crews had cut part of the mountain away for the highway.

There were rock formations on either side of the highway, which created a tunnel for more than a mile. The rock walls were seventy-five feet high on one side, and one-hundred feet high on the other and provided us with the cover for the perfect ambush.

The only traffic in the area were the local farmers from Grantville, Tooele, and Magna.

1900 hours-September 29th, 1994 we picked the UDOT workers, who would die for our cause. Our benefactor's information was so accurate it was frightening.

At exactly 1930 on the nose, the UDOT street cleaners were right where he said they would be. We kidnapped and extinguished four of the State's employees and dropped their bodies in the Strawberry Reservoir near Herbert City.

2100 hours September 29, 1994, Amarillo Texas, Bangman sat the helicopter down after seeing the flashing lights on the truck waiting to refuel the helo. Bangman and Face reported that the theft of the helicopter went off without a hitch. Only three men had given up their souls to the Angel of Death.

As soon as they touched down on the Bonneville Salt Flats, Face traded his flight suit for a UDOT uniform. Bangman waited on the Salt Flats twenty-five miles away to be notified by phone when to make his entrance. Everything was set. Sixty minutes and counting.

"Extinguished ... extinguished, come on Sazzar, what kind of cockadoody horse shit is that?" U.S. Attorney Hughes sprung from his seat, seemingly appalled. "You killed those innocent souls just as sure as John Wilkes Booth popped one in Lincoln's noggin, so let's call it what it is -- murder!"

"We disposed of the obstacles that lay in the way of accomplishing our mission, nothing more, nothing less. It was business, it needed to be done. It wasn't personal." Sazzar's demeanor was numbingly detached.

"Well how's about that one boys and girls? They were obstacles that had to be moved. They were murdered cuz it needed to be done. Whaddaya think Jesus would have to say about that one?" Hughes was up in arms, his tirade coming to an end.

"What difference does it fucking make, Hughes, if they were clipped, murdered, fucked-off, plugged, popped, lullabied, extinguished, or done fucking wrong! Can we please get on with the debriefing."

Miss Corning had to get the shit off her chest.

"Alright, goddammit! What happened after you 'extinguished' those innocent people?"

C H A P T E R   9 3

Babyboss, Badboy, Big Al, K-Nine, Rasheed, Tina, and I
arrived on the scene of the assault around 0400 hours the
morning of the robbery. It was pitch black when we moved
into position without being observed by any of the early-
morning travelers on the highway.

I couldn't tell you if anyone had any misgivings about
what we were doing, we never spoke of it, then, or now. We
had committed ourselves to our cause, a cause this country
would never support. Our livelihood.

We waited, and watched one of God's scenic wonders: the
rising of the sun. However, this placid picture as it was
described in a novel I'd read was 'being brush stroked by the
marauders lying in wait.' The previous evening we had a
serious discussion about the upcoming battle with the guards.
There was a furry of chatter around the table in the safe house,
going back and forth until K-Nine, in a rare show of anger,
burst out.

"I don't believe the shit that I'm hearing around this table!
We are facing a bunch of poorly trained men. The narrow pass
of terrain we've chosen for our assault favors our offensive. No
matter how hard, nor how well they fight back, every last man
in those trucks must die. Our mission is to make sure that not
one of them gets off a single shot. We will not allow them to
turn our theater of operation into a war zone! We will set in
motion, in a few hours, the greatest unsolved mystery in the
history of this country."

Our benefactor's intelligence had placed six guards within
each armored vehicle, and six men each in the lead and trailing

vehicles, all heavily armed.

Elijah and Face took up their positions on the opposite ends of the mile-and-a-half stretch, between the entrance and exit of the short gap that boarders the Great Salt Lake, and the Ophir Mountain Range.

Face allowed the two semis to pass by the roadblock and get set in their positions -- outside of the EMP's range. He pulled the barrier back in place, and stopped all oncoming traffic with a **ROCK SLIDE AHEAD!** sign. Face spoke into his handmic letting Elijah know to cut off his end.

"Already done. Got a couple of farmers pissed off, but they'll get over it," came the reply.

The truckers signaled that they were in position and the road was clear. There was a stunned silence in our earpieces, and then everything came to life with the sound of Big Al's voice.

"It's a go, trucks are on the move! I repeat, it's a go!"

The ETA to the ambush was less than three minutes away. K-Nine's voice sounded in our earpieces.

"This is it. Lack of vigilance will get you killed." He cautioned, his voice sounding like the director of Brook's Funeral Home.

CHAPTER 94

The driver of the lead vehicle turned onto 1-80 and punched the accelerator. His vehicle, followed by the other three, careened down the highway.

He was praying silently to himself, as he'd done before every run, that the law of averages hadn't caught up to him, and something would go terribly wrong. He'd always considered, but never dreamed that in the good old Mormon State of Utah he would be robbed. But last night he had awakened from a dream, sweating from the premonition that he was going to die a bloody, violent death from this fucking job.

Just as he finished his thought, he heard a muffled explosion in the distance, and his instincts told him to stop the vehicle, but his thoughts were interrupted, as he fought to keep his vehicle on the road when the engine shut down.

Right before the assault, everything grew strangely quiet when the EMP activated, detaching us from our surroundings. It was like we were observing rather than participating, as all the vehicles rolled to a stop on the highway. After about thirty seconds, all the doors on the lead car, and the trailing vehicles opened, and twelve armed men began piling out. Again K-Nine called 'good money'. The one hundred-and-five degree heat of the Utah desert played a supporting role, as the doors of the armored cars opened. The plan was when all forty-eight feet hit the pavement, the shooting would began. We settled for forty-four. Two stubborn- ass guards decided to sit in the open door of the armored cars.

We opened fire from our suppressed AK-47's in a

withering ambush from behind the rocks. There was total chaos and confusion on the ground. Two of the twenty-four men lay dead, a third writhed in agony as the others dragged his body to the other side of the vehicle, to what they believed to be safety, only to find that they were surrounded, and trapped.

I sighted my weapon, and every round I squeezed off found its mark. One in the skull, another dead center in the heart, as the subsonic steel-core 7.2/6 x 36 round ripped through his vest. The screams of their deaths were muted due to the elevation we were shooting from. I sighted another, he was praying. Something from Psalms, I read his lips through my scope. I pulled the trigger.

The remaining men reacted by jumping to their feet, whirling around to confront the ambush. Silent gunfire erupted all around them, their bodies torn, and bloodied as the steel-core rounds punched holes through steel, flesh, and the air around them.

One of the guards took off running down the highway, his adrenaline pumping from the silent death raining down on him.

Before his breath, and his ass caught up to his heart, Rasheed stepped from, the rocks, and put a round through his head.

They were scared shitless, but it was over just as fast as it had begun. One lone soul was crawling on his belly, his hands trembling with each painful movement, trying to reach the rocks for cover. Tina stepped from the formations, and shot him at point- blank range. He lay belly down on the side of the highway like all the others, now empty sacks of flesh waiting to be hauled away.

Bangman sat on the Bonneville Salt Flats waiting for his phone to ring, the adrenaline pumping through his veins like ice water. Face saw the flare and dialed the number.

"It's a go, Bangman!" He disconnected the line, not waiting for a response.

Like hooded thugs creeping up on sleeping men, we emerged from the rocks. The terror for those men had lasted less than sixty seconds. The complete and organized disposal of twenty-four men. The smell of their death stayed with me for months, the stench from the desert heat staying in my throat, the smell forever a memory.

C H A P T E R 9 5

Breaking from his commentary, Sazzar turned and faced U.S. Attorney Hughes. "The answer to your question is, yes. We did steal the gold."

"I knew it, goddammit!" He paced the room.

"Don't expect the miracles of dropped clues to the whereabouts of the gold, or the unexpected blessings that were in the belly of those armored cars."

"Unexpected blessings? Three-hundred-million dollars in gold was blessing enough, don't you think?" Asked Special Agent McMurtry.

"There was another four-hundred-million-dollars in those cars."

"In gold, Sazzar?" Mr. Grayford's eyes were bugged out of his head.

"No Carl, bearer bonds."

"Bonds ... there was no report of bearer bonds in those armored cars, only gold." Special Agent McMurtry was adamant.

"I'm sure there wasn't. The bonds belonged to the CIA."

"How do you know that, Sazzar?" asked Miss Corning.

"I was told just like all the others -- by Six. After the robbery, the gold was stored away, not melted down and sold off as originally planned because of the bonds."

"Why gold, Sazzar? Why not deal drugs like all the other thugs?" asked U.S. Attorney Hughes.

"That shit sounds racist. All blacks don't deal drugs to make a living. To answer your question, I asked Six the same question you asked me."

"And his answer was?"

"Six was always quoting somebody. 'He who holds the gold makes the rules.' This may sound crazy what I'm about to say, but it was like Six had a crystal ball. He knew about future events before they would happen. He told us that gold was no longer the currency of the realm. Paper was. Then why steal the gold, I asked him?"

"'Rainy day money. One day America will be a nation printing money at an alarming rate. Nothing short of counterfeiting,' he told me."

"Where gold once protected honesty within commerce, and the nation thrived, in the years to come, the one who prints the money will make all the rules, but he who holds the gold will possess the wealth. Today in 2013 look at what an ounce of gold will cost you."

"This guy is some sick genius. How old was he when he said that?"

"Nearing his seventeenth birthday."

"This is absolutely fabulous, but if my memory serves me correctly, there were no signs of a robbery along that, or any other route those armored cars followed. The FBI even suspected that it was an inside job, being none of the guards ever surfaced." Mr. Grayford repeated the stories of old.

"Six told us that the attention span of the American public is about two weeks. Without a trace of evidence that a crime had been committed, it appeared that the guards just disappeared with the gold. If people of this country are not constantly reminded over the idiot box, or in the newspaper, and there is not an immediate cataclysmic reaction, within two weeks the public will forget anything."

"Was this part of Six's plan?" Inquired Miss Corning.

"Don't know. The American people are asleep at the wheel. Whatever the propaganda machines like FOX feeds them, they believe."

"Why should we believe you Sazzar? Nobody really knows what happened that day. The shit you just fed us could be all bullshit that you just made up to save your ass." Special Agent McMurtry challenged.

"We cleaned up that crime scene, for the lack of a better

phrase, in broad daylight, in front of hundreds of witnesses, so don't tell me I'm serving you shit on a shingle when I'm about to make you famous."

CHAPTER 96

"Walking up on those bodies, my heart was pounding in cadence with my footsteps. The men our benefactor assigned were just as professional as we were.

"Shortly after the flares were fired, those trucks came to a screeching halt. The ramps were lowered, and the forklift driver went to work, lowering a steel-mesh net capable of holding well over thirty tons on a sling-load.

"The gold was fork lifted off the armored cars and placed on the mesh netting. When all the gold was in place, the sling-load cable that ran through the mesh was pulled to the center, and K-Nine stood on the gold waiting for the helicopter.

"Bangman dropped to one thousand feet, and made his approach from a few miles out. The adrenaline was rushing so hard through my body, my heartbeat felt like a bass drum beating as Bangman lowered the bird toward the earth.

"K-Nine hooked the cable to the fuselage of the single-point cargo hook and gave Bangman the thumbs up sign. Bangman made a smooth hovering takeoff, and the mesh netting cradled the gold like a stork carrying a baby. He lifted the bundle easily off the ground, its bottom camouflaged, it looked like a large rock being extracted. The farmers waiting behind Elijah's and Face's barriers were fascinated by the helicopter's ability to lift such a large rock.

"We collected all the guns and bodies and loaded them into the armored cars, attached the winches, and pulled them inside the semitrailer. The same was done with the escort vehicles.

"We climbed inside the back of one of the semi's and the

driver closed the door. All I remember seeing was the bloody after- math of our crime. As soon as we cleared the exit where Face removed the barrier, we could hear the applause. Face told us the people were glad to be moving. Most rock slides made them re-route. Our rock slide was over in twenty-five minutes.

"Glad to be moving, I don't think any of them noticed the two street cleaning trucks that washed away the remains of our crime into the desert floor. Face and Elijah tipped their UDOT hats to each other, as they washed away the blood. Now for the part where I make you famous Special Agent McMurtry."

Everyone in the room sat forward.

"You can find the trucks and the bodies in the deepest part of the Strawberry Reservoir."

C H A P T E R   9 7

"Agent McMurtry, get on this immediately!"

"Already on it, sir." He left the conference room.

"What happened to the gold, Sazzar?" U.S. Attorney Hughes asked.

"Don't know. Bangman dropped the gold, and men went to work loading the dump trucks. That is the last any of us heard about it

"How did you get your cut of the gold?" asked Miss Corning.

"Trust funds!"

"Trust funds?" U.S. Attorney stared at Sazzar incredulously.

"Remember, we were kids. Our benefactor set things in motion a few months after the robbery. Attorneys from around the country contacted us, and told us about a rich aunt or sibling who had died, leaving us a large sum of money in a trust fund."

"How much money?"

"Six wasn't stupid, Carl. The inheritance was for our college educations, off-campus housing, cars, clothing, and general expenses.

"All of us received four-hundred-thousand dollars apiece.

After my twenty-first birthday, as a gift I was given a numbered account in Switzerland."

"If I'm not mistaken, didn't you receive a full ride on a scholarship to the University of Minnesota?" Miss Corning asked.

"Sure I did, worst night of my life. After the robbery we

all went back to school as if nothing had happened, and finished our senior year. All accept Big Al, who was a freshman at Harvard.

"I received a letter from the University of Southern California around the same time I got a letter from a law firm in New York informing me that my great Aunt Edna had passed away, and left me a great deal of money. All this happened a month or so before graduation.

"The night I was in cap and gown, all I wanted was my diploma. You see, the next day I was going to announce at the press conference, and to America that I was going to U.S.C.

"I felt like shit when Mr. Hellman's oldest daughter called me to the stage to announce the winner of the Hellman's Scholarship. Through tears she spoke of her father's legacy and the many recipients of the Hellman's Scholarship.

"Before she presented the award, she expounded a little.

"'This next young man my father loved like the son he never had. In the two years before his death, he would either close down one of the ten stores the family owns- that he may have been working at - or ask one of the employees to work extra hours before he missed a game.

'This young man rushed for over 10,420 yards in his three years of high school. He also scored 84 touchdowns. His GPA earned him High School All American 1st Team. He was also All State Minnesota Twin Cities Division First Team Running Back three years running. This year's Hellman's Scholarship Award, with my father's wish of a full ride to the University of Minnesota, goes to none other than Shanally Lamar Robinson III. You all know him as Sazzar!'"

"I bet you felt like a piece of shit, huh?" Miss Corning asked.

"Worse, I wanted to go to U.S.C. As a matter of fact, I'd told my mother, and the team of U.S.C's scholarship offer. Hell, I walked up on that stage, and even after all the lives that I'd taken, I was crushed when Mr. Hellman's daughter hugged me. 'This is from my dad, I know he's smiling, patting the other angels around him on the back, saying that boy is one hell of a running back.'

"The next day, at the press conference, I announced that I

was going to play football at the University of Minnesota. It was the least I could've done in memory of Mr. Hellman.

"That summer, I spent part of it training on the farm, and the other half running in the backfield of the Golden Gophers. We were on top of the world. Every one of us was attending a major University, and Six's vision was no longer a dream. The GHETTOBOYS had begun, and we all waited patiently for his release from prison.

C H A P T E R   9 8

December 20, 1997, the entire team had assembled back in Minnesota, on the top floor of the Embassy Suites in downtown St. Paul to welcome Six home. He was being released in three days and none of us wanted to miss his homecoming.

Five days prior to his release, a friend from Six's childhood that none of us, not even Tina, knew was processed into St. Cloud. His name was Chuck Ross. Chucky was five-foot-three inches tall, and high yellow with a perm that fell to the middle of his back. Six described him as a pretty boy whose greatest and only aspiration in life was to be the greatest pimp who ever lived.

Six was coming out of the commissary when he heard a voice from his past, and outrageous laughter coming from down the hall.

"Nigga, I am the prettiest, conniving young pimp to ever grace yo' sorry ass presence. I am a master manipulator who'll take that behemoth bitch you call a wife, throw some granny panties on her fat funky ass, and put her in a girl-on-girl sexual comedy. Ugly bitch! She'd catch the clap and herpes, and love me in the morning for it!"

"Nigga, you's a fool!" One of the hecklers shouted.

"Just don't bring yo' bitch around me. I'm ripe for exposure, nigga! A pussy peddling entrepreneur. Tell them ho's to run when they see me coming. I'm a walkin', talkin', livin', breathin' Mack Manual."

"Stop that shit, Chucky 'Alley cat' Ross." Six walked toward the crowd.

"Alley cat! There's only one mafucka in the whole wide world who can call me that. Jeffery, is that you?"

"In the flesh."

"I haven't seen you in eight years." He embraced his friend.

"Still pimpin' I see?"

"As long as my dick stays hard, and my wit's sharp, I'm gonna cross every state line in America and peddle pussy."

"How's Cassandra?"

"You remember her? I had her givin' little niggas' hand jobs on the playground when we were ten. When we were twelve I started fuckin' that no good bitch. To answer your question, she's suckin' more pussy than you or me. I got the bitch into making porn movies. She found out she liked pussy as much as I do."

"Still with her, huh?"

"Till money does us part."

"What are you doing here, Chucky?"

"Got a year and a day for pimping and pandering. I'll be back on the corner slinging pussy in three months. How about you? Word on the street is that you shot a nigga?"

"That was three years ago. I go home in four and a wake-up to a beautiful woman and my first-born son."

"Oh, square-ass mafucka. I always knew you was gonna soft up on me, an' be one of those white-picket-fence, briefcase-carrying nine-to-five bourgeois suburbanite Negros. Congratulations, man.

Is she all dat?"

"Chucky, you could put twenty of your top-flight bitches together and they wouldn't come close to the caliber of my girl.

Is there anything you need?"

"I'm a pimp with ten-prime stock-bitches. Do you think I need anything?"

"Just penitentiary etiquette."

"I'd be in pimp disgrace if I ever let a man give me anything."

"Anything you want, you pretty motherfucker, I'll have it hand delivered to your cell for just a moment of your time."

Punchy walked up behind Chucky and ran his fingers through

his hair.

"Nigga, are you crazy?" Chucky spun around to defend himself. "Jeff, did this nigga just hit on me like I was a bitch?"

"Let it go, Chucky." Six stepped in between Punchy and his friend.

Punchy laughed as they walked away. "Cute face, long, pretty solf, silky hair, and a tight ass. Damn baby, you lookin' good in them institution pants." Punchy shouted after them.

Before Six knew it, Chucky exploded like a rifle shot running toward Punchy. In a surprising display of speed, Chucky hit Punchy with a flurry of punches. To Punchy it felt like he was in a fight with an overtly sexual, delusional bitch. He felt the swell in his loins when he backhanded Chucky, slamming him into the wall, pressing his body against Chucky's like he was trying to burrow himself inside of him.

Six pulled Punchy off his friend and stood between them.

"Back the fuck off, Punchy. This man you got confused is my friend."

"Six, you need to mind yo' business before you get fucked off!"

"Nothing between us but air and opportunity!" Six challenged.

"He don't speak for me, nigga!" Chucky growled. "You done fucked up now, mafucka. I'm a man who's dick swings longer than the gold chain around your neck. You touch me again, nigga, and I'll kill you. You hear me mafucka?" Chucky spat out the words as Six pulled him down the hallway.

"You want me to get some of the fellas together and go get that bitch for you?" Daddy Rat stood next to Punchy.

"Naw, don't trip. In four days time that fine-ass bitch is all mine. His savior won't be around to save him, and I'm going to fuck the shit out of him. Literally."

CHAPTER 99

"Hold still, bitch!" Punchy spoke maliciously as Daddy Rat tied Chucky's hands to the bunk.

"Do you think we should gag this lil' bitch? After all it is some virgin pussy."

"This bitch ain't gonna do too much screaming. I broke his motherfuckin' jaw." Punchy pulled down his pants, and propped a pillow beneath Chucky, raising his naked ass into the doggy- style position.

"Man, this bitch-ass nigga is turning me on. My dick is harder than a sumbitch! Go on and get yo' shit off, nigga, so I can get me some of that pretty yellow ass." Daddy Rat stroked his already hard dick. Chucky felt the solid weight on his back side, then the Vaseline smeared on his asshole. His .pulse quickened, and he howled in complete outrage, as Punchy penetrated his anus. The panic he felt was like a wild animal had been turned loose on him, digging into him until his throat released a desperate cry.

"Gag this bitch now!" Punchy told Daddy Rat, as Chucky noisily grouped for breath beneath him. Daddy Rat ripped the bed sheet, and tied it through Chucky's bloody mouth.

"Yeah, that's right, scream all you want, bitch!" Punchy whispered in Chucky's ear. "I'm picking up the pace." He pumped faster and harder.

"Fuck that bitch, nigga!" Daddy Rat moaned in a low urging voice.

The muscles in Chucky's body tied themselves into a knot from the pain, as Punchy ruthlessly attacked his anus. Chucky began bucking wildly from the muscle spasms that gripped his body. Thinking he was enjoying it, Punchy fucked him harder.

CHAPTER 100

"Jeffery Alexander Lane, report to R&D, now!" Baker's voice commanded over the intercom.

"Well Beloved, this is it. Freedom!" Abdullah hugged his friend.

"For now. How are those lawyers working for you?"

"They are a blessing, Six. They have already discovered several violations that may get me back in court."

"That's nice to hear. You've got my numbers, don't be a stranger."

"Inshalla, Mashalla." Abdullah humbled himself.

"Have you seen Chucky Ross?"

"He said that the oatmeal tore his stomach up, and he was going to the cell to take a 'pimp's dump'. He did say he would be down to see you off."

"Look out for him, Abdullah. Your brother is all over him."

"Yeah, I know. I'll keep him close, Six. I can do that for ninety more days. Now go on, man. Your girl and your son are at the release gate waiting on you."

"I know, but not before I say goodbye to my first friend ever." Six turned away from the exit that would take him to Tina, his son and freedom, and toward the stairs that would take him to Chucky's cell.

* * *

The sensation in Punchy's loins had his heart pumping like a crack head who had just taken a serious blast. His quickened tempo broke into a chorus of moans, sighs and gasps of pleasure. He'd secretly wanted this bitch beneath him to willingly accept this dick, so he could lay him on his back, and feel his nails digging into his back, urging him to fuck harder and faster. The thought alone surrendered his loins, and he exploded his nut deep into Chucky's bloody anus.

* * *

Six walked onto the galley and could see that Chucky's door window was covered. He started to walk away until he heard muffled sounds coming from the other side of the door. Then he heard Daddy Rat's voice.

He yanked open the door, his mind surging with anger. Before he could think he reacted. He placed the front snap kick under Daddy Rat's throat, the impact of the kick forcing him to the back of the cell. Six saw the knife on the locker and in one swift movement grabbed the knife and thrust the knife into Daddy Rat's heart.

Punchy, who had been slumped over Chucky exhausted, stumbled off the bunk trying to pull his pants up from his ankles. Six's kick stood him straight up, and he hit him to the solar plexus with four quick punches before pushing the knife in his neck, which exited from the other side. Punchy slumped to the floor, his blood soaking the front of his sweatshirt.

Six started to untie Chucky's hands, but felt a presence behind him. He turned to defend himself, and standing there in the doorway was Abdullah, looking down at his brother who was fighting for his last breath.

Six untied Chucky and pulled a blanket over his naked body. He had acted violently again, destroying a little more of himself, but that wasn't the worst of it. This act was going to cost him the rest of his life behind bars. His intervention had drawn these two dead mothafuckas to him.

"On my terms." He spoke softly, as he stood to do battle with his friend, whose eyes were focused on his dying brother, his body trembling.

Six watched, as Abdullah knelt down on wobbly legs, and felt the pulse on his brother's neck, which ceased to throb under his touch.

"My brother is dead." His voice was barely above a whisper. "Every soul shall have a taste of death. And only on the Day of Judgment shall you be paid your full recompense.

Only he who is saved from the fire and admitted to the garden
will have attained the object of Life. For the life of this world
is but goods and chattels of deception. Holy Quran, Surah 3,
Al Imran, ayat 185." Abdullah closed his brother's eyes.

Looking up at Six, he spoke in a shaky voice. "I believe in
The Divine Decree of Allah, and it was your destined role to
be the one to take my brother's life. Take off those bloody
clothes." Abdullah closed the door and walked down the
galley. When he returned he handed Six a change of clothing.

"Abdullah?"

"Listen, Six!" He held up his hand. "I believe in you like I
believe in the beat of my own heart. Punchy was my mother's
son, and for her I'll shed a tear. Islam teaches a life for a life,
an injury equal to that given. You are more of a brother to me
than he was. So go home and live your life while you still can."

Six dressed quickly, as the loud speaker boomed, "Jeffery
Alexander Lane, report to R&D now!" Six touched Chucky's
arm and he raised up off the bed. "Be good," he mumbled.

"Six?"

"Yeah, Chucky?"

"Pull the knife out of that nigga's neck and hand it to me."

Six pulled the knife from Punchy's throat and passed it to
Chucky. Walking out of the room, he looked back, and could
see Chucky standing over the two bodies at his feet, saying
something unintelligible due to the fact that his jaw was
broken. To Six, sounded like his friend was both laughing and
crying at the same time.

C H A P T E R 101

"In-fucking-credible!" shouted Miss Corning.

"Now you know what happened to the other brother."

"You're telling us that Six killed those two assholes, and just strolled out of the reformatory?"

"That's exactly what I'm saying, Miss Corning." Sazzar's tone was condescending.

"Kiss my ass. What happened to Chucky Ross?" She was obviously in a state of disbelief as to what she was hearing.

"Chucky had made Punchy a promise. If he touched him again, he'd kill him. When Six and Abdullah walked out of that cell, Chucky stabbed both of them ninety-nine times each. By the time the case was finally brought to trial, defense investigators had acquired written statements from ten plus individuals willing to testify that they had been forced sexual subordinates of Marc 'Punchy' Sutton.

"Although the lawyers Six hired had insisted they could win the case with a defense of justifiable homicide alone, Six bought the jury with the aid and assistance of Ronnie Green, Chucky Ross walked out of Washington County Jail a year later acquitted on the charges of first degree murder, and now resides in Las Vegas, Nevada, where prostitution is legal. Through his company, Alley cat Entertainment, he contracts out two-hundred-and-fifty of the world's finest women working in XXX porn, magazines, and the Internet."

"Let me guess, Six put him in business?" U.S. Attorney Hughes asked.

"Hell no! Well ... not directly anyway, you know Chucky Ross would never accept anything from a man. Six hired a very attractive blond, had her seriously upgraded, and put ten million dollars in a bank account in the Cayman Islands. Her only job was to meet Chucky Ross, fall head over heels in love with him, and as a choosing fee, give him the ten million dollars.

"With one of the world's most gorgeous females on his arm, and choosing him with that kind of cash, Chucky Ross became what he always wanted to be: the biggest, baddest pimp in the game. Chucky told Hugh Heffner at the Playboy Mansion that he was coming for his crown. Hef told him to bring it on."

"And Six?" Mr. Grayford's eyebrows raised.

"We drove him back to the city and celebrated for two straight days. When we finally came off the drunk, we got down to the business of building the GHETTOBOYS. Over the past nineteen years, our ranks have swelled to more than eighty-thousand members. We've financed the educations of some of today's most brilliant thinkers. Our members are in every branch of government, in five major, countries, in banking, in radio, in television, in sports, you name it.

"Right now our members are promoting a youth movement that will take our membership well over a hundred thousand. While the oppressed world is wrestling over their independence and growth, the GETTOBOYS are spending millions educating its members."

"Well, it's time to tie the knot, Sazzar. How does this story you've told us place you in the warehouse?" U.S. Attorney Hughes asked.

The nineteenth anniversary of the shooting of Marcus Taylor on Dunning Field. Six, who owns several radio stations, and the 360 Carpet and Upholstery Cleaning chain, throws a Twin City block party every year on Dunning Field. There are free rides, hamburgers and hotdogs for the kids, and the brightest musical stars Minnesota has to offer. The events that unfolded that evening are the reason why we went to that warehouse."

C H A P T E R 102

August 11, 2013 Nineteenth Anniversary Celebration!

Tina stood facing the mirror, nearly in a state of panic, her heart racing out of control as she replayed the conversation with her doctor in her head.

"Sorry to call you on a Saturday, Tina, but I knew you would want to know the results of the test right away. You have a stage - three tumor that is just a little bigger than five centimeters."

She got right to the point.

"Is it treatable?"

"Yes and no. The tumor has metastasized."

"I know the meaning. Where has it spread?"

"We know for certain to your lymph nodes, but it's also far enough away from your breast to have spread to your bones and lungs.

Even after surgery, and despite the chemotherapy, the cancer may return."

"In my present condition, how long do I have?"

"Less than a year if it reaches your bones and lungs. However, there are breakthrough treatments available. I've scheduled you for surgery to remove the breast and the lymph nodes for the day after tomorrow. You will be back in Los Angeles by then, won't you?"

"I'll be on a flight Sunday evening."

"Tina, this decision to do this is you and your husband's."
If you feel you need another opinion, I'll understand."

"Stop it, Debra. You and I are sisters in the greatest sisterhood ever established. I'll call you tomorrow and give you my answer after I've spoken to Six."

"Sure, Tina. Much love. G.B till infinity." She hung up the phone.

Tina looked in the mirror, and slipped the lightweight Kevlar upper-body vest Six had designed for her over her breast, and pulled it to her waist. She tried to picture herself without one of her twins, or her hair after chemo.

"Rid yourself of cancer first, girl." She spoke to her reflection before slipping into a Baby Phat sundress and her running shoes. She forced a smile at the thought that she'd seen some good looking implants on woman at the beaches in California. Her thoughts were interrupted by a knock on the door.

"Mom?"

"Yes, Tanisha?"

"Dad says to tell you to come on, we're running late. He also says to tell you that you look good enough to appear on the cover of King Magazine, so give the mirror a break."

Tina opened the door and hugged her sixteen year old daughter, who was the same height as she was, and the spitting image of her father, in both looks and personality.

"I'm not suppose to tell you, Mom, but Dad has a surprise waiting for you downstairs!" She smiled excited.

"What is it?" She played along.

"You'll see, come on!" Tanisha nearly dragged her mother down the stairs.

"Surprise!" She yelled, as they walked into the dining room.

Tina felt like crying at the sight of her team members. It had been five years since they were all in the same place, at the same time.

Her smile remained, but her heart was saddened when she didn't see Bangman.

C H A P T E R 1 0 3

J.T. pulled the triple black Range Rover Sport L.L.C. with the 24's front and back into the driveway of his parents' Lake of the Isles home and killed the engine. He smiled at the sight of the BMW M5 with 'NISHA' on the plates, and thought of seeing his baby sister. She had actually paid someone to drive her birthday present from California, so she could sport it around the Twins.

He closed the door, and hit the alarm, and was making his way to the house when he saw a Bentley Flying Spur coming down the street slow and pull in behind his Rover.

"Uncle Bernard!" he moved quickly to embrace Bangman.

"J.T. how's my favorite nephew?"

"All good! Do Mom and Dad know you're here?"

"Your dad does, your mother does not. Six wanted it to be a surprise. I've come with a surprise myself." He walked around his car and opened the passenger door. Out of the car stepped a very attractive white woman with natural red hair. When she took off her sunglasses, J.T. smiled at the emerald green eyes that had to be a legacy from her parents.

"J.T., I'd like to introduce you to my fiancé, Dr. Mercedes English, but you can call her Mercy or Aunt Mercedes, whatever suits you."

"Hello, Mercy. Has my uncle told you that you are absolutely gorgeous?"

"Fifty-five minutes," she looked at her watch, "forty-two seconds ago." She smiled at Bangman.

"Well, come on in. I want to see the look on Mom's face when she sees the two of you." He smiled while fumbling for his house keys. "Mom!" he shouted, as he walked into the house.

"Boy hold down that noise. How many times have I got to tell you not to holler my name when you come into this house." Tina playfully complained, coming to greet her son.

"Surprise!" He shouted.

"Boy, you just left California a few days ago. How was your drive up?"

"Fine Mom, but the surprise is not me." He opened the door for Mercedes and Bangman. Tina and Bangman embraced each other without any awkwardness.

"God, I've missed you!" She exclaimed, relaxing her grip on him.

"Vice versa." He stepped back, and moved Mercedes between them. "Mercedes, this is Tina, the sister I never had, and was blessed to have as a surrogate. Miss Tee, this is my fiancé, Dr. Mercedes English."

CHAPTER 104

"Girl, you have broken the heart of every single female in America by snagging this one." Tina embraced Mercedes. "Congratulations, sister," she whispered in her ear.

"Thanks, Miss Tee. Bernard has told me so much about you, I feel as if I've known you all my life."

"Well, this world renown neurosurgeon has been so busy it must have slipped his mind to send me an invite to the wedding."

"No, not this one. We both wanted to hand deliver it." She pulled an envelope from her purse and handed it to Tina. "Please say that you'll be one of my bridesmaids in our wedding?"

"Only if you tell me how you caught the world's most eligible bachelor."

"I was attending a doctor's conference in Boston, and in walks this guy who had a quiet strength about him. He seemed to make all the men uneasy, and the women salacious." Tina laughed. "I walked over, introduced myself and said, 'I know what you want'. He said, 'What might that be?' I said, 'You want to treat your woman as your equal and not an object.' That did it. We've been inseparable ever since.

"Uncle Bernard, I like this woman." J.T smiled at Mercedes.

"Me too," he replied.

"We better get into the dining room before Six sends out the search party. J.T., show Mercedes to the dining room where she can meet the rest of the fellas and their wives. I need to speak privately with your uncle for a moment."

"No problem, Mom." He took hold to Mercy's arm.

"What's up, Tee?" Bangman noticed for the first time the worry in her eyes.

"It's complicated."

"How complicated?"

"Very."

"Have you spoken to Six about it? He's our go-to-man when things get complicated."

"That's why it's so complicated. You see I have-"

"Bangman!" Six shouted. "Loose that woman of mine and come introduce yours to your family." Six wrapped his arms around the two of them, and ushered them into the dining area.

"Light-skin negro about to speak!" Six shouted to get everyone's attention as they entered the room. Bangman cleared his throat and took his place next to Mercedes.

"My brothers and sisters, please allow me to introduce to you the future Mrs. Bernard Logan, Dr. Mercedes English." Bangman waited for the applause to subside. "Dr. English has taken the lead Cardio Thoracic position here in Minnesota at Ramsey Hospital. Mercy, this is my family. Starting with the guy in the collar, his name is Elijah Cole. He is the head Arch Bishop of the Charismatic Angelican Church. His televised show reaches how many around the world, Arch Bishop Cole?"

"Weekly telecast, over fifty million worldwide."

"Next to him is Professor Emeritus, Michael Williams, and his lovely wife, Kimberly. His field of expertise is Psycho Analysis of teenage children and their behavior. He's lectured all over the world, has four books – all New York Times Best Sellers – and has been nominated for the Nobel Peace Prize twice.

"The guy with the lamplight smile there is Albert Ball, and the woman behind this great man is Carolyn Ball. Albert is sought in the United States, and abroad, as this country's foremost Forensic Criminal Pathologist. If I'm not mistaken, he's just finished his 12th volume of Post-Mortem Analogies.

"This international playboy beside him, is the current President of the Investment Bank of Denmark. This guy has computers on his private jet just to keep him fixed on Nasdaq,

Dow Jones, and the treasury Exchange, he's Albert's older brother Alfred Ball.

"I'm sure you've seen the Senator's face on the television many times, Senator Kenneth Wendell and his lovely wife Tanya. If there is a hope for the Democratic ticket after President Obama, this is our man.

"This next young man just had his face on the cover of National Geographic. He helped to formulate quality mineral lands in Zimbabwe, Argentina, Venezuela, Mexico ... hell, the list is endless. The one and only, Sir Godfrey Frye and his wife Cheryl.

"Of course, you know Sazzar, being a football fan and all. But for the sake of introduction. The soon-to-be retired starting running back for the New York Giants, and next seasons new announcer on ESPN, Shanally Lamar Robinson III and his gorgeous soon-to-be bride and mother of their daughter, Jazz, the super model, Vickie Meyers.

"This guy playing with the Blackberry is Assistant United States Attorney for the State of Minnesota, Ronnie Green and his beautiful wife, who just happens to be Vickie's sister, Pam Meyers- Green. Ronnie has two best sellers on Criminal Attitudes of the Twenty First Century, and two Essence awards for his works as a philanthropist within the black communities across the country helping underprivileged children.

"You've met our sister, Tina, who is the Outreach Director for True Quest. She's helped African-American and other women of color to build businesses worldwide. Not to mention the fact that she has personally taken the lead in several hostile takeovers of large corporations.

"And last, but certainly not least is Jeffery Alexander Lane. He's a Television Baron, who has interest in one hundred radio stations nationwide and four worldwide, with five nationwide television satellite stations and four worldwide satellites. Mercy, these are my brothers and sisters."

"Pleased to meet you all. This family is like the who's who list of the rich and famous." She bubbled with laughter.

"With that said and done, let the party begin. I've got for my beautiful woman, who loves her old school R&B, fresh out of retirement, Alexander O'Neal, Next, Mint Condition, and headlining the show, his royal badness, Prince. For the kids, some rapper who has a hit song that the kids can't get enough of, something about snitches."

"Shall we?" Six pointed at the door.

C H A P T E R   1 0 5

The all-white convertible Bentley cruised down 1-94, its destination St. Paul; its occupants the heads of the most notorious gang in the Midwest. Ice sat back relaxing, thinking about the deal that was going to take his operations to the nine-digit category.

"What's on yo' mind, nigga? You've been awfully quiet since we left yo' crib." Mac Dee turned down the sound system in his new ride.

"Just got my mind on the money," Ice replied softly.

"Sounds like it's more than that. Is that funky-ass jealous bitch of yours who, by the way, wants half of everything you own, starting shit again?"

"Ethel is just being Ethel, Mac."

"That gold diggin' bitch! I remember when she wouldn't even look at yo' ass. Soon as you came up, here the bitch comes. You should have let me put a bullet in that bitch's brain a long time ago."

"You wanting to kill Ethel, was this before or after I married and fathered a child with her?"

"Before, during, and after. She's a trifling bitch, Ice. Look at how she's played you out of millions. If she gets her way with the divorce settlement, she'll get half of everything you own."

"Yeah, I paid two dollars to get her, and fifty million to leave her alone. Fuck her, let her have that chump change. Tonight, we strike a deal that is going to net us a billion dollars over the next three years. You've made all the arrangements, right?"

"Taken care of. I also took care of that other business as well."

"What business?"

"Ethel's chippy."

"This calls for a celebration. Stop by the floral shop in the Midway so I can buy some flowers. What funeral home is he in?" "Brooks."

"Mac, we should invest in funeral parlors and flower shops."

"I'll call Tim first thing in the morning and have him get right on it."

"Mac, I was bullshitting."

"I wasn't.

C H A P T E R 106

"We're out of barbeque sauce!" Mercy shouted.

"No problem, the grocery store is only a few blocks away."

I'll run and grab a case." Tina removed her apron.

"Miss Tee, this is a great celebration, these kids are really enjoying themselves." Mercy passed an adorable little mulatto girl a hot dog.

"Thanks for helping out. Most professional women I know don't care for domestic work."

"I heard that, Tina." Vickie grimaced, as she flipped the dead flesh on the grill.

"Passing out ribs, hamburgers, hot links, and hot dogs to these smiling children is much more satisfying than the night shift in E.R."

"Girl you can't be serious," Vickie chimed in.

"Vickie, you are a supermodel whose last gig was where?"

"The South of France."

"Duh! Last night, I pulled a .38 slug out of a twelve-year-old girl who got hit in a drive-by shooting. I love my work, but sometimes I feel like a doctor on a battle field, and not at a hospital in a major U.S. City. So, this very second, I am very content passing out food to these beautiful children, rather than potassium nitrate."

"My bad. I got a house full of maids. Sazzar doesn't like for me to pour my own orange juice. He's turned me into a spoiled superbitch! But I feel you girl. That's some real shit you're talking."

"Now I know I like you, Mercy. Nobody, and I do mean

nobody, puts Vickie in her place." Tina laughed.

"That's a good thing, right?" Mercy wondered if she'd done something that would offend someone.

"Relax girl, you done good. I need a reality check every now and then. Tina, you forgot your watch!" Vickie shouted after Tina, as she walked toward the parking area.

"Put it in your purse, I'll get it from you when I get back." Tina shouted back.

"Nice watch!" Mercy exclaimed, standing next to Vickie.

"Nice is not the word. This is a Van Cleef & Arpels, Lady Arpels Fairy. This damn thing is set in white gold with diamonds, blue enamel Guilloche dial with a retrograde mechanical movement, and it has an extra feature."

"Extra feature? What else could a girl possibly want?"

"How about a Terra Fix GPS somethin'. Anyway, this thing transmits a distress signal to a global satellite SAR system; brings help in a matter of hours to within shouting distance."

"No shit!"

"Damn, white girl! I'm liking your ass more by the minute.

"In time you'll learn like the rest of us have. These people are serious about taking care of one another."

"Yes, we are." Bangman wrapped his arms around his bride-to-be. "I love you." Mercy turned to face him.

"I love you back. Is there anything I can get for you?" He asked.

"Yes! One of those." She pointed at the cute little mulatto girl.

"We can start tonight, but right now I need to speak to Tina. Have you seen her?"

"She just walked off on her way to the parking lot, she's on her way to the grocery store. You can catch her if you hurry."

She kissed him on the lips.

"Which way?"

"Toward Central High School."

"Girl you are the luckiest bitch on the planet. Bangman is fine as hell." Vickie fanned herself.

"Yeah, I am a lucky bitch." She took another look at the

little mulatto girl.

CHAPTER 107

"Tina, wait up." Bangman ran up behind her.

"Hey, Bangman." She kind of mumbled, as he fell in stride with her.

"Want some company?"

"Sure."

"Where you headed, Miss Tee?"

"To the Midway to buy a case of barbeque sauce."

"My car is right over there. We can ride and talk about what it is that's troubling you."

"I'd like that."

"So what has you feeling so down?" He opened the door for her.

"Bangman, I have cancer." She spoke without hesitation.

"What stage?" He had concern in his voice.

"Stage three," she began, then wisely closed her mouth as J.T. appeared in front of the Bentley.

"Where you going, Uncle Bernard?"

"Just driving your mother to the grocery store."

"Cool, I'll ride with you. I want to tell you about the championship kickboxing match I won in Las Vegas." He hopped in the back seat.

"Already seen it. Your dad sent me a copy of the fight on DVD. Overnight express mail."

"He did?"

"All fifty-seven seconds of it." Bangman started his car and pulled out of Central's parking lot.

"Mom did you know this?"

"First I've heard of it, J.T."

***

"Kiss my black ass! There is a God."

"Nigga, what is you talking about?"

"Nearly twenty years ago, a bitch we both hate humiliated the fuck out of us to the point where we dropped out of school."

"What's the point, Mac?"

"The bitch!"

"What about her?"

"She just rode by in that black Bentley."

"No more sticky bud for you, Mac. The shit has you going out yo' rabbit ass mind."

"Don't play with me when I'm being serious, nigga."

"You're sure?"

"Positive."

Ice flipped open his phone. "Call Slick-B." The phone was answered on the first ring.

"Yeah, Ice?"

"Where are you?"

"Two cars back."

"Get behind us, there's something I need for you to do."

"Do we need those thumpers?"

"Naw, just a severe beat down."

"We'll take care of whatever it is, Ice."

"I know you will." He closed his phone.

...

"Uncle Bernard, I've got seven variations of three kick combinations." J.T. closed the door, and started making his way to the supermarket.

"Damn!"

"What's the matter, Mom?" J.T moved between the crowd to his mother.

"Forgot my clutch purse on the seat. Bangman, let me have your keys."

"Don't worry about it, Tee. I'm rich, remember?"

"I know, but you know I can be stubborn sometimes." She held out her hand.

"Better give them to her, Uncle Bernard. Them Leos have a helluva temper when they don't get what they want." J.T.

grabbed a shopping cart.

...

"That is the bitch!" Ice ran his finger across his lips. Mac Dee pulled the Bentley beside the two Range Rovers, and their windows rolled down slowly.

"See that bitch? I want her barely alive when you finish stomping her ass. Understand?"

"Yeah, Ice, no problem."

...

Tina grabbed her purse, and was locking the door, when from out of nowhere came a spinning-heel kick toward her head. Even at thirty-five she was still limber and fast. She stepped backward and the kick passed harmlessly in front of her face. As her attacker' leg came down she tapped him hard with a roundhouse to the head.

He went down, rattled, but sprang back up. Three more attackers joined him, twirling, and throwing combinations of kicks.

J.T. turned his attention from bragging about his championship fight to look for his mom, and saw several men attacking her. He took off running, knocking over several shoppers, as he ran through the door.

Bangman, trapped by all the people blocking the doorway, looked out the window, and saw Tina fighting. He took a good grip on the cart he was pushing, spun around, and threw it through the window. Making an opening, he quickly jumped through, running across the roofs of parked cars to her aid.

C H A P T E R 108

Tina was hit hard with a vicious backhand to her face. Dazed, she saw through blurred vision the man's body twisting violently, and the spinning heel kick that missed its mark the first time, found its mark on her jaw, and she went down hard on her back. Warm blood filled her mouth, and lights dazzled in her eyes. She felt paralyzed as she struggled up on her elbows, blood flowing freely from her nose and mouth.

"Look bitch!" The 'O' member grabbed her by her hair, and pointed in the direction of Ice and Mac Dee. "Remember them?" One of the others kicked her in the ribs. She fell back to the pavement, and the 'O' members commenced to stomp her as they had been instructed.

J.T. moved unaware of himself. He was fully connected to the bullshit taking place. He ran the last ten feet just as the 'O' members began to stomp his mother, stutter stepping to get the timing he needed. His feet shot out striking the Achilles tendons of the two closest 'O' members, to their left and right heels, jutting them forward.

J.T. jumped into the air, his right leg kicking in a ninety degree backward angle, his left in a jump sidekick the scissor kick striking one of the men on the jaw. He slumped to the ground gurgling, a mouth full of blood. He heard the other's neck snap, as he crumbled, and fell to the ground.

Bangman ran across the rooftops of parked cars concentrating on the two men stomping Tina. Just as one of them raised his boot to stomp her face, he jumped from the car with a sidekick to the man's head. The man crashed hard to the pavement, unconscious.

Stepping left with a side escape, he executed a right

spinning hook kick to the other man's ribs with such speed and force that a broken piece of his rib pierced his lung. Ice pounded on the side of the car, watching history repeat itself.

"Kill that bitch!" he commanded, and an armed gunman slipped out of the Range Rover in a mask. In his hand was a Krinkov 7.62 mm round, Russian Special Ops Pistol.

Bangman lifted a bloodied Tina to her feet, and grimaced at the sight of the bruises on her face. Tina looked behind him, and saw the gunman arcing his weapon at her, its dark metal level with her chest.

Tina positioned herself away from Bangman, ready to take the rounds in her vest. A look of determination on her face caused Bangman to follow her eyes, catching sight of the gunman in his periphery. He threw himself at her using his body to shield hers wrapping his arms around her, he lifted her off the ground, as the gunfire erupted.

The gun's projectiles thudded like a jackhammer into the metal of the car behind her. Her heart was pounding as the bullets began ripping through his flesh.

She felt the first shot as it slammed through his side into her vest through his abdomen. The second entered his lats and exited through his ribs. The third and near fatal shot entered beneath his armpit and exited through his chest above his heart.

Bangman's body going limp, he let go of Tina falling to the ground. J.T. could hear the deafening gunshots and screams of. terror, as people ran for cover from the gunman who was trying to clear his jammed weapon.

The gunman raised his weapon, ready to fire, when it coughed and fired a round into the air as it left his hand, twirling high above his head before crashing to the ground.

J.T. left his feet, the spinning wheel kick sending the man somersaulting to the parking-lot floor. The gunman stumbled to his feet, and fired a series of wild punches that J.T. easily slipped and hit him with a ridge hand to his nose with all of his strength. The blow broke his nose, his cheekbone, and his neck.

J.T. stood over Bangman and his mom. Bangman was wheezing and blood was bubbling in his airway, his chest convulsing, heaving for air. A tear ran down J.T.'s face at the sight of his Uncle lying on the ground, his green eyes on his mother's face, hers on his, staring back in disbelief.

CHAPTER 109

Tina heard the sirens in the distance and looked to J.T.

"Walk away, baby." She maintained her calm.

"No Mom, I'm gonna stay with you and Uncle Bernard." He responded defiantly.

"Remember your training, baby. Walk away. You don't need a murder case."

J.T. knelt down, and kissed his Uncle on the forehead, pressed his hand in his blood, stood, and walked away from the crowd that was gathering.

EMS arrived on the scene and quickly convinced Tina to let them do their job. After cutting his clothing, they rolled Bangman on his side, into the fetal position, examining him for any other rear punctures or lacerations. Satisfied, the paramedic covered the wounds with a heavy gauze before rolling him onto the crash board, knowing that the weight of his body would act as a pressure tourniquet. They placed him in the ambulance, and went about the business of starting an IV, then connecting him to the heart monitor. Tina climbed into the ambulance without protest, and watched the machine project its EKG readings.

"Abnormal with a rapid drop in pulse!" One of them called out.

"Intubate him at 90 percent oxygen 60ML." Called out another as the siren wailed, and they sped down University Avenue.

Tina listened to the paramedic as he radioed the hospital

and asked for trauma team to be paged.

"E.R. Stat. P.T. coming in, blood pressure 98/60, P.O. 30 percent, pupils dilated. Patient conscious but non-responsive."

CHAPTER 110

Trauma One removed Bangman from the gurney, laying him on his stomach, and quickly connecting him to the life support system.

The Chief of the E.R. shouted out, "Call radiology and have them come to E.R. with a portable X-Ray machine stat, and page the Cardio Thoracic Surgeon."

Mercy's pager screamed at her side. She turned her attention from the entertainment on the stage to Six. Is there someone who can give me a ride to the hospital? I have an emergency call."

"I'll take her, Dad." Tanisha volunteered her services.

"Thanks, Nisha."

"No problem, future Auntie."

"Six, tell Miss Tee to enjoy Prince for me. She can give me the 411 later. And please tell my man that I'm in surgery."

"Done." Six watched as Mercy followed his daughter to her car, then grinned, and turned his attention back to the rapper on stage who was giving the audience a serious understanding about the snitch game.

Tanisha pushed the BMW M5 down 1-94, well past the established speed limit, dropping Mercy off at the doctor's entrance in less than five minutes. A few minutes later, Mercy was scrubbed and ready for surgery.

"What do we have, Dr. West?" She addressed the Chief of E.R. as she walked into the operating room.

"Patient with multiple GSW's, with near fatal wounds

entering Infraspinatus puncturing the left lung, missing the heart by two centimeters exiting the Pectoralis Major. The patient's left lung was saturated with blood and other bodily fluids, but the EMT's did a wonderful job clearing the way for us to arrest the bleeding vessels.

"All we are waiting for now is the Hematologist to bring us the three pints of A/B negative blood, and of course, your presence. Which is one of two. Somebody get on the goddamn horn, and get that blood down here." He screamed, making the whole room jump due to his infamous temper.

Mercy looked down at the patient, and a cold chill passed through her body. For some odd reason there was a spark of recognition of his heavily muscled back and shoulders.

"No ... it couldn't be." She dismissed the thought that her man was lying on the table.

"Doctor English?

"Yes, Dr. West?"

"Shall we?" He asked sarcastically.

"Prep the patient for immediate surgery, and page Dr. Trimus." She said as she sprung into her all business mode.

C H A P T E R 111

Tina stood in the bathroom of the hospital's Emergency Room washing the dried blood from her face, and checking the bruises on her face and body. The events in the grocery store parking lot had her killing mad.

She wondered what happened to J.T., Six and the others should been notified and in the hospital by now. Her thoughts of why she hadn't called Six's cell phone helped her instantly excuse her son.

She dried the tears forming in her eyes, leaving the bathroom to find a phone. Midway to the bank of phones, doctors were running toward the operating room where Bangman was. She fell in behind the last nurse, and ran to the entrance of the operating room.

"Beautiful job, Dr. English. His vitals are critical, but our work is done here. May God have mercy on him!" Dr. West pulled the surgical gloves from his hands just before the cardiograph flat lined.

"PT is flat lined! Let's get him on his back." Mercy took up her position for the move. "On three ... one, two, three!" They turned the patient onto his back.

She gasped at the site of Bangman. This shit wasn't happening. She froze, standing stiffly, her hand over her heart which was hammering wildly.

Like a General in the heat of battle, Dr. West, who was so surprisingly casual and controlled, stepped in front of her.

"Potassium 500 ML. Now, goddammit!" He commanded,

grabbing the defibrillator. "Clear!" He shouted when the nurse finished the injection. Seeing the terrified look in Mercy's eyes, a nurse stepped forward and began the CPR. "Breathe!" She pumped his chest.

"Clear!" Bangman's body jumped on the table.

"Breathe, dammit!" The nurse shouted.

"Clear!" Dr. West shouted, as he hit Bangman for the third time. The cardiograph remained flat lined.

"T.O.D." He looked at the clock on the wall. "1830. We're done here people."

His words echoed in Tina's brain and she screamed, causing everyone to look toward the entrance. Her eyes locked with Mercy's as they pulled the sheet over Bangman's head. Tina slammed her fist into the wall, and took off running down the hallway. Just as she ran out of the hospital's front entrance, running hard toward University Avenue, Six, her son, and her team entered the Emergency Room door.

C H A P T E R 112

Mercy waited for everyone to walk out of the O.R. before she pulled the sheet from Bangman's face. "You promised me a life." Tears streamed down her face. "Damn you, Bernard, we had a great life, goddammit!" She pounded on his chest. "You can't die on me, you hear me? You can't die!" She laid her head on his chest.

She lifted her head when she thought she felt him quiver.

She turned on the cardiograph, it beeped a few times and went flat. She grabbed a syringe and filled it with 200 ML's of potassium nitrate and turned on the defibrillator.

"Fight, Bangman, fight for your life. Fight for our love. Fight for our life together!" She injected him with the potassium nitrate. She grabbed the defibrillator, and held it in her hands, waiting for the charge.

"Live!" She sent the current to his heart.

* * *

"Bernard Logan, what operating room is he in?" Six asked the Emergency Room receptionist.

"The doctors who operated on him are coming down the corridor now, sir. You can speak to them if you like," she replied.

"Doctor?"

"West. May I help you with something?" He looked over the large entourage behind Six.

"Are you the doctor who operated on Bernard Logan?"

"One of them, yes."

"His condition?"

"Are you immediate family?"

"Yes!" Six was barely able to control his temper.

"Mr. Logan died at 6:30PM. I'm sorry for your loss. Now, if you'll excuse me." Dr. West walked toward the doctors lounge.

"Who did this?" Six angrily inquired of his son.

"It was the 'O', dad."

"Every last one of them is going to die. Fan out, find Tina."

Mercy sat with tears in her eyes, watching the cardiograph.

"Who are the bastards who did this to you, baby?" She watched the cardiograph's readings grow stronger. "For your protection, baby you are officially dead." She signed the death certificate. Mercy reached for the phone on the wall and called the morgue. It was answered on the third ring.

"Morgue."

"Cliff, this is Dr. English. I need a favor, but you're going to have to break all the rules on this one."

"What's the favor, Doc?"

"I need a body of a John Doe if you have one."

"Doc there are at least twenty of 'em down here. Any particular race, shape, size, color?"

"African American, preferably one of fair complexion, six-one in height."

"What are you up to, Doc?"

"Saving a life, Cliff. I promise no one will ever know. You will be rewarded handsomely, and I will carry our little secret to my grave with me." She pleaded.

"Stop that, Doc. We're friends, and what are true friends for, right?"

"Yes Cliff, we are friends."

""Then I got yo' back. If anyone asks, I'll show them the paperwork, and let them figure it out."

"Thanks Cliff. You're a sweetheart."

"Doc?"

"Yeah, Cliff?"

"You want me to switch the dental records and the

fingerprints of your guy and the John Doe?"

"You can do that, Cliff?"

"I'm not as dumb as I look, Doc. I've learned a few things over the years working in this basement."

CHAPTER 113

"Don't worry about the cab fare ma'am, it's on me." The cab driver told Tina as he pulled into her driveway.

"No, I couldn't ..." she paused, looking at his identification, "Gary. I'll just run in the house and grab the money. Really it's not a problem."

"Please, my gift." He shut off the meter that displayed the thirty-dollar fare.

Six, snatched open the door, and made both of them jump. "You alright, Tee?" He looked at his badly bruised wife.

"I'll live." She answered him.

Six dropped two hundred-dollar bills in the cab driver's lap and helped Tina out of the cab, taking her nervously trembling hand in his. Halfway up the walk to their house she asked. "Have you located them yet?"

"Vehicles are loaded and ready. We were just waiting for you. They're in a warehouse on Selby and Milton in St. Paul."

Her lips began to quiver, and her throat tightened, as she ripped open the top of her dress to show him what had caused the serious internal damage that killed Bangman, and was now lodge in her vest.

"I can still see his eyes, Six. Even bleeding to death in my arms, they were sending me the message that he was proud to give up his life to save mine." She ran her hand over the slugs. Her voice cracked, as she vehemently spoke in rage. "Six, those niggers killed Bangman!"

Six kissed her, running his fingers over her bruised and

swollen face. "Look at me, Tee! The joy I have, this world didn't give to me, and this world can't take it away. Bangman died so that you could live. Keep his memory close." He touched her heart.

"My last memory of him was the doctors pulling the sheet over his head." Her bruised facial features showed a heartache and anguish that made Six want to just hold her, but he had other plans.

"We can stand here a little longer, and I can hold and comfort you, or you can get suited and booted, and we can go kill those mothafuckas responsible for his death. You wanna go now?"

She nodded her head, "Yeah, right now!"

Six opened the door, and heard his team arguing in the dining room. "Just stay here Elijah. You don't need to be mixed up in this shit" Rasheed loaded his AK-47 clips with armor-piercing rounds.

"He's right, Elijah. If you go tonight, you'll be responsible for murder by your own hand. Up until now, we've kept you out of the killing. It's the way we all wanted it." Tina entered the room ahead of Six.

Elijah leveled his eyes on her bruised face. Biting on his knuckled fist, he could barely contain his anger. "Tina, killing Bangman, and the beating they gave you, they all deserve to die.

I'm in, and there'll be no more rap about it. Understand?" He looked everyone in the eye, as he screwed the suppressor on his forty-five.

"I'm in too." J.T. was still amped up.

"Stay out of it, J.T." Six admonished his son.

"Dad, I'm already in it, remember, I was there. They killed Uncle Bernard in front of me. "I've already killed two of them, but that's not enough for my uncles' life." He loaded a two-hundred- and-fifty-round can with armor-piercing, incendiary, and green- tracer rounds.

"Stay in the car, and don't get involved unless you absolutely have to. Those are my terms, son. Take 'em or leave 'em." Six handed him the PKS.

"Yeah, Dad." J.T. agreed, not really thrilled that he wasn't going into the warehouse. According to my contact at the police department, the warehouse is more like a clubhouse for the Organization. Motorcycles, parties, strippers, the whole nine yards." K-Nine reported the Intel he received.

"It's going to be their casket in an hour." Tina pushed the clip in her AK.

C H A P T E R 1 1 4

We arrived at the warehouse at 2200 hours. J.T. parked the Escalade on Dayton and Milton, and watched, as his heavily armed parents exited the vehicle.

"Inexhaustible people prepared to die about their own," J.T. whispered to himself.

"Big Al set his eyes on top of the building across the street, the night concealing his presence to the men outside the warehouse. Babyboss moved into position with the thermal imaging device with the infrared video camera attached, aiming it at the warehouse.

"Big brother, you copy?"

"Loud and clear, baby brother."

"Big Al, we're in position. What's the deal?" Six and his team moved between the houses and buildings, taking up strike positions.

"Installation heavily guarded with puppet soldiers. Is everyone in position?" Big Al checked.

"Five seconds," Elijah replied, as he Rasheed, and Face made their way from Hauge and Milton.

"Big Al, Babyboss, it's your show,"

"Copy that, Six." Babyboss took over. "Here's the situation. The monitor shows twelve bodies inside, all appear to be armed.

Half of them are clustered together, the others are scattered about the room. Looking to other areas of the warehouse, it appears to be all clear."

"Checking the field of fire." Big Al's voice rang in their ears. "We're going to need six firing positions. There are six men standing on different sides of the building on the Selby and Milton side. All appear to be carrying concealed weapons."

"What does the entrance look like?" Big Al inquired.

"The entrance is a steel fire door in a steel frame, probably deadbolt locks. My guess is the back door is the same. The whole warehouse is brick, and the few windows have steel grills over them to keep out the would be thieves. And there's an added plus."

"Talk to me."

"State-of-the-art alarm system."

"Won't mean much in five minutes."

"You've got that right, Six. They'll all be dead. I've got the one nearest the door on the west end of the building," Big Al declared.

"The one firing up his last blunt on the edge of the building on the Selby-Milton cross is mine," whispered Badboy.

"The three walking what looks like post, I've got the tall one." Buzzed Elijah.

"The one in the middle is mine." Tina's tone was venomous.

"They're all dead. I've got the last one." Six was ready to move.

"Kiss my ass, we rehearsed this damn scenario hundreds of times over the years. All head shots, people." Big Al fingered his trigger, as he spoke.

"Everybody got their man?" Babyboss queried the team.

"Yeah, we got 'em," came the replies in his earpiece. "On my command, take aim ... ready ... fire!" Six clean head shots hit their marks simultaneously. All the men dropped to the ground with a thud.

"Just like we practiced." Babyboss stepped from his cover.

They quickly gathered the bodies, and placed them inside of two cars on the Milton side of the building. I placed C-4 beneath the two cars with the bodies in them , and more under a Benz on the Selby side, then set the timers for fifteen minutes.

Elijah moved to the door to set the charge. "Entry in ten seconds."

CHAPTER 115

"Mac, have somebody check on security. You know those fools tend to lax because they in the hood." Ice commanded

"Problems ?"

"No amigo, no problems."

"My men can help if you're having security problems. Their all prior military." The Mexican looked at his men.

"Don't worry, Mario. There is plenty of security around the building to protect our investments."

"Then why are we wasting precious time. I suggest we get down to business." Mario gestured toward the three Econoline vans that were parked inside the warehouse.

"Cash-Money, go check on those niggas and put their asses in line and on point while you're out there."

"Sure, Mac." Cash-Money spun off like an obedient soldier, and walked the final steps to the end of his life.

Elijah was about to set the charge to blow the door when he heard it unlock, he moved with the door as it opened. Cash-Money stepped out, closing the door behind him. His scream remained silent as the blade slid smoothly through his throat, his blood pulsing violently from his neck, as his heart rapidly played its last beats.

Elijah pulled him inside the doorway, the rest of the team moved in quickly behind him.

Two flash bang grenades went off simultaneously inside the warehouse. Ice could hear men crying out, as silent gunfire erupted around him. Mario's men were cut down instantly.

Through blurred vision, Ice could see the remaining men sinking slowly to their knees, as the gunfire stopped.

"Stand the fuck up!" Six commanded, as he strolled toward Ice, Mario, and Mac Dee. The three of them rose on wobbly legs. "Which one of you mothafuckas is the leader of the Organization?" Six stood in front of the three men.

"He is!" Mac Dee pointed at Ice.

"Then that means you're useless!" Babyboss stepped forward, placed the .45 to Mac's head, and pulled the trigger.

The round hit Mac just above the temple, taking a quarter of his skull with it, blood and brains splattering in Ice's face. Thick dark blood and brain matter dripped from his chin, as his body trembled out of control.

"And who are you?" Six trained his weapon on Mario.

"I'm Special Agent Mario Enriquez with the FBI, and I'm working undercover to bring down the drug trade between members of the St. Paul Police Department and the Organization. It's taken us a year to get all the players of this conspiracy into one room."

"Guess what, Special Agent Enriquez? You're a dead FBI Agent." K-Nine fired two silenced bursts into Mario's chest. Blood rushed from his heart, as he stared at the holes in his chest, not believing that anyone would kill an FBI Agent.

"Look, my man, you don't have to do this. There is plenty of money for all of us to make here. Robbing me is nothing compared to what we can do together." Ice suggested in a desperate attempt at self-preservation.

"So your dumb ass thinks this is a robbery?" Six asked incredulously .

"Isn't it?" He responded.

"Fuck no, fool!" Rasheed shouted.

"Look man, not here." Ice pleaded. "This is my city, you guys can be my new friends, my new partners. I can work for you if you like. Man, we could own the whole Midwest drug trade and make bill-"

"Friends?" Six questioned.

"Sure man, friends, I protect my friends, and they protect me. Trust me, I can fix whatever the problem is between us." Ice spun the three suitcases around on the table and opened them. "One-hundred and-fifty-million dollars. You can have it all." Ice pushed the money toward Six.

"When you change sides, nobody trusts you." Face stepped forward.

As he came into focus Ice felt a sense of relief. "Assistant United States Attorney Green. Man, am I glad to see you," he blinked his eyes to clear his vision.

"You know this piece of garbage?" Elijah asked.

"Yeah, this fucking yard nigger shuffles for the DEA and the FBI. He's a rat." Face breathed the words in Ice's face.

"You're a bucket of soft warm shit." Six slammed Ice into the wall. Before he could catch his breath, Six pressed his forearm against his throat, cutting off the much needed air.

"Tee come on in." Six spoke into his handmic.

C H A P T E R 116

Tina walked into the room, and Ice's eyes rolled straight back in his head, from fear taking hold. Six let him go, and he began to babble incoherently.

"What's wrong, you don't recognize me all beat up?" She came and stood before him.

"She asked you a question." Elijah moved Tina out of the way, and punched Ice in the chest. The blow came with so much force, Ice slumped over and fell to the floor, his body convulsing, as if he were having a seizure. Elijah stepped over him and repeatedly slapped the shit out of him. When Ice opened his eyes, Elijah grabbed his arm, twisting it behind his back nearly to the breaking point before he placed his .45 to his head.

"Elijah?"

"I can't hear you right now, Six. I'm suffering from a temporary case of multiple personality disorder."

"That's too good for him. This bitch-ass nigga, and his gang like to mark their territory with a big red 'O' after a kill, or an act of violence. Well I like to mark my kills on the battlefield as well."

"You're right, Six." Elijah let go of Ice, who fell to the floor, lying like a broken board.

"Nice stage you're building here!" Elijah walked onto the stage and picked up the nail gun lying in the corner.

"What is this, oak timber from Germany?" Rasheed asked.

"Yeah, it's nice." Tina kicked Ice hard in the ribs.

"His bladder let go as they snatched him off the floor, and carried him to a wooden walled area off the stage. K-Nine and Six stretched Ice's arms out against the wall, as Elijah placed the nail gun against his flesh. Ten thuds in each limb pinned him to the wall as his bones began fracturing and separating at the sockets under the weight of his body.

K-Nine stepped aside, gesturing like an usher at New Hope Baptist Church, as Tina walked toward Ice. The air around him reeked of shit and piss, she thought, as she pulled the same blade from her boot that she'd used to cut the X through his lips nearly twenty years earlier.

"This is for my friend that you had murdered." She slammed his head against the wall, and tilted his chin back to where she could see the long muscle in his throat, then sliced the blade through the seat of his voice, turned and walked away.

CHAPTER 117

"Pay attention, people. While you guys are in there having fun, we have a situation developing out here."

"What is it, big brother?" Babyboss asked.

"Three police cruisers just pulled up and parked in front of the warehouse. Each of the cars are full, it looks like there are at least five officers in each car, fifteen total."

"What are they doing?" Six asked.

"Right now, nothing, just sitting in their cars. Wait a minute. Two of them are getting out and heading your way. ETA to the front door ... ten seconds."

"I'll take care of it." Elijah stepped quickly to the front entrance.

"Man aren't you glad we came on board with the Organization?" Officer Crawford asked his partner.

"Shit pays the bills ... and other things." His partner fired up his Cuban cigar.

"After tonight, we'll be able to retire early in any part of the world we like; fuck being a pig in this funky ass town. Besides, I'm starting to enjoy this criminal lifestyle a bit more than police work."

"Why, because it's profitable?"

"Beats the fuck out of thirty grand a year!" Officer Crawford spat just before he slipped and fell. "Goddammit! What the fuck?"

He stared at the blood on his hands.

"Should I call for backup?" His partner put his hand on his weapon and radio.

"Use your fucking head. There are fifteen of us here already.

Do you want to explain to the entire St. Paul police force what's inside that warehouse?"

"You've got a point there, Crawford." He pulled his weapon and stepped toward the door that was slightly ajar.

    * * *

Approaching the entrance, Elijah pressed his body against the wall, adjacent to the door, which was slowly creeping open. Keeping all the years of his training in mind, Elijah slipped the knife from his belt. He took a deep breath, as the barrel of the officer's weapon cleared the doorway, slowly sweeping from side to side.

Elijah timed the sweeping motion, and used the steel door frame to break the officer's wrist. He managed to get off a round, chipping the wall. He felt something impact his chest, and all of his fears released, as they drained down Elijah's blade.

Gunfire erupted as Officer Crawford let off round after round into the doorway of the warehouse, which was rapidly closing before him. Big Al stopped his assault with a round to the back of his head.

"Body down, the rest of the officers are taking up positions and calling for backup. I can hear the sirens in the distance.

Timers go off in exactly one minute thirty seconds. Wait for my signal."

The pounding in my heart settled down to a smooth idle when Big Al started the countdown. "In five, four, three, two, one!" Explosions shattered the still darkness, as the cars blew up, and flames, debris, and body parts littered the streets.

"Now!" Big Al shouted into his handmic, as he let loose several smoke grenades to mask our getaway.

"When we stepped out of the warehouse it felt like it was one- hundred-and-thirty degrees from the burning vehicles. Liked dazed prize fighters taking a serious ass whupping, the police were trying to find cover from the burst of gunfire coming from our weapons.

I was pulling up the rear. As soon as I cleared the

doorway, I slipped and fell, rolling into the street. When I stood up I'd lost sight of the others in the smoke. There was a silence that I felt was suffocating me until I heard Six's voice in my earpiece.

"Sazzar, where are you?"

"I've got my back against the wall of the warehouse on the Milton side."

"Move toward the alley. We're coming to get you."

I started to move through the smoke, and was rammed hard by a police cruiser. I hit the ground, then stood up, and was hit five times in my vest. When I hit the ground, I hear four shots ring out. I blinked my eyes, and Six was standing there, his Beretta smoking. The two police officers were lying on the ground dying.

Gunfire erupted from the police, and the team responded. Visibility was down to yards, and live rounds were hitting the ground in front of me, forcing me to crawl away from Six.

The police had Six trapped behind some vehicles and concentrated their fire on his area. Six's voice came through our earpieces in a heavy gasp.

"Taking fire ... no way to move." Six broke off his communication as he analyzed his possibilities. Left with no other choice, he issued the order. "Escape and evade!"

Big Al made his way quickly off the rooftop, and slammed the door on the Escalade, then J.T. pulled away speeding down Dayton Avenue to Victoria. Several police cruisers raced by him, and turned down Selby Avenue toward the warehouse. J.T raised his hand to his face, as he raced across Selby and Victoria headed toward Hauge.

"Dad, if you can hear me get ready to move. My ETA to your position is less than five seconds. On my mark, move!"

"Copy that," came the reply.

J.T. slammed on the brakes, grabbed the PKS, and stepped out of the Escalade. "Now Dad, move!" He conveyed into his handmic, as he walked down Milton, and unloaded the two-hundred-and-fifty-round can.

That's all I remember, other than the fact that the kid let loose two-hundred-and-fifty well-placed rounds in less than six seconds. By then I was on the move.

C H A P T E R   1 1 8

"Looks like our boy is telling the truth. They haven't been on the scene an hour, and the divers have already located the trucks." Special Agent McMurtry spoke as he walked into the conference room.

"It was all done on the hush as we requested?" asked U.S. Attorney Hughes.

"Agents and locals have formed a protective and restrictive cordon around the reservoir, sir."

"And the press?"

"Shut out until you give the go-ahead for the carefully prepared statement that was faxed down from Director Mueller himself. He handed his boss the paper.

"Thanks, McMurtry. Well done. Sazzar, I owe you an apology." U.S. Attorney Hughes humbled himself.

"So do I," added McMurtry.

"You wanna throw me a party, or are we done with this debriefing? Either way, I'm cool, with it," Sazzar sat back rubbing his eyes.

"We've been here for hours. I'm sure all of us could use a break." Miss Corning stood and stretched.

"Not quite!" Sazzar spoke in a somewhat urgent voice. "Now it's time for a reality check. Everything I've just told you is going to be useless come 9:30AM." Sazzar apprised them.

"Why the urgency?" McMurtry asked.

"Ronnie Green will show up for work at nine, and I can guarantee he'll see right through the bullshit. Once he alerts

Six, the game will be over."

"You talk like this guy is some kind of demagogue, Sazzar." U.S. Attorney Hughes' tone was arrogant as usual.

"Don't get it fucked up! He's a leader who is championing the cause of his people, and if you piss him off he'll put your lives in so much danger and darkness that your every waking moment will be filled with terror. So be afraid, not only for yourselves, but for your families."

"As soon as we get arrest warrants, this guy, and your crew will be cooling their heels behind bars, waiting to be lethally injected." McMurtry wasn't a true believer yet.

"And how long do you think that will take?" Sazzar asked.

"By the end of the day, tops." U.S. Attorney quipped sharply.

"By then, all of them will have disappeared, forever if they wanted to. But they won't run. Even if they're captured and sent to death row, they'll retaliate."

"That's comforting." Miss Corning's eyes widened from fear, and the disbelief that doing her job had put her in danger. "I can't believe this shit!" She screamed.

"Believe it. But things get worse."

"What now, Sazzar?" asked Mr. Grayford.

"You are going to need a SEAL team, and every member of the Twin Cities Swat Teams to arrest them."

"Sazzar, the FBI is capable, along with the local authorities of bringing these criminals to justice." McMurtry laughed at Sazzar' suggestion.

"Have you forgotten what they did to the police at the warehouse?"

"Luck shines on a dog's ass some days." McMurtry snickered.

"You think their exit from the warehouse was luck?"

"Absolutely!"

"What if I could prove to you that there was no luck in the equation?"

Sazzar looked at a book of matches lying on the table from the Egg and I. "You like that eatery agent ... Sorry, I don't know your name."

"Bradley. My name is Bradley, and yeah they serve a

mean steak and egg breakfast."

"You a betting man?" Sazzar asked.

"Depends on the bet."

"I'll bet you the cost of breakfast that in less than sixty seconds, all ten of you will be unconscious, and twenty minutes later, after I stroll out of here like I have keys to the building, I'll be sitting in the Egg and I having breakfast."

Over the laughter, McMurtry shouted, "Sazzar, that is the most absurd thing that you've said. There are ten Agents and Marshals' highly-trained in self-defense in this room. At best you'll get wrestled to the floor, you'd have to be the equivalent of Jason Bourne to make it out of this room." McMurtry gave his two cents just before his body went painfully vertical, hitting the wall, and sliding down blood flowing freely from his broken nose. Several pairs of hands tried to grab Sazzar, but he quickly fulfilled his promise, and filled the room with unconscious agents.

"You've proven your point, Sazzar." Mr. Grayford watched Sazzar grab Miss Corning's car keys and parking permit from the table.

"Not quite, Carl." He stepped toward U.S. Attorney Hughes, whose whole body shuddered at the presence standing over him. "Get on the phone, Hughes, call whoever you have to, and make this happen. You have less than five hours, and tell McMurtry when he wakes up, there are eleven more just like me." He gathered up radios and cell phones.

U.S. Attorney Hughes laughed tonelessly, as his star witness walked out of the conference room, closing and locking the door with a pair of handcuffs on the other side of the door.

CHAPTER 119

"Oh my God! John, you will never guess who just walked into our restaurant."

"Sonny Bono?"

"No silly. Sazzar!"

"NFL running back, Sazzar? You're kidding."

"I wish I were. Sazzar, can I help you with something?" The large-breasted waitress escorted him to a table.

"Yes. Let me have the steak, well done, eggs scrambled with cheese, bell peppers, and onions, home fried potatoes, and Texas toast."

"Coffee, tea, or me?" She leaned over showing off her cleavage.

"Sazzar made sure he took a good, long look, as if he were contemplating her offer, sighed, and gave her a wink. "Just the orange juice for now." He left her offer on the table.

"Be just a minute. Would you like a cup of coffee while you wait?"

"Sounds good." Sazzar watched the convoy of police cars as they approached the restaurant.

"Just one more thing, Sazzar." She spoke in a real sexy voice that made Sazzar think of one of those phone sex girls.

"What's that?"

"Would you autograph my breast? I'm going straight to the tattoo parlor, and make your signature permanent." She bared her breast.

"Sure, why not. Do you have a pen?" He watched as the

parking lot was flooded with lights. Sazzar signed the waitress's breast, wondered if they were hers, sipped his coffee, and waited as FBI Agents and SWAT stepped cautiously into the Egg and I.

"On the ground, now!" McMurtry commanded.

"Do it now or you're a dead man!" Added the SWAT leader.

"Fuck it, shoot me!" Sazzar erupted calling their bluff.

"Hold your fire! Stand down!" U.S. Attorney Hughes walked into the restaurant with Mr. Grayford and Miss Corning in tow.

"But sir?"

"Do it, McMurtry! Sazzar, everything is in the mix. All we need is the whereabouts of these individuals." U.S. Attorney Hughes took a seat across from Sazzar.

"I'll give you the rundown over breakfast." He picked up his fork and wiped it with a napkin to make sure it was clean.

"You can't be serious?" Huffed Miss Corning.

"As a mothafucka! I'm starving. Besides, I deserve a hot meal. I've broken a code of trust against one of the most powerful organizations in the free world, one that can never be traced, nor identified. At least I'll die with a full stomach, before all of our screams echo like Miss Corning's voice in the courtroom."

She gasped. "Okay Sazzar, I'm scared shitless, okay!" She was emphatic, obviously in a state of panic.

"Don't worry, Fanny. A massive force of law enforcement officers, and military personal is being mobilized, and will be waiting back at FBI headquarters to be briefed. They have assured us that everyone associated with the prosecution of this case will receive round-the-clock protection for as long as we need. With the General's help who's come on board, arresting personnel will be ready to strike in any area of the country, if need be, simultaneously, to apprehend these criminals, and make the mission a success."

"But Mr. Grayford, what about leaks?"

"Trust me, Fanny, there'll be no leaks of the arrest until each one of them is in custody." He assured her. Seeing her relax, he turned toward Sazzar.

"You talk about urgency, Sazzar, and how our screams will echo at death, yet you sit here waiting to eat breakfast. Don't you think it's time to bring this thing to a close?"

Sazzar took a gulp of his orange juice, wiped his mouth with a napkin, and called for the waitress, then told her to make the order to go, and give the bill with a generous tip to the agent with the swollen jaw.

"I have a question, and feel free to correct me if I'm wrong." Miss Corning stared out the window.

"What is it, counselor?" U.S. Attorney Hughes gave her a quizzical look.

She composed herself. "With all these people here, in and around the restaurant, how are you going to contain a leak to the media, when a WCCO truck has just pulled into the parking lot?"

"No problem!" U.S. Attorney Hughes quipped. "McMurtry?"

"Yes, sir?"

"I want complete media blackout, and I don't give a flying fuck who we piss off. And as of this moment, every person in the immediate area, who is not arresting personnel, will be sequestered by the FBI until this mission has been accomplished. No exceptions."

Jeffrey L Barnes

C H A P T E R 120

Sazzar stared into the eyes of the high-ranking General, who wore a clean, starched uniform, and beautifully shined boots. Ignoring the fact that Sazzar was sitting there dog tired, and still wearing those filthy-ass overalls, the General stepped to him with another man Sazzar recognized, by the bars on his shoulders, to be a Captain.

"Mr. Robinson, I'm General Larry Brantley, and this is Captain Barr. The Captain will be the senior advisor on the ground. We have been briefed that in less than three hours, we have to coordinate the arrest of some of America's most infamous domestic terrorist." Sazzar nodded his head. "Time is wasting, so I suggest that we get down to business. Captain Barr?"

"Thank you, General Brantley. Due to the urgency of this operation, I need Intel on just who it is that we are dealing with."

"You are up against an enemy who is not only dangerously clever, but deadly. Currently he and his team are holed up in a safe house in a residential neighborhood in the 1300 block of Marshall Avenue."

"How many in the house?" Captain Barr asked.

"Ten, maybe less."

"What can you tell us about the house?"

"The house has been fortified to withstand a direct assault. There are steel doors in steel frames at the front, back, and side entrances. Armor plating four-feet in either direction around all window frames, as well as, a bulletproof glass behind all panes."

"Weapons?"

"In the attic window facing Marshall Avenue, M-60 .308 belt- fed 250 rounds; Attic window facing the alley, M-249 .223 belt-fed 250 rounds, Second floor, front and back windows, M-240G-7.62 x51 belt-fed 250 rounds, and MK-19 40mm grenade launchers. Off their shoulders M-16's, Ak-47's and more than two hundred-thousand rounds."

"Who the fuck are these people?" One of the SEAL members asked.

"I know your use to fighting in the jungles, and not the heart of an American neighborhood, but I promise you that Six will make you adapt very quickly. As for who they are; think of them as going against the best the SEAL's have to offer from their own ranks."

"As good as SEAL Team 6?"

"That good or better." Sazzar held his eye contact with the SEAL.

"You said he would make us adapt quickly. How so?" The SEAL asked.

"By the number of casualties that are going to take place if you storm the house. I can guarantee you that within minutes of the assault, you will be eating death."

"Nonsense, Sazzar. This offensive is predicated on the use of all available law enforcement in the Twin Cities, which includes both Minneapolis and St. Paul SWAT Teams, FBI, and Captain Barr's SEAL Team. I'm confident that the combined forces, working together, will take immediate control of the situation. Taking down that house will be child's play, considering we have 150 trained professionals assembled here." U.S. Attorney Hughes was confident without doubt.

"Mr. Hughes, unless you want a repeat of Selby Avenue, this operation will have to have the element of surprise on its side," Sazzar warned.

"What do you suggest we do to hold down causalities and assure success, Mr. Robinson?" Captain Barr ignored Hughes' rambling.

"Assemble several surveillance teams to follow them from

the house. All of them have lives: jobs, families, and reservations on commercial flights leaving Minneapolis-St. Paul International Airport. Except Albert Ball, who has his own plane, and AUSA Ronnie Green, who'll be in a domestic capacity, they will not have any weapons on them. You can arrest them without firing a shot, except Six."

"And Six?" asked U.S. Attorney Hughes.

"My guess is he's going to claim Bernard Logan's body, to take back to California where he'll be buried next to his father and mother."

C H A P T E R 121

Daybreak, Safe house 0730

"Anybody hear anything from Sazzar?"

"Nothing, Six. He's probably back in New York by now. He's been on the move now for twenty-four hours." Face poured himself a cup of coffee.

"K-Nine, what is your take on Sazzar?" Six's tone was leery.

"Something is wrong, or he would have contacted us by now.

"There is no reason for him to be playing his freedom this close to his vest. He knows our protocol when we've been separated."

"Well, we know he's not dead. If he were, the news of his death would be on every news station around the globe." Rasheed added.

Elijah peeked from behind the newspaper he was reading: "What if he was arrested?"

"He understand our code of silence. Besides we have an army of lawyers on retainer who can find loopholes in any case. Assured Big Al.

"Somehow that sounds like betting on a penitentiary football ticket with bad odds." K-Nine joked half serious.

Six swiveled in his chair, clasped his hands behind his head, and locked eyes with K-Nine. "You sound like you don't think Sazzar will hold his water, Nine."

"The price to pay if we're wrong, Six, is painfully too

high. Think about it. Anyone from our inner circle, if turned, would destroy us."

"Face?"

"Yeah, Six."

"Use our connections in the Justice Department to find Sazzar."

"As soon as I get to my office, I'll get right on it, Six."

C H A P T E R 122

Captain Barr walked into the command center and faced the team leaders. "I want to set the stage for the surveillance. Our man on the pole has confirmed movement in the house at 1310 Marshall Avenue. However, we do not have confirmation that all of the suspects are in the house.

"Presently our people at the airport are reporting that there has been only one change in their flight reservations. It seems Mr. and Mrs. Lane are departing this afternoon, and not on the 9:00AM flight that was previously scheduled. All of the suspects have first-class reservations on different flights leaving for several U.S. locations, with the exception of Alfred Ball whose private jet has filed a flight plan. There are fifty officer on the surveillance team that will follow the suspects from the house to the airport, Federal Building, and the morgue.

"SWAT and SEAL Teams are already in place in those locations to arrest the suspects upon their arrival. As a word of caution to the teams, there is a standing order: no matter what happens, should the suspects decide to stop at a brothel on their way to the airport, they are to be observed and followed. Do not, and I emphasize, do not attempt an arrest before they have made it to their destinations. Am I understood?"

"Yes, sir."

"Let's move out! Agent McMurtry, would you like to accompany my team to the morgue?"

"Thank you, sir. I would be honored."

CHAPTER 123

Six pulled out his cell phone, "Call Tina." He listened to the phone ring as he watched the limo driver load his team's bags into the trunk. The four rings it took for her to answer, and the grogginess in her voice indicated she had been asleep.

"Hey, baby."

"Hey yourself."

"How are those nasty bumps?"

"Swollen, and black and blue last time I looked. These cracked ribs don't make moving around to easy either, and there is nothing attractive about me right now."

"How did Fate and Vee take the sight of you?"

"Nothing, except uneasiness." She drew a deep shuddering breath.

"Not a word, huh?"

"You know them, they mind their own business until you ask for their help. Besides being extremely happy to see their grandchildren, all Vee said was 'make sure you make it to old age, you hear?'"

Six laughed. "God, I love her."

"Me too. She's made us so happy over the years. Especially Fate."

"Listen Tee, call the airport, and make arrangements for shipping Bangman's body."

"I did it last night, flight leaves at noon. J.T. and Nisha don't have to be back in school for a week, so they decided to spend the week with their grandparents before they go back to

California."

Six could tell she was fighting off the tears so he cut the conversation short. "Well, I gotta go. I told the mortician I would meet him at the hospital morgue at 9:30AM. I love you, and I'll see you at the airport by eleven.

"I'll be there. I love you back." She disconnected the line.

Six slipped his phone in his pocket, and walked toward the limo. "I'll see all of you in California day after tomorrow, so we can pay our respects to Bangman. K-Nine, I'll get at you tonight with what I find out about Sazzar. I know you have to be on the Senate floor by noon, and will probably be there late into the evening."

"I'll put my phone on vibrate. When you get the news, call." K-Nine rolled up the window.

CHAPTER 124

"Captain Barr, our man on the pole has confirmed they're on. the move. A limousine has just left the rear entrance of the home. Seven suspect have been identified as being at that location. Five are enroute to the St. Paul-Minneapolis International Airport. The female nor her children have yet to be identified as being on the property. Do you want to abort the mission, sir?" The SEAL Team member asked.

The Captain turned back to the board he was studying, and for a brief moment remained silent. When he turned around, he issued instructions." Leave some men on the house, just in case the female and her children are on the property. The arrest of the others will proceed as planned.

CHAPTER 125

K-Nine, Rasheed, Badboy, and the Ball Brothers' rode to the airport in silence, other than the tapping Rasheed was doing on his Blackberry, and occasional grunts from Big Al, as he checked the updates of the stock market after the opening bell was sounded.

The driver, a big corpulent man in his mid-to-late fifties, rolled down the partition. "Not much traffic, gentlemen. We should be arriving at the loading area in five minutes, tops."

When they arrived, they could see that the loading area was congested. Unmarked SWAT vehicles rigged to look like airport service vehicles were everywhere. The driver pulled the limo to a halt, popped the trunk, and proceeded to open the rear door for his passengers. K-Nine and the others stepped out and surveyed the area. Snipers began to appear all around them, resting their high- powered rifles over the roofs of their vehicles, while others with automatic weapons, locked and loaded, walked toward them shouting deadly instructions. K-Nine looked into the eyes of the men surrounding them, their eyes said it all, they wanted to kill them right then and there. Like all the other members of his team, he slowly knelt down on one knee, and then the other, interlacing his fingers behind his head. All he could think of was Sazzar.

C H A P T E R 126

Assistant United States Attorney Ronnie Green's secretary smiled courteously, as she stood and walked from behind her desk. She was a petite woman with a friendly, eager face.

"Mr. Green, how are you this fine, wonderful morning?"

"I'm fine, Gwen. I've already exceeded my limit on caffeine for one day."

"Well if you need anything don't hesitate to buzz." Gwen had put on a great show of indifference, as she waited for the armed men in the other room to burst through the door, and arrest her boss.

She snuck a quick glance in his direction as he closed the door to his office.

Face sat at his desk, turned on his computer, and began flipping through his rolodex for the number of the FBI Agent whose education they had financed when the door to his office burst open, and United States Attorney Hughes, and several armed men quickly filled his office.

"Ronnie Green, it saddens my heart to do this, but you are under arrest for the robbery and deaths associated with the First Bank of Minnesota, The bombing of the St. Paul Police Department, the Utah armored car robbery, and the killing of a federal agent, and local law enforcement officers. Read him his rights." U.S. Attorney Hughes spoke with disdain, as the arrest team handcuffed Face.

CHAPTER 127

"Our target has just turned onto the hospital property, remember, let him enter the morgue, where we will take him down. Hancock, Ramsey, and Central, you'll come in from the corridor.

Any questions?" Captain Barr asked.

"No, sir."

"Let's get this thing done. Take up your positions."

Six pulled his Jaguar in behind the hearse at the entrance to the morgue at Ramsey County Hospital. The driver of the hearse approached the entrance, flashed his credentials, the doors opened and he drove inside. Six pulled his car into the parking space, killed the engine, and walked to the entrance of the morgue.

As soon as he opened the door, he saw an armed man in a flak jacket and cap, bearing a SWAT emblem, duck behind a pillar and then reappear. "Don't move! Don't move a goddamn muscle, you cop-killing motherfucker!" The officer's wide open eyes were darting back and forth, his weapon steady, as he called the others. "I've got him, sir. In the corridor!"

"The entrance to the morgue opened, and five armed men Six immediately recognized as Navy SEALS with scowls on their faces came out, demanding that he kiss the concrete.

Defiant and ready to die, Six stood his ground. When he didn't move, Ramsey stepped forward, his weapon trained on Six's head, and reached out, taking his hand off his weapon to try and force Six to the ground. As soon as his hand touched

Six's shoulder, he quickly stepped into him taking him to the floor.

Ramsey pulled the trigger on his weapon, ripping off several rounds in succession at the same time. Six grabbed his weapon, and directed its fire in the direction of the others. Several rounds hit above their heads as they instinctively sought cover.

Six yanked the weapon from Ramsey's hand just as its clip emptied. He looked down at the useless weapon in his hand, then at those pointed at his chest, and slowly raised it over his head. Captain Barr stepped up from behind him, and hit him to the base of his skull with the butt of his weapon.

Six laid on the floor semiconscious, as legs began to appear and disappear all around him. He could fell himself being handcuffed. Agent McMurtry and one of the SEAL members lifted him to his feet.

"Look at me, asshole! I'm with the FBI, and your murderous ass is under-"

Before McMurtry could finish his sentence Six head-butted him in his broken nose, and he howled like a bitch.

Captain Barr escorted Six to the transport vehicle, and roughly tossed him inside. All he could think of when the door closed was finding and killing Sazzar.

C H A P T E R 128

"Grandpa, telephone! It's Judge Davison." Tanisha shouted, not knowing that her grandfather had just walked into the room.

"Baby girl, what did I tell you about all that yelling?"

"Sorry, Grandpa." She gave him the long face.

"Go on honey, before you melt this old man's heart. I love you." He called after her when she walked out of the room.

"I love you too, Grandpa." She yelled back.

"Judge Davison, how the hell are you my friend? Calling to confirm our fishing trip this weekend, or are you-backing out because you know I'm going to catch more fish than you?"

"Lafayette, I'm afraid I'm going to have to permanently cancel our fishing trips."

"What's wrong, Colonel?" Fate asked with concern for his old friends health, as he took a seat prepared to hear the news that troubled his friend.

"Lafayette, you've made a wonderful life for yourself, Vee, and your family through hard work, sweat, and intellect. Your wife is the finest woman I know, outside of my own."

"All of this praise is for nothing, Colonel.. I'm sure you didn't call me to tell me how great my family is."

Judge Davison held the warrant for Fate's farm in his hand. "Lafayette, have you been watching the news stories about the deaths of the undercover federal, agents, and St. Paul police officers?"

"Yes, Colonel, it's damn near on every local channel. Why

do you ask?"

"This is the hardest decision I've ever made in my life, and after I've said my piece I'm going to resign from my position on the bench."

"Nonsense, Colonel. You're up for the position on the Eight Circuit Court of Appeals, and one step closer to your dream of being appointed to the Supreme Court. Why in God's name would you want to do something like that?"

"I am about to violate my oath of office, Lafayette. At seven o'clock this morning, I signed several warrants for the persons responsible for the murders of those officers. Seven of them are already in custody."

"How is this a bad thing, Colonel? It's what you do."

Fate wondered where this was going.

Judge Davison sighed heavily into the phone. "The arrest warrants were for your son, daughter, grandson, and others." Fate was silent as he stared blankly at the wall.

"Lafayette?"

"Yes, Colonel?"

"It gets worse."

"How so, sir?"

"They wanted an arrest warrant for you as well. I told them that although the evidence against you sounded incriminating, it was circumstantial at best, and I needed more. That was my stall tactic. Tomorrow morning they take the case before the grand jury. From the evidence I've heard and seen, along with the public outcry for justice, you will be indicted, and stand trial with the others. I'm sorry, old friend."

"Me too, sir. Thank you, Colonel. How long do I have before they come for me?"

"My official last act before I resign will be to sign a 'no knock' nighttime warrant for your home on Clinton, and the farm.

I'll find some reason to delay the signing until tomorrow, give you some time to figure out what you need to do to protect yourself."

"That bad, huh?"

"That bad."

"Again, thank you, sir."

"Lafayette?"

"Yes, Colonel?"

"Take your wife and disappear. Go to that place we always spoke of, and I'll find you there, and keep you informed.

"Colonel, you've already done enough."

"I've always wanted to find a way to repay you for saving my life."

"You just did, sir." Fate hung up the phone, his mind racing to fast to think straight.

Vee entered the room and saw the look of gloom on her husband' face." What's the matter, honey? The Colonel backing out on the fishing trip?" She gave him a hug from behind.

"Everything is going to be alright, honey, just as soon as I have a serious conversation with Tina and my grandson."

CHAPTER 129

"Mom, it's Aunt Mercy." Tanisha handed her mom her cell phone

"Hello." Tina spoke softly, her voice choking.

"I've been calling your cell, and sending you emails for hours Miss Tee. Where have you been?"

"Besides losing one of my phones, I had some unfinished business to: tend too. Mercy, I'm sorry about Bernard, you know how much I loved him. I've been wrestling with how I was going to tell you how he lost his life."

"Before you do that, there's something I want to talk to you about as well. But first there is something I want you to hear." There was a slight pause over the line, and then a very weak voice spoke.

"Miss Tee, how is my favorite sis?"

"Bangman?" She shouted into the phone.

"Nope, he's dead. I've got a new identity. Right now I'm dog tired, but Mercy will fill you in. I love you."

Tears were running freely down Tina's face, she could barely contain the joy she was felling.

Mercy came back on the line. "Isn't that the sweetest sound you've ever heard?"

"How Mercy? I saw him flat line and the sheet being pulled over his head, he was dead."

"Man's plans are sometimes interrupted by the Almighty's. How's that Islamic saying go? 'Man plans and God plans but God is the best of planners.' God gave me my man back,

Bernard Logan is dead, and his body is lying in a morgue waiting to be buried."

"His body?"

"Yes, Miss Tee. Fingerprints, dental records, height, weight, the whole nine yards."

"Mercy, how did you pull this off?"

"A beautiful friend, but if I tell you who I'll have to kill you." She joked.

"You can fill me in as soon as I get there. What room is he in?"

"I had him transferred to North Memorial Hospital under the name Demetrius English."

"Nice name.

"Yeah, he's going to be my husband one way or the other," she uttered laughingly.

"We'll, be there, all of us, before noon. Right now I have to call Six and the others, and give them the good news." Mercy?"

"Yeah, Miss Tee?"

"Bless you, sister." She smiled at the sound of Mercy's laughter, as she disconnected the call.

"Everything alright, Mom?" Tanisha looked a bit confused at her mother's behavior.

She raised he sore body from the bed. "Everything is just fine, baby."

Fate knocked and opened the door at the sound of their voices. "Tee, we need to talk!" The look in his eyes said it all.

CHAPTER 130

Fate and Vee sat listening to Tina and J.T's account of the events surrounding Bangman being shot, and the assault on the warehouse, and their escape afterwards. When they took a breath, Fate told them of his conversation with Judge Davison, then he dropped the bomb. He told them that Six and the others had all been arrested.

Tina shook her head in disbelief, and wondered if she'd heard him correctly, so she had him repeat it. When she finally acknowledged him, she was unequivocal in her assessment. "Fate, we have to disappear, all of us, if we want to help Six and the fellas."

"How Tee? If we run, won't that be a sign of guilt?" Vee asked.

"Vee, I have a plan." She picked up her daughter's phone. "Call Mercy." After a few rings, a cheerful Mercy came on the line.

"Mercy, this is Tina. Sister, I'm in serious trouble, and I need your help."

"Anything for you, Miss Tee. How can I help?"

"I need the aid and assistance of your special friend. Tell him or her that for what I want done they can name their own price.

"I'll arrange a meeting. Just say when."

"Right now, Mercy! Right now!" After she hung up the phone, she turned to her son. "J.T., there's something I need for you to do for me, baby."

"Whatever it is, I can handle it, Mom."

"I know you can, baby. Fate?"

"Yes, Miss Tee?"

"Gather up the fellas."

"I don't even know what the plan is, but if it involves my men, we're in." Fate picked up the phone.

CHAPTER 131

"Gangster, there's a lil' nigga at the door, says his name is Nino, he claims that he's Cuzzo's cousin from Detroit."

"What does the nigga want? Cuzzo's ass is dead."

"He wants to speak to you. He says it's important."

"Bring the lil' mothafucka in."

"What it do though, Gangster?" Nino asked the highest ranking member of the Organization, and soon-to-be new leader.

"Speak yo' mind, lil nigga. I'm a busy man." He fired up his blunt.

"My cousin, Cuzzo, was a loyal member of the 'O'. When I wanted to join he brought me to Ice. After a serious conversation with Ice, he declined me membership as a soldier, said he needed lawyers not shooters on his team. With my grades tight, he paid for a full-ride for me in USC's legal program.

"Yeah nigga, that's all fine and good, but Ice's ass is dead too."

"That's why I'm here. I know where the people are who killed Ice and my cousin."

"So do I. My mans at the police department tells me all the niggas responsible are on lock. Tell me somethin' I don't know." Gangster rose from his seat, and made his way toward Nino.

Nino waited until they were eye-to-eye before he continued. "The bitch who killed Ice, and her son who killed my cousin are holed up at a farm in Albert Lea, Minnesota."

"How do you know this?" Gangster searched Nino's eyes for a motive to the shit he was spittin' out of his mouth.

"The dude who murdered my family member, his name is J.T. We went to high school together, and now share a spot off campus at USC. Every summer since, we spent time on his grandfather's farm."

"What makes you thing the bitch who killed Ice is there?" He took a long pull on the blunt.

"He called to let me know that he was going to be in the Twins a few more days, said he was at his grandfather's place with his mom."

"Why come to us?" He blew a cloud of smoke in Nino's face.

Nino remained calm. "Because I want in, I want to avenge Ice and my cousin, I wouldn't be shit if it wasn't for them." He took a deep breath, and slowly blew the air in his lungs in Gangster's face.

Gangster smiled at Nino's boldness. "L-Dog, take some of the fellas and them thumpers and kill that bitch and her son."

"No guns."

"Why the fuck not?" Gangster snapped.

Nino could smell the garlic and Cush on his breath, as Gangster stepped so close to him their noses were touching. Not wanting to show any signs of fear, Nino held his ground.

"Small town, black faces, one hundred-and-sixty mile drive, eighty there, and eighty back. As soon as those good nosey country white folks hear gunfire, you'll have law enforcement officers, and every oakey with a shotgun on our asses. It'll be like white folks chasing down runaway slaves. Besides, what if we're pulled over with all that heat in the car? You want us to shoot it out with the police?"

"I like this lil' nigga, he can think." Gangster stepped back and looked Nino up and down. "Alright lil' college boy, wantin' to be grimey nigga. What do you suggest?"

"One weapon, silenced, which I have. And enough explosives to destroy the evidence of our crime. By the time the authorities put out the fire and discover the bodies, we'll be back in the Twins chillin'."

"L-Dog?"

"Yeah, Gangster?"

"Make it happen. And L-Dog, don't come back if you fail."

"Gangster, you know me. I never fail."

C H A P T E R   1 3 2

Nino sat on the passenger side of the Chevy Impala, as it sped down 35W South toward Albert Lea, trying to put all the shit that was happening into perspective. What he was about to do felt completely insane to him, but it was for his family. And nobody was gonna fuck over Nino's family.

Although he'd told Gangster that he could pull this thing off with two men and himself, he sent five. 'Strength in numbers, the 'O' never fail in a mission.' He told him. Now here he sat, silent for the past twenty miles, after arguing with these slow-ass mothafuckas about the best way to approach the farm. Rookies! These broke-down-ass drive-by shooters wanted to just pull up in the front yard.

"And do what?" He'd asked. "Knock on the front door and say 'sorry for the home invasion but we're here to kill you?"

Sheisty, Lil' Cox, Snaps, and Pep-Talk looked to L-Dog, with his lame leading ass, for their instructions.

"Let's hear this nigga out! Fuck it, however we get in the house, that bitch and her son are gonna die, even if we fuck around and get caught up. Understand."

After Nino finished giving them the rundown, L-Dog nodded his head vigorously. Sounds like that's the plan, my nigga."

The Chevy bounced off the exit and drove past miles of cornfields. Four miles in they all wondered whether Nino knew where the fuck he was going, as they looked into the pitch-black cornfield, when he told the driver to make a hard left in what appeared to be a patch cut through the corn. They rode for another half mile before

Nino had them park behind some underbrush a quarter mile from the farm. They exited the Chevy, and quickly made their way to the main house.

Nino saw a girl sitting in a car and removed the .45 from his waistband and screwed the silencer in place. With a nervous anticipation, he moved toward his unsuspecting victim.

Tanisha sat in her BMW listening to Deborah Cox CD 'The Promise' when she thought she saw something moving in her rearview mirror.

She turned down the sound, and checked the side mirrors. Nothing.

"Hell of a delusion you're having here, girl. You are officially tripping! Now you're seeing things." She mumbled to herself as she killed the power silencing the CD player. Peeking around in the darkness one last time, she took a deep breath to calm herself, and stepped out of the car to walk the thirty five yards to the house.

Nino eased up behind her, and clasped his left hand firmly over her mouth to muffle her scream. Terror stricken, she struggled to free herself. She immediately ceased when she felt the cool steel pressed against her temple.

"How many people in the house?" Nino growled in her ear, shifting his grip from her mouth to her throat.

"Just three. My mom and my grandparents."

"Where's your brother?" He snapped in her ear, causing her to spasmodically shudder. She tried to respond to his question audibly, but had trouble with the words.

"Did you hear me?" He added pressure to her throat.

"Yesss!" She whimpered. "He's at the arcade in town playing Grand Theft Auto."

"Fuck!" Nino cursed. "Do they have any weapons on, or near them in the house?" He signaled the others.

"No, they're just watching a movie in the family room." Her body shook at the sight of the other men.

"Let's finish this shit!" L-Dog walked up, and grabbed Tanisha by the chin.

Nino released his grip on her throat, and snatched a handful of her hair, then nearly dragged her to the front door, at which point she led them to the family room where Fate, Vee, and Tina sat watching 'Soul Men'.

Tanisha screamed when they entered the room.

"Oh my God, please don't hurt my baby!" Vee wailed reaching for Fate. "Oh my God!" She whimpered, her sobs dying only when Fate touched her hand.

Tina looked on in disbelief at what she was seeing. "Nino, is that you?"

"Shut up, bitch!" He snapped.

"Nino, what is this about?"

"You know what this is about. You and your fucking son killed my cousin and Ice, and now all you mothafuckas are going to die."

He pressed the gun against Tanisha's temple.

"Nino, please don't do this." Tina pleaded. "You're like a son to us, an extended member of our family."

Ignoring her pleas he shouted. "Move!" Pointing the .45 toward the rear of the house. "L-Dog, have them fools set the explosives while I take care of business."

"Crazy mothafucka!" L-Dog turned to the others. "Set the C-4." He commanded.

"Damn Dog, I need to get my nuts out of hock, and these bitches is looking pretty damn good. Even that old bitch! We got all night, we can fuck these hoes and make the old man watch before we kill them, and still make it back to the city before morning." Sheisty chimed in, looking hard at Tanisha and Tina.

"Unless you wanna die with them, I suggest you set the C-4 nigga, cause in five minutes there ain't gonna be nothing left of this house or the pussy!" Nino growled angrily over his shoulder.

"Nigga! Yo' ass don't run shit here! Do he L-Dog? This is our shit, 'O' business, and I say that we get some of that sweet pussy from shorty, and those old bitches before we kill 'em." Sheisty burst into laughter while reaching for Tanisha.

Just as Sheisty grabbed Tanisha's arm, Nino slapped him on the top of his head with the .45, and he dropped to the floor, a lump quickly rising on the crown of his head.

"Nigga, who the fuck do you think you're talking too? One of these gutter-mouth mothafuckas? I'll leave yo' bitch-ass stinkin', too!" Nino shouted in an indignant rage as he pressed the .45 to Sheisty's head. "What do you wanna do?" Nino asked, the threat of death dripping from his words.

"Finish the business we came here to do, man. Damn!" Nino pulled the gun from his head, and he bolted to his feet, storming out of the room like the checked bitch he was.

In a voice laced with pure anger Nino shouted. "Move, goddammit. He quickly herded them down the hallway to a room at the rear of the house, pushing them inside. Releasing his grip on Tanisha, he spun her around, and shot her three times at point blank range.. She fell to the floor, eyes wide open, mouth opening and closing, as blood began rushing from the holes in her body.

Before the screams of her death faded, Nino shot Vee and Tina. Fate rushed him in the small room, and Nino pulled the trigger, ripping off several rounds in succession before Fate grabbed the gun. L-Dog, thinking that Nino needed his aid and assistance, bolted down the hallway prepared to crush the old man when the gun fired again. L-Dog stood frozen, as a bloodied Fate stepped back, and fell into the room.

"Damn nigga!" L-Dog looked in the door at the pool, of blood, and bodies that littered the floor. "What the fuck? ... I thought the plan was to duct tape them, end let the explosion kill them?"

"Changed my mind, L-Dog." Nino watched Fate crawling toward his wife, using the last of his strength to pull her close to him, as his eyes closed, and he struggled to take a breath.

"That old nigga ain't gonna make it," L-Dog laughed. "Set the timers, mothafuckas. You've got five minutes to get the fuck out!"

He commanded, taking control of the situation. They quickly set the timers on the four eight-pound C-4 explosive devices and ran back to the Chevy.

"What about the son?" L-Dog asked, as he closed his door.

"I'll, find a way to kill him when he comes back to school." Nino spoke in a menacing voice.

"You're one crazy sumbitch, Nino, but I like you." L-Dog fired up the Chevy.

"Yeah, I've been told that." Nino checked the timer on his watch. "Five, four, three, two, one, BOOM!" Nino counted down as L-Dog sped through the cornfield while a ferocious blast shook the ground beneath them.

C H A P T E R   1 3 3

Thomas Shaw sat down for his first cup of coffee, and his customary half-hour of watching CNN News before he headed off to the office. The biggest case of his career was about to start and he was completely prepared. The best legal team the world would ever know had been assembled, and would be waiting to be briefed at 10:00AM in the conference room at Thomas Shaw and Associates.

He accepted his coffee and danish from his long-time live-in lover, Brenda, kissed her tenderly on the lips, and settled in to watch the news. His attention was drawn to the screen, as a live report was just coming in about an explosion that left ten dead in Albert Lea, Minnesota.

Thomas and Brenda both watched in horror, as they recognized the name of the farm on which the ten body bags were laying under. Thomas pulled out his cell phone and pushed the speed dial. His lead investigator answered on the third ring.

"David, are you watching this?"

"Not only am I watching, Thomas, I've got my old academy buddy on the line, who just so happens to be the Chief of Police in Albert Lea, and it's confirmed. It's Lafayette, his wife, both grandkids, their mother, and the five members of his squad from Vietnam who lived on the farm. He said they must have put up one hell of a battle because there are shell casings, thousands of them, lying all over the ground in various locations around the outside perimeter. A fucking war zone, Thomas!"

"This troublesome-ass case just gets more complicated by the minute. David, stay on top of this, and get back at me within the hour."

"Sure, Thomas. I got one more piece of information that has been verified. There was a big red 'O' spray painted on the ground in front of the house."

CHAPTER 134

Thomas stood when his client was escorted in chains to the visiting area. "Are the restraints necessary?" He asked the guards who took up post in the room.

"Very, sir." One of them answered.

"I'm his attorney!" Thomas began to protest but Six cut him off.

"They're assigned to me, Thomas. U.S. Marshalls. They wait on me hand and foot. What happened to the arraignment at one o'clock?"

"Postponed by my request until tomorrow morning."

"Postponed?"

"Yeah Jeff, something terrible has happened. I don't know how to tell you this, so I'll just spit it out. Your family, all of them have been murdered."

"How, Thomas?" He asked in a casual voice.

"There was a gun battle at the log cabin home on the farm. Thousands of rounds from various weapons were everywhere. FBI and other authorities have confirmed that there were as many as thirty shooters around the house. After they were killed, the bad guys blew the building. It took fireman hours to put out the flames because there was a bunch of tires in the cellar."

"What about Fate's men?"

"All killed, Jeff. I'm sorry for your loss. I know how you loved them."

"Have the bodies been identified?"

"Yes Jeff. Tina, Tanisha, J.T., Lafayette, and Vee's bodies although burned terribly were identified by dental records. Fate's men were identified by the dog tags they wore around their necks. Before I came here, I went down and checked personally, because I wanted to be absolutely positive before I brought you the news."

Six sucked in a breath, and a hush fell over the table.

"Again Jeff, I'm sorry to bring you this news."

"Me too, Thomas. I know how you loved my family." Six rose from his seat. There was a slight tremor in his bottom lip before he spoke. "Thomas, please arrange for the burial of my family."

"Brenda has been on it all morning."

"Thomas ?"

"Yeah, Jeff?"

"Do they have any idea who did this?"

"Right now the investigation is centered around a big red 'O' that was spray painted on the ground." Six rolled his eyes toward the ceiling, but said nothing, turned toward his escorts who opened the door, then exited without saying a word.

CHAPTER 135

The next morning, sitting on the steel benches in the federal courthouse holding cell, Six looked at his chained and black-boxed comrades. They were all far from the traditional stereotypical black men that the world had come to know. These were men who had climbed to the highest levels of economic success, and he refused to allow their work to go out in disgrace.

"Fellas, I've got something to say, and I want you to hear me out. Over the next few months, the U.S. Attorney is going to depict us to the American public, and the world as a group of angry black domestic terrorist and murderers. Fuck all the things we've accomplished, and the good we've done around the world. They will paint a grotesque scene of the robberies, using vintage film footage, through the media to condemn and convict us. I say we take the sensationalism of a trial and jury verdict from them."

"And how do you suggest we do that, Six?" Face asked.

"By pleading guilty at the arraignment."

"I'm sure that would be a shock to the prosecutor, the judge, and the army of talking heads we saw lined up when they drove us into the underground parking area this morning." Elijah admitted.

"I'm with you, Six. Fuck promoting that type of image of our legacy to our families, and the world, just so those bitches can up their television ratings." Rasheed was on board.

"Six, as a former prosecutor and defense counsel, I have to

ask you to consider what it is that you are asking us to do. I understand the pain that you are going through because of the loss of your family. Hell, they were my family as well, and I'm suffering from the same grief. However, we have assembled the greatest legal minds this world has to offer, and an army of investigators to find Sazzar. In my professional opinion, this case will never make it to trial once we've located the government's only witness." Face turned and faced the bars of the holding cell.

"Sounds to me, Face, like you actually believe our people are going to find Sazzar." K-Nine flashed a smile of understanding.

"Any and all things are possible, Nine." He replied.

"Sazzar could be any place in the world right now. I doubt, with all that he knows, and has already told the authorities, that they would even keep him in the U.S." Babyboss surmised.

"Yeah, that no-good rat sumbitch has probably got a seat on the next departing space shuttle." Rasheed laughed.

"Look at the positions that all of us hold in this American society. Unlike some of these street corner thugs, our trial will be a media event before the world. Trust me, as a prosecuting attorney, I suggest we at the very least give this thing a few weeks to see how the evidence against us develops. And," he raised his chained hand to stop any questions before he finished, "Give our people some time to investigate. Maybe even get lucky and find Sazzar's location."

"Sounds to me, Face, like you think our status is going to come to our rescue, along with lady luck." K-Nine was being sarcastic.

"Nine, you are a United States Senator in good standing with the Senate."

"Face, what I am, is a black man who happens to be a Senator. Regardless of my position in this life, I'm still a nigger in the eyes of the two-hundred-and-forty-million white folks who make up the judging, voting, and jury duty majority who will simply say, 'He must be guilty of something, otherwise he wouldn't be on trial for his life.'"

"After all that we've accomplished, Nine, and the history

that we've witnessed with our own eyes in 2009 and again in 2013 of the first election and reelection of the first African American President, I'm sorry to hear you speak that way."

"Don't be, Face. It is what it is. If you were prosecuting this case with a witness as knowledgeable and cooperative as Sazzar, who just happens to know the complete inner workings of our society, how would you proceed with the investigation and prosecution of the case?" Six asked.

"I would gather intelligence on the working order of the society, its strengths, and its weaknesses. I would bring super ceding indictments against some of the smaller players in hopes of bringing down the entire network." Face paused, as he thought about what he'd just said. "You're right, Six. We can't allow that to happen. The GHETTOBOYS must survive. How's that old quote go? 'Never have so few owed so much to so many.' And for the race card that you played, K-Nine, you're probably right. With all the information that Sazzar will provide, we will all be found guilty."

"No ifs, ands or butts about it. Will be lethally injected." Big Al stated with definitiveness.

"I agree with Six and Rasheed. Why should we put our families through the burden of a lengthy trial, and countless appeals that will surely be denied, and only prolong the inevitable. Besides, this way there'll be no public record of the evidence presented during a trial. Right, Face?'" Badboy asked.

"Just our guilty pleas." He smiled.

"What's with the grin, Face?" Six asked.

"Got to die from something, might as well be on my own terms. Here's how we do it. We have our attorneys agree to waive the reading of the indictment and proceed straight to the pleas. Agreed?"

"Agreed." They spoke in unison.

CHAPTER 136

Six was the first to shuffle his chained feet into the courtroom, followed by the others. Slowly, he edged himself into a seat positioned next to Thomas. For a moment, Six felt like the kid who met this brilliant man all those years ago, and his eyes suddenly warmed and he smiled.

"Hey, Thomas."

"Hey, Jeff. You're awfully upbeat considering the situation."

"Can you recall what Muhammad Ali said when he knocked out Sonny Liston?"

"I'm not a boxing fan, but I believe he said 'I shook up the world!'" Knowing Six the way he did, Thomas mused. "Jeff, what are you up to?"

"I'm going to shake up the world, Thomas. I want you to waive the reading of the indictment, and proceed directly to the plea."

Thomas started to ask why, but decided against it, then moved from the table to speak with U.S. Attorney Hughes. Hughes seemed delighted with what Thomas was saying, and vigorously nodded his head in agreement.

"Done." Thomas reported taking his seat.

"One more thing, Thomas."

"Now what, Jeff?"

"No matter what you hear come out of our mouths, do not object."

"Jeff, whatever you are about to do, don't. Let your legal

team work things out."

"Thomas, trust me. It's for the best, old friend."

"All rise! The Honorable Judge Judith Staples presiding." Bellowed the court deputy.

"You may all be seated. Well Mr. Hughes, I feel honored with your presence.

"Likewise, your Honor. It's been years since I've tried a case before you. Before we get started, Your Honor, counsels for the defendants, and I have reached an agreement to waive the reading of the indictment, stipulating that the charges contained therein are accurate enough to proceed to the plea portion of this arraignment hearing."

"This is very unusual. However, I'll allow it because all parties to this case agree. Will the defendants please stand? After having stipulated to the charges in the indictment that contain a maximum sentence of death if you are found guilty, Jeffery Alexander Lane aka Six, how do you plea?"

"Guilty, Your Honor!"

Pandemonium swept through the courtroom, as Judge Staples banged her gavel to restore order to her court.

"Dog-gone-it! This will be my only warning. Any further outbursts of any kind and I will clear this courtroom. Is this understood?"

The silence in her courtroom provided her with the answer.

The court, as well as those in attendance, listened in shock as each defendant entered guilty pleas. When she reached Ronnie Green, she spoke to him addressing him by his official title.

"Assistant United States Attorney Ronnie Green, aka Face, how do you plea?"

"Guilty, Your Honor. And may I address the court?"

"You may."

"We also stipulate to the death penalty phase of the trial, and moved the court to pronounce a sentence of death by lethal injection as soon as a date is available on Your Honor's calendar."

"Mr. Hughes?"

"Huh?" He was in complete shock that his trial of the

century had started and ended in one fell swoop.

"Do you agree with the defendants request?"

"Doesn't seem like I have much of a choice in the matter, does it Your Honor?"

"From where I'm sitting, not much. Due to the defendants' pleas of guilty on all charges, and a waiver of the death penalty phase, they will be sentenced to death by this court." She checked her calendar. "One week from today. May God have mercy on all of your souls. This court is adjourned!"

C H A P T E R   1 3 7

"Sazzar, what the fuck is going on? These agents storm into our hotel suite, drag me and our daughter out kicking and screaming without any explanation, then bring us here. And on top of all this shit, Tina, the kids, and their grandparents have been murdered." Vickie had been crying, her face tear stained.

"I know, baby. I've heard." He moved to embrace her.

"Don't touch me!" She cautioned. "What is going on?" She screamed.

"Right now you are under the protective custody of the FBI, at least until things blow over.

Her heart dropped. "Protective custody? For what?"

Sazzar dropped his head, and then raised it slowly, his eye resting on hers. "I'm a witness against Six and the others in a federal murder investigation."

"You're a fucking rat? Wow nigga, am I surprised to hear some shit like that coming out of your mouth."

"Vickie?"

"Vickie my ass. What the fuck does telling on your family, you stupid cocksucker, have to do with me?"

"I'm just protecting you, Vickie. You of all people know who it is that we are dealing with."

"Are you serious? I'm not running and hiding from shit, Sazzar, you are!"

"To get to me, they'll do something to you or our daughter."

"Bullshit, Sazzar. The further I am away from you and

these toy cops is how I'm going to stay alive. You want to be a rat, you can do that shit without me and Jazz. Come on baby, we're out of here." She grabbed her daughter's hand.

"Sorry ma'am, we can't let you leave." The agent stepped in front of her. Her heart pounded in her chest, as her anger rose, and she began throwing everything within reach at the agents blocking her path.

Sazzar wrestled her to the floor as the agents stood over them, threatening to press charges for assault against a federal agent if she continued on the path she was on. Vickie calmed herself down, and slowly raised herself off the floor.

Grabbing her purse, she politely asked, "What room am I staying in?"

Sazzar pointed toward a room at the back of the suite, and she strolled off with the same grace she used on the runway.

Sazzar smiled and bent down to scoop up his daughter and she shrank back from him. "What's the matter, baby girl?"

"You hurt Mommy and me, Daddy." She replied.

"I promise you I'll make it all better, baby." He took her little hand in his.

"I thought you told me never to tattle on anyone, Daddy?"

"I know I did, baby, but this is different. Tattling to save your life is okay. You understand?"

Jazz snatched her hand from his, and her beautiful little face flushed with anger. "Daddy, tattling is tattling!" she hissed out the words before she ran to the bedroom that her mother had entered. Once in the room she climbed on the bed, sitting with her arms crossed next to her mom.

"Are you alright, Mommy?" she asked with a hint of anger lingering in her little voice.

"Mommy will be fine in a minute, baby." Vickie dumped her purse on the bed looking for her aspirins. At the sight of Tina's watch she smiled, lifted it off the bed, and looked at her daughter.

"You want to leave this place, honey?"

"Um-huh!" She nodded her head.

"Do you see this fairy on the watch?"

"Yes, Mommy, it's pretty."

"Well, it has magical powers. All you have to do is press

this button."

"Can I do it, Mommy?"

"Sure, baby. But first we have to make a wish." Vickie and Jazz both closed their eyes, and their lips moved silently.

"Did you make a wish, baby?" Vickie asked when she opened her eyes.

"Yes, Mommy."

"Alright. Baby all you have to do to make our wish come true, is to push this button." Vickie handed her daughter the watch.

"Like this, Mommy?" Jazz pushed the button.

"Yes, baby, just like that."

CHAPTER 138

The Sergeant's eyes fluttered open, and took only a moment to focus in on the beep on the screen. "Impossible!" He muttered to himself refusing to accept what his eyes were seeing.

Uneasiness wrapped around him, as he made his way to the outer room, where the rest of the team sat discussing the latest developments of Six and the others' criminal trial.

"Kiss my ass!" He grumbled as he entered the room.

"Hell of a way to enter a room, and start a conversation, Sergeant. What seems to be the problem?"

"Tina's distress signal."

"What about it?"

"It was just activated, Cap."

"Impossible, she's dead."

"Well, then, it's being activated from the grave because it's definitely hers, sir." Both men twisted their heads to the lone figure sitting in the corner.

"Care to explain how the dead are speaking, Nakia?"

"The dead are not speaking, Cap. The living are reaching out for help. Where is the signal coming from?"

"Downtown St. Paul. Give me a few minutes, and I'll have the exact location.

"Thanks, Sarge. Cap?"

"Yeah, Nakia?"

"You ready to suit up and boot up? We're going on a rescue mission."

"I thought you'd never ask."
"Cap?"
"Yeah, Nakia?"
"Bring Tony!"

CHAPTER 139

Sazzar walked to the door which stood slightly ajar. He hesitated, then called out in a whisper. "Vickie." She gave no reply.

He eased the door open, and could see his daughter was sleeping on the bed, her mother sitting at the desk writing.

"What are you writing?" He whispered.

"You don't have to whisper, she sleeps like a rock. It's called the spoken word." She continued writing without looking up.

"Does it have a title?" He asked, glad that they were talking.

"Yes it does. She turned to face him. When their eyes met she spoke. "Was it worth it."

"Was what worth it, baby?"

"It wasn't a question, Sazzar, it's the name of the spoken word." Drops of guilt dripped in his veins from her stare like he was hooked to an I.V.

Sazzar pulled up a chair. "Can I hear some of it?"

"Sure, why the fuck not! After all, it's all about you anyway." Vickie walked to the window, facing her reflection she began.

"You jump at shadows, and hearing footsteps at night. Scared to death, so you sleep with a gun and a knife. Living your life with a price tag on your head, going Through hell cause you wanted to tell. Your losing your Mind because you think people are following you, you're hated by all, even your family disowned you. All alone Cause of the shit you've done, now you're useless and Weak, can't even look me in the eyes, so you stare at You' feet. Now it's known that you were scared to fight,

And here I thought your bitch-ass was true to this life. Maniacs hate you, even cowards despise you, the Prosecutor You told, don't even like you. Still you all on his dick, You a suck without help, a bitch without a trick. It's too Late to try and change now, no one will, let you, you done Jumped off a cliff, and praying' someone will, catch you. You're wishing for forgiveness and mercy that no one is Given' If I had a gun, I'd be the one to stop you from living'.

Before he could say a word Vickie asked. "With all the power the GHETTOBOYS hold, why didn't you just stand up and be a man, Sazzar. I would have stood beside you until God took my life."

CHAPTER 140

Tony was the team's 'Black-Bag-Man.' Surreptitious entry, and extraction were his specialty. Four figures in black stood on the nearby building, and watched the shadowy figure make his way through the entrance at the rear of the Embassy Suites.

Close observation revealed that the signal was coming from a suite on the top floor, at the west end of the building. Thermal imaging showed eleven male figures, ten armed, a woman, and a child. They waited patiently for the signal.

A ripple of laughter came from the Security Control Room, as Tony pushed the hose beneath the door, and turned on the gas canister of Methyl that snaked its way around the room. The odorless gas shut down the uplifting conversation about reconnecting with an old flame, and the room fell silent.

Tony opened the door, his silenced weapon leading the way.

The guards were sleeping peacefully, slumped over the control panel.

"Situation contained. Use backdoor entry, I'll be waiting in the service elevator." Tony looked at his watch. "You have ninety seconds. I suggest you move people!" He went about the business of disabling the security surveillance system.

Sazzar sat on the hotel-room floor playing UNO with his daughter, and couldn't help yawning, as he contemplated whether to allow Jazz, who had nodded off, to sleep on the floor. As his vision clouded, he watched through dazed vision, as the agents and Marshalls slumped to the floor, and five masked figures enter the room. They all stopped in their tracks at the sight of Sazzar lying on the floor.

"This is not a sightseeing mission, people. This gas is going to wear off in thirty minutes. Pick up his snitching ass off the floor. We'll bring him with us." Tony began checking the other rooms. When he came to the master bedroom, he called for Nakia."

"What do you want to do with her, Nakia?"

Nakia stood in the doorway holding Jazz in her arms and saw the sleeping woman lying unconscious on the bed. "Grab her, Tony, and be gentle. She's a friend."

CHAPTER 141

The Town car slowed and parked in front of the Miami Federal Courthouse, and a beautiful brunette exited the vehicle, and strutted into the building like she owned it, her dark hair bouncing off her shoulders. She had the look of a federal prosecutor, as she made her way to the judge's private chambers. The judge's private secretary was leafing through some files when she appeared at the door.

"Excuse me, I'm from the federal prosecutor's office, and I need for Judge Edmonds to sign off on these Federal Writs for appearance in his court. Is he in?"

"Just left. He won't be back until tomorrow. Sorry." She turned back to the papers she was going through.

"Fuck!"

"Excuse me?"

"Sorry about the profanity, but it's been a long day, and I need to get these writs stamped and filed." She shoved the documents out in front of her. The secretary shrugged somberly, and motioned for her to come behind her desk.

"Busy?" She made small talk, as she passed the papers over.

"Very! All these damn federal crack cases from low level drug dealers are giving me the blues. If you ask me, you guys at the prosecutors' office should be sentencing these dope heads to ten years in a drug treatment center, and not prison. But what the hell's the use in complaining? Is this all I can do for you, honey?" She looked at her imploringly.

"Well, there is one other thing."

"Come on, spit it out. I don't have all day." She shifted her large frame in her seat.

"I need all seven of these defendants in Judge Edmonds Court before the close of business on Friday."

"Are these defendants over at Dade County?"

"No, they're in St. Paul, Minnesota."

"So, you're going to need long distance transport?"

"Yes."

"No problem." She pulled out a rubber stamp.

"You won't get into trouble for doing this, will you?"

"Rubber stamping a document? Honey please. How long have you been working in the prosecutors' office?"

"A year, almost to date. Why do you ask?"

"Around here, honey, we rubber stamp everything. Judges are too busy." She stamped the paperwork. "I'll hand-deliver it to the Marshall's office on my way out. There's this guy who just loves to watch all this ass move who's working tonight, and I could use some company, if you know what I mean." She gave her a wink.

"Thanks, you saved my career. I owe you one."

"I'll remember you said that. The defendants will be here this Friday to appear before Judge Edmonds at," she checked his calendar, "1:30PM Friday afternoon. Is that good for you, madam prosecutor?"

"Absolutely wonderful." She spun on her heels and headed for the door. Mercy adjusted her skirt, flipped open her phone, and hit the digits of the phone number she'd memorized.

"All done."

"Problems?" The voice on the other end asked.

"Everything went exactly like you said it would."

"Then walk out like you walked in."

CHAPTER 142

"Lane, turn your face to the wall of your cell, and get down on your knees, fingers laced behind your head. Do it now!" The Marshal commanded through the door. Six did what he was told, as the Marshals who were suited and booted for the occasion with shotguns and shields in hand entered the cell.

"What's the deal?" Six asked the Marshal's as they began the procedure of shackling him. "Today is only Wednesday. I don't get sentenced to death until Monday."

"Escorts are here to take you to Florida to answer for several murders before a federal court. That's all I know. It appears that someone else in your network is singing." The Marshal attached the black box to Six's handcuffs. Inside the escort vehicle they all sat quiet, as they made their way to the airport, and the waiting Marshal transport plane.

C H A P T E R 143

"We've been sitting in this filthy-ass roach and rat infested jail for two nights now, and nothing. From the looks of things we'll have to sit here until Monday." Rasheed played the queen of spades."

"Doesn't matter. I'll bet you part of the sleep-inducing drug from the lethal injection that our asses will be back in Minnesota bright and early Monday morning for sentencing." Face played the king of spades and took the book.

"Rasheed, it's only 9:00AM, and the court will be going on all day. Maybe we'll find out who it is that we've murdered today." Baby boss played a card.

"Don't matter. Whoever it was, we're pleading guilty to the charges anyway." Rasheed played his last trump card.

"Fry, Ball, and Williams. Y'all know the drill. They're here for you." The Marshal shouted through the door of their three man cell.

"Guess we'll find out who we killed now." Rasheed mumbled in Face's ear, as the Marshal's led them down a long corridor.

Face climbed in the van. "What the hell is going on, Six?"

"Don't really know. All we got out of these assholes is one word."

"And that word is?"

Six adjusted himself on the metal slab. "Mistake!"

"This is different. The Marshals who dropped us off seemed to have their own personal press core. Hell, for a while there I thought we were making a documentary for the fucking Discovery Channel without our permission." Big Al suggested in an attempt at humor.

"All I know, and care about is that we're out of that nasty mothafucka. We should get a message to our people and have this fucking place burned to the ground." Badboy climbed inside the van.

"You guys are going to think I've lost my mind, but I'm going to enjoy getting back to those clean-ass cells in the Washington County Jail." Elijah firmly stated as he took a seat on the slab, and the Marshal closed the sliding door behind him. The slamming of the door caused Six to look to the front of the van.

"What happened to the regular?" He asked the driver.

"Probably having their second cup of coffee. No disrespect, fellas, but right now I need for all of you to be quiet for a minute. Not a sound. Understand?" The Marshal started the van, and moved, as the two escort vehicles, one in front the other trailing, drove out of the prisoner loading area of the Dade County Jail

CHAPTER 144

"Fucking aye! That was some intense shit!" The Marshal shouted at his partner when they entered the expressway.

"Yeah, that shit went off just as planned. Alright fellas, you can talk now, but before you do." He turned in his seat and faced them. "I need to know if you guys like old school R&B?" When nobody answered he turned to his partner. "Nakia said they wouldn't say a word. I owe her a grand." He pushed the Dramatics Greatest Hits CD.

Six began to laugh hysterically, as The Dramatics 'Bottom Line Woman' began to play. Six inhaled the words Ron Banks sang.

When he finally calmed down he asked the Marshal. "How is she?"

"Alive and well!" He shouted over the music.

"Six, what the hell is going on?" K-Nine asked.

"Nakia is what's going on."

"What and who the fuck is Nakia?" He looked beyond puzzled.

"Freedom, K-Nine, freedom!"

"Not for another four miles." The Marshal driving the van lied over his shoulder.

CHAPTER 145

The van pulled next to another van which was identical to the one they were riding in, parked next to a refrigerated truck.

The driver shut down the van. "Listen up! After we uncuff you, we're going to have to work together. In that truck are your body doubles, so you're going to have to strip off those orange jumpsuits, and put them on your replacements."

"How so?" Rasheed asked.

"They're all dead, and propped up in a sitting position, so I'm sure rigor mortis has set in," He opened his door and quickly began to unchain them, and they went about the business of exchanging their clothing with their body-doubles.

Six carried his body-double to the van, and peeked at the Marshals who were sitting in the front seat. Both of them had been shot in the back of the head. He smiled at the coffee in the cup holders.

"I like your style." Six complimented the fake Marshal.

"I had nothing to do with it. It was all Nakia's idea."

"Even the bodies?" He asked.

"That was the fun part. All these stiffs are Organization members. The morgue bodies wouldn't work because they were in a vertical position, and we needed them in a sitting position, so Nakia and Fate came through with these poor fucks, Those old men put in major work." He laughed, and pulled the C-4 and a timer from a bag. "She's a resourceful one that Nakia is,"

"That she is, and old soldiers never die."

"I'll say, and by the way, do you remember me?" The fake Marshal asked.

"Can't say that I do."

"Nakia said you wouldn't. I'm Gary Pennick. I was recruited by Bernard Logan, and have been an initiated G-B for seven years now."

"Now I remember you, Gary. We met after you graduated from the FBI Academy. You still a fed?"

"No Six, I'm with the CIA now. When Nakia called me, and told me about her plans, I assembled a team at the Director's request. Nakia wanted to pull off the greatest unsolved mystery this world will ever know." He attached the C-4 beneath the van. "If you want my take, she has."

C H A P T E R   1 4 6

After the doors on the van were secured, using a remote control, Gary started the van containing the body-doubles, and made a few practice runs around the immediate area.

"What's the plan?" Six asked.

"We are all about to die. Our remains will be discovered, and after several weeks of checking dental records it will be conclusive that the men in the van are in fact you, and your notorious friends, along with the convoy of Marshal's assigned to escort and protect you." He laughed again.

Gary steered the van into a wooded area near the swamps, and pushed the detonator. The explosion sent a fireball into the air that could be seen for miles.

"I guess we should get out of here. The authorities will be here in a few minutes. Gary put the van in gear and drove away.

CHAPTER 147

They rode in silence taking in the Florida countryside, and after several miles Six asked Gary when he would get to see his family. Gary smiled.

"Technically, you've been with them for the last five miles. You see those two expensive Motor Coaches in front of us?"

"You're bullshittin'!"

"I bullshit you not, Six. In those coaches are every member of your teams family member, even the dogs and cats." He pulled off the expressway behind the Motor Coaches, and into the rest area.

Six and the others watched, as the motor coaches pulled over and parked. His heart skipped a beat when he saw Andre and Fate sitting in front of one of the coaches. As soon as they came to a halt, the door flew open, and Tanisha bolted from the door and hit the ground running, and right into Six's arms.

"Dad, when we get settled into our new lives, I know exactly what I wanna do for a career. I wanna take acting lessons. You should have seen my performance on the farm, dad. I was great!"

"Yeah, she gave an Oscar winning performance, Dad. When the special effect that my friend from the Ordway Theater put together for us, I nearly stopped to check to see if I had mistakenly put live rounds in the .45, the blood flowing from the holes looked so real." J.T. agreed as he walked up, and joined his sister and father.

"I'm sure she did, Son." He pulled both of them close, not wanting to let go of either of them.

"Dad?"

"Yeah, J.T.?"

"I'm not J.T. anymore, he's dead. From now on just call me Nino."

"Does Nino have a father?"

"Of course."

"Then I hope he won't mind if I call him son

Andre stepped from the motor coach, and approached the six men who had posed as the Marshal's, then he stood before Gary. "As we agreed, Gary, your boss's manifest. He handed over the leather case. "Six, my friend." Andre extended his hand. "How are you?"

"Never better, Master Gunnery Sergeant." He replied.

"I take it you've met Gary?"

"Absolutely."

"He's a very persuasive fellow. He convinced the Director of the CIA to aid and assist in the return of their property. Of course, we happily agreed to their terms, and here you are."

"Your idea to return the manifest?" Six asked.

"Heavens no! After nearly twenty years I finally cracked the code, but don't tell Gary. Serious information in that book, Six, it was worth whatever they had to do to retrieve it." Andre looked around at the men behind him, and mouthed the words, "I managed to liquidate hundreds of millions before I returned it." Six laughed.

"You know I want my cut?" He mouthed back.

"Andre smiled. "As I was saying, it was all Nakia's idea to return the manifest. She's a keeper, that one is. Now come on, I have a boat - or is it a ship? - waiting in the harbor to take you to Belize."

Tina stood in the doorway of the coach, watching the smiles on her teams faces, as they embraced their families. She saw Six walking toward her and found herself running to him. He scooped her up in his arms, and they kissed passionately.

"You seem really glad to see me, Six." She tried to say it with a straight face.

"You damn right I am. I thought I'd lost you to death." He embraced her tighter.

"Not yet. Boy, have I got a few surprises for you!" She tried to be coy about it.

"Tee, that's what you said when you told me you were pregnant with Tanisha."

"This surprise is running neck and neck with the birth of our children." She dragged him to the motor coach and to its rear compartment. "You ready for this?"

"It's a bedroom, Tee. You damn right I'm ready."

"Six get yo' head out the gutter, boy." She playfully punched him in the arm.

"If not the wonders of your sex, then what?" He quizzed.

"Someone I want you to meet. His name is Demetrius English."

"Doesn't ring a bell." He shrugged his shoulders. Tina opened the door and sitting in a hospital-style bed, complete with the tubes in his arm, was Bangman.

"How?" He asked, the shock on his face apparent, as he made his way to the bed to embrace his friend.

"I asked the same question, so I'll tell you the same answer I was given: 'Man plans and God plans and God is the best of planners'."

"What are the other two surprises you told me about?"

"One is waiting for you on the boat. The other is something I need to speak to you about in private."

"If they're anything like this, I can't wait." Six embraced Bangman and Tina again.

CHAPTER 148

Sazzar was suddenly jarred awake by the constant rocking motion to find that he was enshrouded in total darkness. Shivering and disoriented, he thought. Where am I? The surface that he was lying on told him that he was no longer on the plush carpet of the suite in the Embassy Suites Hotel. He tried to sit up, but his limbs were unresponsive. He screamed into the overbearing darkness. "Let me the fuck out of here!"

Just as he was trying to make sense of what was going on he heard the pounding of rapidly approaching footsteps, and his dark space was flooded with light.

"This blood clot has finally awakened," The man with the dreadlocks shouted and slammed the lid, and the darkness once again wrapped itself around him.

His anxiety began to subside and a strange contentment swept over him, as the realization of his situation manifested itself.

He was a captive.

He heard the sound of several feet urgently approaching and his heart rate quickened as they grew nearer. The lid was once again pulled back, and it took several minutes for his eyes to adjust to the bright light. He could see the silhouette of several figures standing around him. For two anguish-filled minutes Sazzar experienced a helpless frustration, as his captors said nothing while they waited for his vision to correct itself.

As his sight slowly came around, he could see that Aunt Jean's prophecy had been fulfilled. There were ten men and two women standing in front of him, the sun blaring, distorting their faces. He willed himself to ask the question he had dreaded the answer to.

"Who are you?"

Someone bent down and placed a pair of sunglasses over his eyes and seconds later their faces came into view. For a second he thought he was dead.

Bangman, Tina and J.T. stood together, as Sazzar panned past them, and looked at the other members of his team he saw an additional person, Vickie. Unaffected by the sudden turn of events, and with a surprising calm he spoke.

"Six, I see you and the others came out on top."

"What did you expect?" Six paused before adding. "The fate you had in store for us?"

Sazzar attempted to speak, but Six's words cut sharp as a knife through tender meat. Before he could form a sentence he heard Tina's voice.

"Sazzar, we drew straws amongst the team to decide who would have the privilege of taking your life. You sold out everyone who ever loved you, and anyone who would ever do such a thing deserves to die at the hand of someone who loves them." She stepped aside and Vickie replaced her, screwing the silencer onto the .45.

"Bishop Cole, would you please say a word for this sinner?" Vickie requested.

"Anything in particular?"

"How about John 15:13."

"Excellent choice. 'Greater love have no man than this, that a man lay down his life for his friend'."

"Just in case you're wondering, Six pulled the short straw, but I asked him for it, Sazzar." Vickie placed the .45 to Sazzar's head. She looked him directly in his eyes. "I loved you like the husband I never had." She pulled the trigger.

E P I L O G U E

Ngoro Ngoro Conservation Area, Tanzania, Africa Six Months Later.

Over the past six months Tina had her breast and lymph nodes removed. Six took her to some of the best cancer specialists in the world, but the results were always the same. Stage four recurrent breast cancer. The tumor had now spread to her bones and lungs.

Tina laid in her bed in a mud-brick bungalow with a banana leaf roof, the interior brimming with African and European influences. She had insisted that if she was going to die, she wanted to die and be buried in the Motherland.

She shivered uncontrollably, as her nurse covered her with a comforter. "I'm sorry, Mr. Six. We've done all that we could do to make her comfortable, but her time has come." The nurse who had been taking care of Tina day and night for the past three months walked out of the bedroom to give the family their privacy.

Tanisha, who refused to leave her mother's side, yearned for some way to ease her suffering. Her heart plummeted when all of Tina's vital signs started falling, and the doctor told her to say her goodbyes to her mother. Death, he said, was ready to claim her. She laid down next to her mother on the bed and snuggled against her. When Tina spoke, her words were quiet, loving and reassuring.

"I'll always be with you, baby. Remember that you've

given me sixteen wonderful years of joy and happiness, and I've loved every precious second of it." A sharp intake in Tina's breathing caused Tanisha to bolt upright in the bed. The pain on her mother's face let loose the floodgates in her tear ducts, and she sat there crying, trying to deal with the relentless pain that had gripped her heart.

J.T. bent over and kissed his mother on her lips. He was all cried out. Now he was admiring her remarkable courage at death, and her fierce love for her family. He defied his desire to join his sister in tears, and instead smiled at his mom. Tina had always told him about the first time she saw his face, about how his extraordinary good looks, and smile had captured her heart. That's how he wanted her to remember him, so he smiled, and told her how much he loved her.

"I'm dying now, Six." Her voice echoed, as he knelt by her beside. A sinking sensation gripped his stomach, as an inexplicable shiver shook her. He traced the lines on her face, just as he'd done so many years ago the first time she'd laid her head in his lap on the beach. The pain in her eyes would haunt him forever, and with a weak trembling hand she touched his face, wishing she could erase the heartache in his eyes.

"Have I told you how happy you've made me, Tee?"

"Once or twice." She teased, just before a wave of pain seized her, and she struggled to breathe. Taking her last breath, her heart ached for him, as she watched his face dwindle, and then disappear

"Take with you into death the fact that you were the only woman I ever loved. I love you Tina." He promised breathlessly, closing his mouth over hers, inhaling her dying breath.
***

Six, Bangman, K-Nine, Babyboss, Big Al, Badboy, Face, Elijah, and Rasheed stood over Tina's grave and watched as the dirt filled her final resting place.

"What now, Six?" K-Nine asked.

"We have some unfinished business in America."

"And what might that be?"

"I promised my woman that by 2016 one of our own would be in the most powerful seat America has to offer, and I never go back on my promise."

"So be it. The rise of the GHETTOBOYS!" K-Nine grabbed a handful of dirt from Tina's grave and wrapped it in his handkerchief, and placed it in his pocket, the others did the same.

Six knelt down and placed of handful of dirt in a handkerchief.

"Rest in peace, Mrs. Tina Lane."